AF559915

# Breakpoint

# Breakpoint

## The Crisis of the Middle Class and the Future of Work

Saurabh Mukherjea

With Nandita Rajhansa and Sapana Bhavsar

juggernaut

JUGGERNAUT BOOKS
C-I-128, First Floor, Sangam Vihar, Near Holi Chowk,
New Delhi 110080, India

First published by Juggernaut Books 2026



10 9 8 7 6 5 4 3 2

P-ISBN: 9789353452254
E-ISBN: 9789353458515



Typeset in Adobe Caslon Pro by R. Ajith Kumar, Noida

Printed at Thomson Press India Private Limited

*For those who did everything right and*
*still felt the ground shift beneath their feet*

# Contents

# Introduction

## A Million (Middle-Class) Mutinies Now

*Breakpoint is a scoring situation during a tennis match when the player receiving the serve is one point away from winning the game. The 'break' refers to the player breaking the server's hold on the game, an advantageous situation to be in and one that can significantly shift the momentum of the game.**

### India at the Breakpoint

In a darkened control room in Navi Mumbai (previously Bombay), 100 agents monitor 30,000 ATMs across India. Their cameras, sensors and bots do the work that 60,000 security guards once did. As shareholders in India's best-run banks, we take comfort in the cost savings. As investors wanting to see the Indian economy thrive, we feel fear.

In a small town near Bhilwara, Rajasthan, a 27-year-old BTech graduate named V.S. lost ₹13 lakh – nearly all his

---

* 'What Does "Break Point" Mean in Tennis?', *Basha Tennis*, 10 January 2025, https://tinyurl.com/bd6298kc.

family's savings – trading Futures and Options (F&O) in the stock market. Seduced by influencers on YouTube promising easy money, he now earns ₹14,000 per month as a freelance salesperson. He is one of 9 million Indians who collectively lose over $12 billion annually in F&O trading – nearly as much as the Government of India's (GoI's) entire education budget.

In Mumbai's suburbs, Sharad Chandra, a well-dressed CFO earning ₹60 lakh annually, took 30 personal loans in two years. Drowning in debt after losing money in F&O trading, he eventually embezzled over ₹1 crore from his employer and fled the city, leaving behind a padlocked apartment and unanswered questions.[1]

These are not isolated incidents. They are symptoms of a profound crisis gripping India's middle class – the 40 million income tax filers, earning between ₹5 lakh and ₹1 crore per annum, who form the backbone of India's economy.

## The Middle Class at a Crossroads

India's middle class today faces its most vulnerable position since economic liberalization in 1991. This book tells the story of how the Indian middle class reached this breakpoint – a moment when the old certainties of secure employment and steady consumption-driven growth are collapsing under the weight of technological disruption, demographic pressures and structural economic shifts.

The middle class is often defined by its attitude towards education and employment – the belief that a university degree is the gateway to prosperity. Yet a disturbing paradox has emerged: While India produces over 8 million graduates annually, becoming a graduate now actively reduces both earnings and employment prospects. The unemployment rate for graduates stands at 29.1 per cent – nine times higher than for illiterates. At elite IIT Bombay, minimum salaries have been slashed from ₹6 lakh per annum to ₹4 lakh per annum, while 8,000 of 21,500 IIT graduates nationwide remain unemployed.[2]

## The Triple Squeeze

Three forces are simultaneously crushing middle-class prosperity:

- **Jobs are disappearing.** White-collar job creation has plummeted from 11 per cent annual growth before 2020 to just 1 per cent today. India's IT services sector – the country's largest graduate employer with 8 million workers – is in retrenchment mode as AI (artificial intelligence) replaces coders and call centre agents. The country's leading IT firms laid off over 1,00,000 professionals over 2024 and 2025. Meanwhile, banks have become reluctant to finance new business projects after the 2015 Asset Quality Review, choking off private sector job creation. Small and medium enterprises, which employ 90 per cent of India's workforce, are being crushed by regulatory overload and competition from larger, more capital-intensive firms.[3]
- **Wages are stagnating.** For employees of Nifty 50 companies, real wages (after adjusting for inflation) have

fallen over the past nine years (FY2016 to FY2025).[4] The average income of India's middle class – those earning ₹5 lakh to ₹1 crore – was ₹10.23 lakh a decade ago. Today it is ₹10.69 lakh. Meanwhile, the cost of a typical vegetarian thali is rising at 11 per cent annually, medical costs rise at 14 per cent and the true cost of middle-class living doubles every eight years. The government has compounded this by shifting tax burdens from corporations to individuals, with personal income tax as a percentage of GDP (gross domestic product) rising from 2.5 per cent to 3.6 per cent.[5]

- **Debt is exploding.** India's non-housing household debt as a percentage of income now exceeds that of the United States (US) and China. Nearly half of Indian families have taken personal loans, with 67 per cent having availed of them before age 30. For borrowers, nearly 40 per cent of annual income goes to debt servicing. This borrowing finances not productive assets but consumption – holidays, smartphones and, increasingly, essential expenses like education and healthcare. Between 5 and 10 per cent of retail borrowers are caught in a debt trap, using multiple loans to finance day-to-day living.[6]

## The Social Media Catastrophe

In 2016, Jio launched almost-free mobile data. Within months, hundreds of millions of Indians – particularly young men in their twenties – had unlimited Internet access for the first time. What followed was a psychological and financial catastrophe.

Anxiety and depression medications now grow twice as fast as other pharmaceutical categories.[7] Young Indians spend hours on social media, bombarded by curated images of wealth they cannot attain. The psychological toll has contributed to a doubling of suicide rates at IITs since 2015.[8]

But the damage isn't just psychological. As mentioned earlier, egged on by influencers promising easy money, 10 million Indians have plunged into F&O trading. Over three years (FY2022–FY2024), they've collectively lost ₹3 lakh crore ($33 billion) to institutional investors and brokers – more than the government spends on social welfare.[9] The typical F&O trader is a 30–40-year-old small-town male who loses a lakh annually in a country where per capita income is just over ₹2 lakh.

## The AI Disruption

As middle-class Indians gamble away their savings, the same AI tools glamourizing trading on social media are eliminating their jobs. The NITI (National Institution for Transforming India) Aayog estimates that by 2031, AI could reduce IT services sector employment from 8 million to 6 million, and customer experience jobs from 2.5 million to 1.8 million – a loss of 2 million middle-class jobs.[10]

The CEOs of India's most profitable companies tell us they're aiming to use AI to reduce salary bills by up to a third. Everything from human resources to underwriting to call centres will be automated. For a country where 8 million new graduates enter the workforce annually, watching existing jobs disappear is devastating.

## The Consumption Crisis

The combined impact of scarce jobs, falling real wages and soaring debt has jammed India's consumption engine. FMCG (fast-moving consumer goods) volume growth has slowed from 11 per cent 14 years ago in FY2011 to 3 per cent in FY2025. Car sales are actually shrinking. Consumer durables growth has collapsed from 11 per cent to 1–2 per cent.

This matters profoundly because consumption accounts for 60 per cent of India's GDP. Unlike export-driven East Asian economies, India's post-1991 growth model was built on middle-class consumption creating demand, which created jobs, which further created more consumption – a virtuous cycle. However, that cycle has broken.

## Structural Vulnerabilities

The crisis didn't emerge overnight. For decades, India has churned out graduates through a system focused on rote learning rather than creative thinking. The shift from descriptive to multiple-choice questions in IIT entrance exams has eroded quality. Only 43 per cent of graduates in India are employable, with most lacking problem-solving skills and creativity.[11]

Meanwhile, automation has been hollowing out middle-skill jobs since 2000. Research shows that routine cognitive work – clerical jobs, bookkeeping, sales – has been disappearing for the past 20 years.[12] A generation before AI arrived, middle-skill jobs were already losing share in the labour market.

The middle class's political disenfranchisement has left

these problems unaddressed. With just 40 million income-tax payers among 970 million voters, the middle class is politically insignificant. Politicians prioritize the poor for votes and the elite for funding, using middle-class tax payments to finance subsidies for others.

## The Silver Linings

Nevertheless, within this crisis lie opportunities. By late 2025, the government finally responded with ₹6.3 trillion (US $70 billion) in stimulus – income-tax cuts, GST (goods and services tax) reductions, interest rate cuts and a ban on online gambling. The Diwali 2025 shopping surge showed that when taxes fall, the middle class spends.[13]

More fundamentally, India is witnessing an entrepreneurial renaissance. New company registrations have surged, with a quarter-million Indians annually setting up formal businesses and over a million creating micro-enterprises. The gig economy already employs 8 million people with meaningful income. Artificial intelligence, while destroying jobs, is also creating opportunities in data labelling, bot training and tech R&D (research and development), with estimates suggesting 100 million new jobs possible by 2030.

The transition from secure employment to entrepreneurial uncertainty will be painful. But firms like NJ in Surat – which grew from two college graduates selling mutual funds in 1994 to India's largest private mutual fund distributor with ₹2.7 trillion (US $30 billion) in assets – show what's possible when entrepreneurial ambition meets India's vast market.

## The Road Ahead

This book is about change – a profoundly disruptive economic and social change rippling through 40 million middle-class Indians. The old model of university education leading to stable employment and leading to consumption-driven growth is breaking down. What replaces it will determine India's place in the twenty-first century.

The middle class must adapt, developing an entrepreneurial mindset focused on continuous learning rather than credentials and status. The government must cut the red tape strangling small businesses and rebalance taxation away from individuals and towards corporations. The labour market needs liberalization to match the sophistication of India's capital markets.

Most urgently, middle-class Indians must stop gambling their futures away and instead embrace disciplined financial planning – double engine compounding of both livelihoods and investments to weather longer, more uncertain careers and extended retirements.

India stands at a breakpoint. How it navigates this transition will echo through generations. The middle class's mutiny has begun – the question is whether it ends in rage or renaissance.

*Disclaimer: The authors, their families, Marcellus Investment Managers and the firm's clients may have a beneficial interest in the companies mentioned in this book. The material in this book is neither investment research nor investment advice.*

# Section I

# The Crisis of the Middle Class

# 1

# Who Are the Middle Class Anyway?

*The middle class is a section of society between the upper and lower classes. It is a group characterized by a certain income level, education and lifestyle. This class is essential for a country's growth and development, demand and job creation.**

## Mr Jha and Mr Kumar

Manoj Jha is a 50-year-old insurance professional in Patna who earns ₹6.5 lakh per year and struggles to make ends meet. He says, 'We have stopped travelling, going for movies or attending social functions.'[1]

According to Mr Jha, not only has the rise in prices of essential goods inflated his own household budget, but the rise in medical costs, and therefore insurance premiums, has also

* Shivani Giri and S. Subramanian, 'The Middle Class in India: Trends and Patterns', *Ecomomic & Political Weekly*, Vol. 60, No. 23, 7 June 2025, https://tinyurl.com/y6wd5ykr.

affected his livelihood. His clients are reluctant to renew their policies because of how expensive these have become.[2]

Kandivali is a thriving Mumbai suburb, 1,800 km away from Patna. The Kumars (names changed for anonymity) from Kandivali are clients of Marcellus. Vivek Kumar is a middle management employee at a leading private-sector bank in Mumbai. His wife, Anjali, worked in the underwriting team of a private-sector insurance firm in the same city. Their total net (i.e., post-tax) household income is ₹50 lakh per annum. Their savings comfortably exceed the minimum of ₹50 lakh required to become a Marcellus client. Yet, when the Kumars first reached out to us two years ago, they gave us the following numbers for their annual earnings and expenditure (Figure. 1.1):

**Income and Savings**

| **Income** | |
|---|---|
| Annual takehome of Mr. Kumar | ₹ 35 lakhs |
| Annual takehome of Ms. Kumar | ₹ 15 lakhs |
| **Total net Household Income** | **₹ 50 lakhs** |

| **Expenses** | |
|---|---|
| Home expenses | ₹ 12 lakhs |
| School fees & tuition etc | ₹ 8 lakhs |
| Home loan EMI | ₹ 12 lakhs |
| Pune flat investment EMI | ₹ 6 lakhs |
| Car loan EMI | ₹ 4 lakhs |
| Travel & vacations | ₹ 3 lakhs |
| **Total net Household Expense** | **₹ 45 lakhs** |

| **Total Annual Net SAVINGS** | **₹ 5 lakhs** |
|---|---|

**Investments**

| **Real Estate** | **₹ 2.05 cr** |
|---|---|
| Residential House | ₹ 1.30 cr |
| Plot | ₹ 75 lakhs |

| **Debt allocation** | **₹ 80 lakhs** |
|---|---|
| FD | ₹ 25 lakhs |
| PPF EPS | ₹ 35 lakhs |
| Debt mutual funds | ₹ 20 lakhs |

| **Indian equities** | **₹ 65 lakhs** |
|---|---|
| Small cap stocks | ₹ 30 lakhs |
| Flexi cap mutual funds | ₹ 20 lakhs |
| ESOP | ₹ 15 lakhs |

| **Total Assets** | **₹ 3.50 cr** |
|---|---|

**Figure 1.1:** The Kumars could barely save anything after accounting for all expenses

**Source:** Marcellus Investment Managers

Superficially, the Kumars' seemingly comfortable metropolitan lifestyle seems a world apart from the life that Manoj Jha lives in Patna. However, as we will discover in this book, the underlying drivers of the challenges both families face are very similar.

## The Butterfly Effect

Chaos theory became very popular when Saurabh Mukherjea was in high school in the 1980s. In particular, one facet of this theory – the Butterfly Effect – was a staple of school quizzes in that era.

The founder of chaos theory was a meteorologist and mathematician called Edward Lorenz (1917–2008). During the 1950s, Lorenz searched for a new means of predicting the weather, realizing that linear models were useless when it came to prediction.

In a now famous experiment to model the weather, he entered the initial condition as 0.506 instead of 0.506127. The result was surprising: a radically different prediction. From this, he deduced that a tiny change in the initial conditions had enormous long-term implications.

In 1963, he crystallized this idea in an award-winning paper titled 'Deterministic Nonperiodic Flow'. In it, Lorenz theorized that weather prediction models are inaccurate because a tiny change in the initial conditions can throw off the results. He then began to use the butterfly analogy to make the concept understandable to non-scientific audiences. He said that each wing flap of a butterfly represents tiny atmospheric changes. By itself, these wing flaps don't create typhoons. But as these small changes compound within complex systems, they can have massive implications. One such complex system is India's job market.

According to the GoI's income tax data for the financial year (FY) 2022–23, about 40 million Indians earn more than ₹5 lakh per annum. These Indians account for ~70 per cent of income tax paid in India. As we explain ahead, these 40 million Indians are the primary driver of non-agricultural employment and consumption in India. Electorally, these 40 million Indians are relatively insignificant given that India has nearly 970 million adults registered for voting. However, economically, this class of Indians are like butterflies. When these Indians start flapping their wings, they can generate a typhoon. How so?

To understand the full dynamic of how middle-class butterflies flapping their wings in India can cause a typhoon, consider the following waterfall of numbers:

- India has nearly **970 million** adults registered to vote.[3]
- Around half of India's working age population works in agriculture.[4] This implies that around **500 million** Indians are part of the non-agricultural workforce.
- Of these 500 million Indians, nearly 80 million are registered as members of the Employees' Provident Fund Organisation (EPFO).[5] Since EPFO membership is mandatory for Indian employees who work in firms with more than 20 employees, this number gives us visibility on part of the workforce that is in regular salaried employment. Around 50 million Indians work in firms with less than

20 employees. We also have to add to this around 15 million Indians who are either state government or central government employees.[6] Therefore, around **150 million** Indians appear to be in regular salaried employment.[7]

- Of these 150 million Indians in regular salaried employment, we can see from the income tax data that India has **40 million** income-tax payers earning more than ₹5 lakh to ₹1 crore per annum. As mentioned, these tax payers constitute 70 per cent of the government's income tax collection and account for a third of India's GST collections.[8] As you can infer from the preceding bullets, these income-tax payers are clearly very affluent people in the context of India's job market. However, in the context of the super-affluent class described in the next bullet point, this constituency falls bang in the middle of the income tax payment. Hence, this is our definition of the 'middle class', and it is this constituency's wings whose flapping can create typhoons.
- Approximately **2,30,000** income-tax filers in India earn in excess of ₹1 crore per annum.[9] This is India's 'elite' and, as described in the Indian media on a daily basis, they are flourishing. They have large investments in real estate and in the stock market. They also own the most profitable of the 1.5 million companies registered to pay corporate tax in India. In many cases, they are also related to the political and bureaucratic establishment which runs India. Entrepreneurial and hardworking, these tiny class of around 2,30,000 families (assuming one income tax filer per family) are the kings and queens of modern India.

Leaving aside income tax payments, why are the 40 million Indian families who make up the middle class so influential? Note that the above waterfall of numbers implies that there are around 350 million Indians who are part of the non-agricultural workforce but not in regular salaried employment (Figure 1.2). Let's call them 'working-class' Indians. So how do they earn a living? Answer: by working – directly or indirectly – for the middle class.

Firstly, most middle-class families in India tend to employ a cook, a cleaner and a driver. Let's call this 'direct employment' and let's apply a multiplier of 2.5 on this, i.e., thanks to each middle-class family, another 2.5 working class Indians gets to earn a living.[10] However, the story doesn't end there.

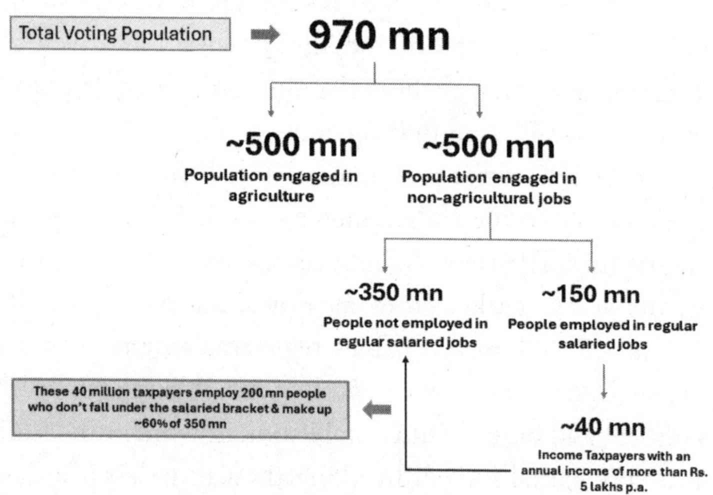


**Figure 1.2**: India's 40 million tax payers offer employment to another 200 million

**Source**: Marcellus Investment Managers

Each middle-class family spends money on shopping, driving, entertainment, travel, education, etc. Their spending pays the wages of millions of waiters, security guards, shop assistants, delivery agents, truck drivers and owners of unorganized businesses. Let's apply a multiplier of 2.5 to this as well and label this 'indirect employment'.

Therefore, the earnings of the 40 million middle-class families in India also pays for the livelihood of another 200 million people in India. In other words, the majority of working-class India (200 million out of 350 million) are dependent – directly or indirectly - on the middle class. Leaving aside the centrality of the middle class to the government's tax collections, the middle class is also the largest employment engine for the non-agricultural sector in India.

## Tightly Defining the Indian Middle Class

Consider that you had just five citizens in an economy. Their incomes (ranked from richest to poorest) in rupees were 78, 30, 25, 20 and 2 lakh per annum. In this fictional economy, who would you deem to be the middle class? Would it be the individual earning ₹25 lakh? Strictly speaking, the ₹25 lakh earner does sit in the middle of the income distribution, but he represents just one-fifth of the citizenry of this fictional economy, and just 16 per cent of the income generated in the economy.

We believe that a more apt definition of the middle class in this fictional economy would be the three individuals earning ₹30 lakh, ₹25 lakh and ₹20 lakh. Why so? Because not only do

**Table 1.1:** Income and Filer Distribution Using the Income Tax Department's Data (2023–24)

| Income Categories in ₹ | Midpoint of Income Categories (in ₹) | Number of Filers (in million) | Gross Total Income (₹ billion) | Average Income (in ₹) | Cumulative Number of Filers (in million) | Cumulative Total Income (in ₹ billion) |
|---|---|---|---|---|---|---|
| >150,000 and <= 2,00,000 | 1,75,000 | 1.4 | 241 | 1,76,192 | 1.4 | 241 |
| >2,00,000 and <=2,50,000 | 2,25,000 | 2.7 | 617 | 2,32,090 | 4.0 | 858 |
| >2,50,000 and <= 3,50,000 | 3,00,000 | 5.6 | 1,712 | 3,03,347 | 9.7 | 2,570 |
| >3,50,000 and <= 4,00,000 | 3,75,000 | 4.0 | 1,485 | 3,75,498 | 13.6 | 4,055 |
| >4,00,000 and <= 4,50,000 | 4,25,000 | 5.9 | 2,526 | 4,25,867 | 19.6 | 6,581 |
| >4,50,000 and <= 5,00,000 | 4,75,000 | 12.5 | 6,017 | 4,80,910 | 32.1 | 12,598 |
| **>5,00,000 and <= 5,50,000** | **5,25,000** | **6.1** | **3,176** | **5,21,805** | **38.2** | **15,774** |
| **>5,50,000 and <= 9,50,000** | **7,25,000** | **20.4** | **14,255** | **6,98,673** | **58.6** | **30,029** |
| **>9,50,000 and <= 10,00,000** | **9,75,000** | **1.1** | **1,034** | **9,74,659** | **59.6** | **31,062** |
| **>10,00,000 and <=15,00,000** | **12,50,000** | **6.2** | **7,507** | **12,05,338** | **65.8** | **38,569** |
| **>15,00,000 and <= 20,00,000** | **17,50,000** | **2.4** | **4,166** | **17,16,378** | **68.3** | **42,735** |
| **>20,00,000 and <= 25,00,000** | **22,50,000** | **1.2** | **2,654** | **22,24,606** | **69.5** | **45,389** |
| **>25,00,000 and <= 50,00,000** | **37,50,000** | **1.8** | **6,243** | **33,86,971** | **71.3** | **51,632** |
| **>50,00,000 and <= 1,00,00,000** | **75,00,000** | **0.5** | **3,475** | **67,50,528** | **71.8** | **55,107** |
| >1,00,00,000 and <=5,00,00,000 | 3,00,00,000 | 0.2 | 3,744 | 1,77,68,273 | 72.0 | 58,851 |

| Income Categories in ₹ | Midpoint of Income Categories (in ₹) | Number of Filers (in million) | Gross Total Income (₹ billion) | Average Income (in ₹) | Cumulative Number of Filers (in million) | Cumulative Total Income (in ₹ billion) |
|---|---|---|---|---|---|---|
| >5,00,00,000 and <=10,00,00,000 | 7,50,00,000 | 0.0 | 706 | 6,79,57,587 | 72.0 | 59,557 |
| >10,00,00,000 and <=25,00,00,000 | 17,50,00,000 | 0.0 | 660 | 14,86,75,056 | 72.0 | 60,217 |
| >25,00,00,000 and <=50,00,00,000 | 37,50,00,000 | 0.0 | 369 | 34,25,89,044 | 72.1 | 60,586 |
| >50,00,00,000 and <=100,00,00,000 | 75,00,00,000 | 0.0 | 303 | 69,40,27,523 | 72.1 | 60,888 |
| >100,00,00,000 and <=500,00,00,000 | 3,00,00,00,000 | 0.0 | 481 | 1,83,44,57,252 | 72.1 | 61,369 |
| >500,00,00,000 | – | 0.0 | 183 | 7,96,50,91,304 | 72.1 | 61,552 |

**Note:** Emboldened figures indicate our definition of the middle class. Average income for each category calculated as gross total income divided by the number of filers for that category; *CAGR: Compound annual growth rate

**Source:** Income Tax Department, Ministry of Finance

they sit in the middle of the income distribution (like the ₹25 lakh earner), they also a fulfil a more desirable criteria – they account for roughly half the income generated in this fictional economy (75/155 = 48 per cent).

For the analysis of the middle class to be relevant for the broader economy, we believe two criteria have to be fulfilled:

- The middle class has to sit in the middle of the income distribution, and
- They should account for at least half the income earned in the country (which allows them to be a critical driver of the economy).

Linking this to our definition of the Indian middle class, **53 per cent of the Indian population that files non-negative tax returns (as of 2023–24) and earns between ₹5 lakh and ₹1 crore per annum** (see Table 1.1). But how does our definition of the middle class compare with that of others?

Hundreds of academics and marketing professionals have tried to arrive at who *exactly* is the middle class in India. In fact, a flourishing cottage industry specializes in this very subject. For example, the National Council of Applied Economic Research (NCAER) defines middle-class households as those earning between ₹5 lakh and ₹ 30 lakh per year.[11]

In recent years, the most authoritative analysis on this subject has come from Rama Bijapurkar. Her book, *Lilliput Land: How Small Is Driving India's Mega Consumption Story* (2024), includes a long and data-rich discussion on this issue. Bijapurkar looks at GDP divided into four equal categories, or quartiles. According to the World Bank's methodology:

- 10 per cent of Indian households fall into the global rich category,
- 20 per cent of households fall into the global upper middle income,
- 20–30 per cent of households fall into the global middle income, and
- 40–50 per cent of households fall into the global low income.

The top 10 per cent of all households (31 million in number) account for 36 per cent of India's income, just a bit more than a quarter of Indian households' routine expenditure and two-thirds of the total surplus income (see Table 1.2). If we take the Indian middle class to be those whom the World Bank's methodology has defined as 'Upper Middle' and 'Middle', then the annual per capita income of the middle class would span from ₹3 lakh to around ₹20 lakh (see Table 1.3).

**Table 1.2**: Income, Expenditure and Surplus Income Share of Each Group (2021–22)

| % Share of All Indian Households | | | | |
|---|---|---|---|---|
| **World Bank–Defined Global Income Class** | **Income Share** | **Expenditure Share** | **Surplus Income Share** | **Million Households** |
| Rich | 36 | 27 | 68 | 31 |
| Upper Middle | 31 | 30 | 32 | 62 |
| Middle | 17 | 19 | 8 | 62 |
| Lower | 17 | 23 | -8 | 154 |

**Note:** All India nominal GDP taken as $3.38 trillion; component of all India GDP resident in each income group

**Source**: Rama Bijapurkar, *Lilliput Land: How Small Is Driving India's Mega Consumption Story*, Penguin, 2024.

**Table 1.3**: Household Income Levels Based on GDP for Each Global Income Class (2021–22, Nominal)

| Size and Average Income of Each Income Class Based on GDP | | | |
|---|---|---|---|
| World Bank–Defined Global Income Class | % of Households | Million Households | Average Household Income (₹ lakh/year) |
| Rich | 10 | 31 | 27 |
| Upper Middle | 20 | 62 | 12 |
| Middle | 30 | 92 | 6 |
| Lower | 40 | 123 | 2 |

**Source**: Rama Bijapurkar, *Lilliput Land: How Small Is Driving India's Mega Consumption Story*, Penguin, 2024.

While we agree with Ms Bijapurkar's analysis of where middle-class India lies on the spectrum, and how to identify them, we believe that this methodology also needs to be applied to data which is available on an annual basis, so that we can track the evolution of the middle class over time. With this in mind, we decided to use the income-tax filers' data reported by the Income Tax Department, Ministry of Finance, each year. Even though this data is not all-encompassing – as the number of people earning an income is unfortunately far higher than the number of people who file returns – this is the closest proxy for incomes that we could find for this exercise.

We then segmented India's income tax payers into quintiles (five equal segments) using three different methods: (1) quintiles using the number of income-tax filers in the database, (2) quintiles using gross total income as reported by the income tax filers and (3) quintiles using percentile ranks on gross total income (see Table 1.4).

**Table 1.4**: Quintiles Made Using Income Tax Filing Data (2023–24)

| Quintiles | Using Number of Income Tax Filers (Method 1) | | Using Income (Method 2) | | Using Percentile Rank of Income (Method 3) | |
|---|---|---|---|---|---|---|
| | Lower Bound of Annual Income | Upper Bound of Annual Income | Lower Bound of Annual Income | Upper Bound of Annual Income | Lower Bound of Annual Income | Upper Bound of Annual Income |
| Q1 | More than 0 | Less than or equal to ₹3.5 lakh | More than 0 | Less than or equal to ₹5 lakh | More than 0 | Less than or equal to ₹4 lakh |
| Q2 | More than ₹3.5 lakh | Less than or equal to ₹4.5 lakh | More than ₹5 lakh | Less than or equal to ₹9.5 lakh | More than ₹4 lakh | Less than or equal to ₹9.5 lakh |
| Q3 | More than ₹4.5 lakh | Less than or equal to ₹5.5 lakh | More than ₹9.5 lakh | Less than or equal to ₹25 lakh | More than ₹9.5 lakh | Less than or equal to ₹25 lakh |
| Q4 | More than ₹5.5 lakh | Less than or equal to ₹9.5 lakh | More than ₹25 lakh | Less than or equal to ₹50 crore | More than ₹25 lakh | Less than or equal to ₹10 crore |
| Q5 | More than ₹9.5 lakh | – | More than ₹50 crore | - | More than ₹10 crore | - |

**Source:** Income Tax Department, Ministry of Finance

The most interesting insight from Table 1.4 is the fact that the distribution of incomes and number of filers are both heavily skewed. Two-thirds of the return filers (66 per cent) sit between the ₹5 lakh to ₹25 lakh income category, with the highest income categories consisting of barely any filers (as would be expected in one of the fifty poorest nations in the world if measured by per capita income).

As a result, if we create quintiles based on the number of filers (Method 1) then most of them are concentrated in Q1–Q4, leaving a long tail of (very rich) filers clubbed into Q5 or the top 20 per cent. However, Q5 here also includes the uber rich, i.e., those earning beyond ₹100 crore per annum. As a result, making quintiles using the number of filers (Method 1) does not yield much benefit to our analysis. Simply put, in a poor country, just looking at the number of income tax filers does not get you very far if you want to understand where the real economic action lies.

Quintiles made using gross income – our Method 2 – solves this issue to some extent, as relatively more weight is given to the categories of income beyond ₹9.5 lakh (due to the size of the income reported therein). This method for quintiles works fine until we reach the threshold of ₹25 lakh. Beyond this, the income distribution gets further skewed, with the amount of income reported under each category increasing at a far slower pace from one category to the next, leading to the clubbing of incomes beginning from ₹25 lakh to ₹50 crore under Q4.

Due to this skewed natured of this data, any kind of analysis that includes Q4 becomes distorted, and analysing absolute values in this regard also becomes meaningless. This is where the percentile ranking – Method 3 – comes in handy. This method transforms the data into a relative scale (between 0 and 100), especially to understand the underlying distribution. The ranks by themselves help create far more 'equal' splits of the data into five parts. This is what the final two columns of the previous table show. However, even with this treatment, the range for Q4 is quite large – from ₹25 lakh to ₹10 crore – but it is still smaller than the range ₹25 lakh to ₹50 crore for Method 2.

Now, coming back to the question of what constitutes the middle class, we try to arrive at the answer using the data and methods explained above. We do this by clubbing Q2, Q3 and Q4 together in order to put the middle class in the absolute middle of the distribution, and also in order to ensure that the majority of the income generated in the economy is being captured. Under the two usable methods explained above (Methods 2 and 3), we get to the percentage of filers, percentage of total income and weighted average income for this category (as shown in Table 1.5). Under Method 2, Q2–4 span income tax filers earning ₹5 lakh to ₹50 crore. They account for 78 per cent of the income generated and for 53 per cent of the filers, thus satisfying our definitional criteria.

However, there is one problem with defining the middle class as those earning as much as ₹50 crore per annum. As we can see in Table 1.4, even using Method 3, Q4 extends all the way to the seventy-eighth percentile of the income tax paying population. The fact that the upper bound is extending to ₹10 crore of annual income for middle-class India is a little hard to digest.

**Table 1.5:** Definition of Indian Middle Class Using Income Tax Department's Data

| Quintile Groups | Gross Total Income (₹ billion) | | | Number of Income Tax Filers (₹ million) | | | Weighted Average Income (₹) | | |
|---|---|---|---|---|---|---|---|---|---|
| | Using Filers | Using Income | Using Percentile Rank | Using Filers | Using Income | Using Percentile Rank | Using Filers | Using Income | Using Percentile Rank |
| Q2+Q3+Q4 | 27,549 | 47,988 | 55,502 | 48.9 | 40.0 | 58.4 | 6,14,985 | 7,64,282 | 6,83,433 |
| As a % of total | 44% | 78% | 90% | 65% | 53% | 78% | | | |

***Note:*** Weighted average income calculated using weights derived from number of filers in each category of income multiplied by corresponding average income (which is simply gross total income/number of filers)

**Source:** Marcellus Investment Managers, using information from Income Tax Department, Ministry of Finance; Rama Bijapurkar, *Lilliput Land: How Small Is Driving India's Mega Consumption Story*, Penguin, 2024.

Therefore, we need to make the upper bound more reasonable than ₹50 crore while not relenting on the conditions that define middle class in India. In other words, they should be literally in the middle of the income distribution and account for bulk of the representative data.

Since the number of income tax filers earning more than ₹1 crore but less than ₹50 crore is just 227k, we decided to cap the upper bound of the middle-class category at ₹1 crore of income. To be clear, our decision to drop the upper bound from ₹50 crore to ₹1 crore does not exclude a significant number of income tax filers because India has so few high-earning tax payers.

**Our definition of the middle class is therefore those earning between ₹5 lakh to ₹1 crore per annum**. These bounds contain 53 per cent of India's income tax filers and ~70 per cent of the income earned by all filers. In the chapters that follow, we follow the economic fortunes of this stratum of Indian society, which pays the bulks of its income taxes and is the main driver of consumption (which in turn accounts for 60 per cent of economic activity in the country).

Our definition is different than the more traditional definitions of the Indian middle class, which range from ₹5 lakh of annual income as the lower bound and around ₹25 lakh as the upper bound. Such a definition would encompass majority of filers, but it wouldn't account for majority of the income generated by India's income tax filers (thus defeating the whole purpose of analysing the fluctuating fortunes of this segment of India's economy).

## Returning to Mr Jha and Mr Kumar...

At the beginning of the chapter, we highlighted the financial struggles of Manoj Jha, the 50-year-old insurance professional in Patna who earns ₹6.5 lakh per year, and the Kumars from Kandivali (Mumbai) who are upwardly mobile financial services professionals pulling in ₹50 lakh per annum. Both are middle class on the basis of our definition. Moreover, as can be seen in Table 1.6, like other Indians earning between ₹5 lakh to ₹1 crore, their incomes have stagnated in nominal terms over the past decade (which means that after adjusting for inflation, their real incomes have shrunk over the past decade).

In the chapters that follow, we will see how five common sets of forces are making things difficult for all sections of the middle class. First, a seemingly endless supply of graduates is undermining the bargaining power of these professionals in the job market (Chapters 2 and 4). Second, technology is undermining the value of such professionals by replicating much of what they do but at a fraction of their cost (Chapter 3). Third, the rapid rise in the cost of living is all but ensuring that in real terms – after adjusting for inflation – their income barely grows (Chapter 5). Fourth, professionals such as these are taking on excessive debt to cope with the financial and social pressures that they are facing (Chapters 6 and 7). Fifth, social media is creating angst among such professionals as they see – on social media, if not in the real world – others in their peer group seemingly pulling away and living the good life (Chapter 8).

**Table 1.6:** Growth in Average Income over FY2014–24 for Each Category of Income Tax Filer

| Income Categories (in ₹) | Midpoint of Income Categories (in ₹) | Number of Filers (in million) | Gross Total Income (in ₹ billion) | Average Income (in ₹) | Cumulative Number of Filers (in million) | Cumulative Total Income (in ₹ billion) | 10Y CAGR in Avg Income |
|---|---|---|---|---|---|---|---|
| >150,000 and <= 2,00,000 | 1,75,000 | 1.4 | 241 | 1,76,192 | 1.4 | 241 | 7.8% |
| >2,00,000 and <=2,50,000 | 2,25,000 | 2.7 | 617 | 2,32,090 | 4.0 | 858 | 2.2% |
| >2,50,000 and <= 3,50,000 | 3,00,000 | 5.6 | 1,712 | 3,03,347 | 9.7 | 2,570 | 3.2% |
| >3,50,000 and <= 4,00,000 | 3,75,000 | 4.0 | 1,485 | 3,75,498 | 13.6 | 4,055 | 2.4% |
| >4,00,000 and <= 4,50,000 | 4,25,000 | 5.9 | 2,526 | 4,25,867 | 19.6 | 6,581 | 1.3% |
| >4,50,000 and <= 5,00,000 | 4,75,000 | 12.5 | 6,017 | 4,80,910 | 32.1 | 12,598 | 1.3% |
| **>5,00,000 and <= 5,50,000** | **5,25,000** | **6.1** | **3,176** | **5,21,805** | **38.2** | **15,774** | **0.9%** |
| **>5,50,000 and <= 9,50,000** | **7,25,000** | **20.4** | **14,255** | **6,98,673** | **58.6** | **30,029** | **2.9%** |
| **>9,50,000 and <= 10,00,000** | **9,75,000** | **1.1** | **1,034** | **9,74,659** | **59.6** | **31,062** | **3.4%** |
| **>10,00,000 and <=15,00,000** | **12,50,000** | **6.2** | **7,507** | **12,05,338** | **65.8** | **38,569** | **2.1%** |
| **>15,00,000 and <= 20,00,000** | **17,50,000** | **2.4** | **4,166** | **17,16,378** | **68.3** | **42,735** | **3.6%** |
| **>20,00,000 and <= 25,00,000** | **22,50,000** | **1.2** | **2,654** | **22,24,606** | **69.5** | **45,389** | **2.6%** |
| **>25,00,000 and <= 50,00,000** | **37,50,000** | **1.8** | **6,243** | **33,86,971** | **71.3** | **51,632** | **4.3%** |
| **>50,00,000 and <= 1,00,00,000** | **75,00,000** | **0.5** | **3,475** | **67,50,528** | **71.8** | **55,107** | **7.3%** |
| >1,00,00,000 and <=5,00,00,000 | 3,00,00,000 | 0.2 | 3,744 | 1,77,68,273 | 72.0 | 58,851 | 10.1% |
| >5,00,00,000 and <=10,00,00,000 | 7,50,00,000 | 0.0 | 706 | 6,79,57,587 | 72.0 | 59,557 | 14.2% |

| Income Categories (in ₹) | Midpoint of Income Categories (in ₹) | Number of Filers (in million) | Gross Total Income (in ₹ billion) | Average Income (in ₹) | Cumulative Number of Filers (in million) | Cumulative Total Income (in ₹ billion) | 10Y CAGR in Avg Income |
|---|---|---|---|---|---|---|---|
| >10,00,00,000 and <=25,00,00,000 | 17,50,00,000 | 0.0 | 660 | 14,86,75,056 | 72.0 | 60,217 | 8.3% |
| >25,00,00,000 and <=50,00,00,000 | 37,50,00,000 | 0.0 | 369 | 34,25,89,044 | 72.1 | 60,586 | 8.9% |
| >50,00,00,000 and <=100,00,00,000 | 75,00,00,000 | 0.0 | 303 | 69,40,27,523 | 72.1 | 60,888 | 7.4% |
| >100,00,00,000 and <=500,00,00,000 | 3,00,00,00,000 | 0.0 | 481 | 1,83,44,57,252 | 72.1 | 61,369 | 11.2% |
| >500,00,00,000 | – | 0.0 | 183 | 7,96,50,91,304 | 72.1 | 61,552 | 17.6% |
| >5,00,00,00,000 | >5,00,00,00,000 | 0.0 | 6,71,00,00,000 | 7,96,50,91,304 | 1.7% | | |

**Note:** Emboldened figures indicate our definition of the middle class. Average income for each category calculated as gross total income divided by the number of filers for that category; *CAGR: Compound annual growth rate

**Source:** Income Tax Department, Ministry of Finance

# 2

# Education: No Longer a Fail-Safe Option

*Around 75 per cent of IIT Bombay students secured jobs this year, a drop from last year's 78 per cent, and the minimum wage has been cut from ₹6 lakh to ₹4 lakh. Nationwide, the situation is more severe, with over 8,000 out of 21,500 IIT graduates remaining unemployed, a significant increase from the previous year's figures.**

The middle class is often defined by its attitude towards education and employment – in their belief that a university degree is the gateway to prosperity and social mobility. Yet, in contemporary India, a disturbing paradox has emerged: While the country produces more graduates than ever before, they are less able to find work or see meaningful rises in income.

India churns out over 8 million graduates annually, yet becoming a graduate now actively reduces both your earnings

* 'IITs Witness Drop in Placement Rate and Minimum Pay, 8,000 IITians Remain Unemployed', *APAC Media*, 5 September 2024, https://tinyurl.com/4mk3bun2.

and your chances of employment. The unemployment rate for graduates stands at 29.1 per cent – nine times higher than for those who cannot read or write. Even 90 per cent of the latest batch of engineering graduates failed to secure jobs.[1] As mentioned earlier, in elite IIT Bombay, minimum salaries of graduates passing out have been slashed from ₹6 lakh to ₹4 lakh, while thousands of IIT graduates nationwide remain unemployed.[2]

This chapter examines how India became a nation where education undermines employment prospects – a perfect storm of oversupply, deteriorating quality, skills mismatches, sectoral slowdowns and relentless automation threatening the very foundation of middle-class aspirations.

## Education: A Battlefield with Few Victors

Released in 2025, *Homebound* is a Hindi film written and directed by Neeraj Ghaywan, based on a *New York Times* article written by Basharat Peer in 2020. Peer's article in turn was about the heartbreaking true story of two friends, both factory workers in Surat (Gujarat), caught in the Covid-19 lockdown of 2020.[3] *Homebound* stars Ishaan Khatter, Vishal Jethwa and Janhvi Kapoor. It follows two childhood friends who attempt to pass the police constable exams. The film was selected as the Indian entry for the 'Best International Feature Film' for the ninety-eighth Academy Awards, i.e., the Oscars 2026.

Saurabh's favourite scene is the train journey where *Homebound*'s protagonists – Shoiab (Khatter) and Chandan (Jethwa) – travel from their native village to a major city in northern India to appear for the police constable exams in their state (police constable recruitment is, by and large, a 'state' subject in India and is, therefore, managed by state governments). During that train journey, we learn from Shoaib and Chandan about the unbelievable level of competition for these police constable jobs that pay around ₹6 lakh per annum, almost 3x India's per capita income.[4]

We also learn from the protagonists that millions of Indians sit for these exams each year for a few thousand vacancies. For example, in the state of Uttar Pradesh (UP), in August 2024, 48 lakh (4.8 million) aspirants competed for just 60,224 constable vacancies, i.e., 1 job for every 80 aspirants. The director general of police for UP 'visited several exam centres, monitored with drones and equipped with CCTV cameras and mobile jammers to prevent unauthorised communication. To ensure a cheating-free environment, magistrates were appointed at each centre. Over 2,100 buses of UPSRTC [UP State Road Transport Corporation] were deployed for ferrying students to exam centres.'[5]

In the movie, as Shoaib and Chandan stand in the corridor of a packed express train transporting aspirants to the exam centre, Chandan looks across the sea of young men and women swotting feverishly for the exams and asks Shoaib a rhetorical question that sums up the life of many young Indians: '*Exam deney ja rahein ya jung ladney ja rahein hain* (Are we going to give an exam or are we going to fight a war)?'

While Bollywood movies tend to dramatize the challenges of middle-class life in India, the situation for most of India's graduates is similar to the challenges that Shoaib and Chandan face. In fact, the overwhelming majority of India's freshly minted graduates are not getting jobs. In October 2024, as mentioned earlier, about **90 per cent of the latest batch of engineering graduates did not get jobs.**[6]

The Parliamentary Standing Committee on Education, in its March 2025 report, cited data to note that 'there is an unusual decline in placements in IITs and IIITs between 2021–22 and 2023–24'.[7] A TeamLease report from October 2024 estimated that only 10 per cent of engineering graduates would secure jobs that year.[8] Another survey, published in March 2025, revealed that 83 per cent of engineering graduates have no jobs.[9]

More worryingly, even India's most elite universities – the ones that millions of students spend years trying to enter – are being afflicted by the unemployment virus as evidenced by the newsclip cited at the beginning of the chapter regarding unemployment among IIT graduates. To be specific, over 8,000 out of 21,500 IIT graduates remained unemployed, which was a major increase from the previous year's (2023's) figures.[10]

Part of the challenge appears to be the traditional attitudes that push the Indian middle class towards first pursuing undergraduate education and then towards an office job. While none of the authors are sociologists, all three of them have grown up in households where the *dharma* was to become a graduate and then an office worker; anything else would be seen as deviant behaviour. When Sapana Bhavsar was in Class X, she vividly remembers her mother silently wishing, '*Mere teeno bacche doctor banenge* (All three of my kids will become doctors).'

The default level of ambition and aspiration in an Indian home is that the children will graduate from an elite university and make their parents proud. This aspiration is firmly embedded in the minds of Indian students by the time they enter their teens. Then begins the endless hours of work – much of it involving rote learning and regurgitation of the study material in the exams – that defines the most formative years for most students (including all three of the authors of this book).

All this pent-up family ambition builds an aspirational mirage of employment and success that is disconnected from the reality of what sort of jobs are available and what sort of skills are required in the marketplace. In fact, a plethora of economic data suggests that it is a *really* bad time to be a graduate in India.

## No Country for Graduates

There are two dimensions along which graduates appear to be severely disadvantaged relative to others in the Indian workforce: the first is earnings and the second is the likelihood of gainful employment.

Rama Bijapurkar's *Lilliput Land* contains data on just how significantly graduation reduces one's earnings profile in India. In figure after figure (see, for example, the row titled 'Graduate' in Table 2.1), Ms Bijapurkar teases out data which shows, among other things, how graduates suffer in comparison to those who have simply passed their Class XII exams. Ms Bijapurkar notes in her book that 'even in the richest 10 per cent of households [...] **one-third only have graduate or above degrees**, another third have stopped studying after school finals and a quarter have very little schooling.'[11]

**Table 2.1**: Graduates are Underrepresented in the Richest 40 per cent of Indian Households

| **% of Each Quintile with CWE (Chief Wage Earner) at Each Education Level** | | |
|---|---|---|
| **Education Level of CWE** | **Richest 20% (Q5)** | **Next 20% (Q4)** |
| Low or no literacy | 11 | 18 |
| Some schooling | 23 | 37 |
| **Finished schooling (class 10/11/12)** | **37** | **36** |
| Technical/ diploma | 9 | 2 |
| **Graduate** | **23** | 7 |
| Postgraduate and professional | 6 | 1 |
| Total | 100 | 100 |

**Source**: ICE360° data; table taken from Rama Bijapurkar, *Lilliput Land: How Small Is Driving India's Mega Consumption Story*, Penguin, 2024.

Moving from earnings to the probability of getting a job, multiple layers of data now show that becoming a graduate actually reduces one's employment prospects (see Figure 2.1). 'The jobless rate for graduates was 29.1 per cent, almost nine times higher than the 3.4 per cent for those who can't read or write, a new ILO report on India's labor market showed. The unemployment rate for young people with secondary or higher education was six times higher at 18.4 per cent.'[12]

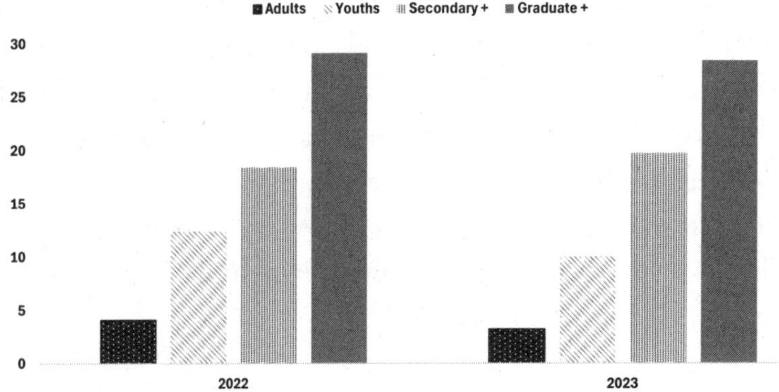


**Figure 2.1**: Unemployment climbs with education level in India

**Source**: Marcellus Investment Managers; Periodic Labour Force Survey and India Employment Report 2024

Why does university education reduce both the earnings of graduates and their probability of getting a job? We can see five sets of forces at play, each of which is squeezing the earnings and employment prospects of Indian graduates. While most of these forces have been at play over several decades, we point to evidence (in the sub-sections that follow) that the intensity of adversity has ramped up over the past 10–20 years.

## Excess Supply of Graduates

For several decades now, India has churned out millions of graduates each year. However, since demographically the country is still getting younger, these numbers are continuing to rise. For example, a record number of students – 1.2 million – appeared for the IIT joint entrance exams in January 2024.[13] Unsurprisingly, therefore, the Indian university system is producing graduates in ever larger numbers. Although, tellingly, there is no consensus on how many graduates India produces each year, relying on the All India Survey on Higher Education (AISHE) – the most exhaustive source of data for higher education in India – we reckon that more than 8 million students graduate out of India's university system each year.[14] The result is that the graduate pool in India is burgeoning rapidly, as shown in Figure 2.2.

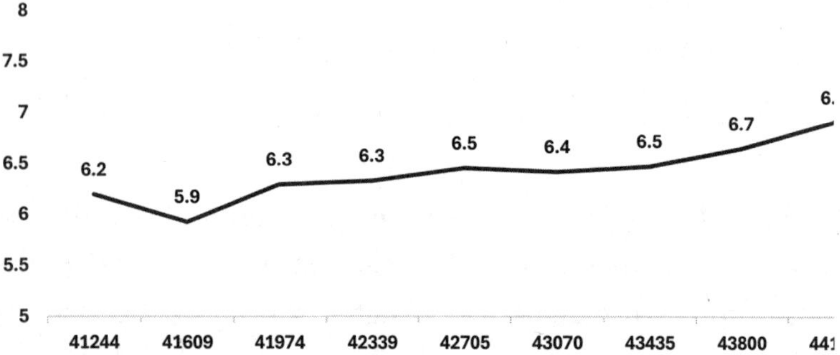


**Figure 2.2**: India's number of graduates has grown by 25 per cent+ in the last nine years

**Note:** Values in millions; data pertains to enrolment in both government and private colleges

**Source**: Marcellus Investment Managers, data based on surveys conducted by AISHE each year

However, demographics aside, there is another factor that has pushed up the supply of graduates – entry into the university education system appears to have been made easier over the past couple of decades. Whilst the administrators and leaders who run India's education system have sought to democratize access to higher education for all the right reasons, as explained ahead, not only have their efforts jacked up the supply of graduates (thus allowing employers to squeeze their wages), but have also reduced the quality of the graduates.

Some of us in Marcellus have been recruiting Indian graduates fresh out of university for over two decades. Over the past decade, we have seen a sharp dip in the quality of graduates emerging from India's universities, including from the elite IITs and IIMs. Speaking to friends in other firms, we find that the situation is similar across a range of industries. Recruiters in pharma, FMCG and IT Services are just as bewildered about how the quality of Indian graduates has deteriorated so sharply.

As far back as 2011, doyens of the Indian software industry, such as N.R. Narayana Murthy, were highlighting the steady decline in the quality of students emerging from India's elite institutions of higher learning such as the IITs. An important factor behind this decline, say some of our colleagues in Marcellus, was the change in the format of the IIT entrance exams. Chukka Ramaiah – a member of the Legislative Council of Telangana and an eminent educationist, with nearly three decades of experience of training IIT aspirants – says that before the turn of the century, students had to attempt descriptive questions, where the method in which they attempted a question was also examined alongside the answers. This resulted in the IITs enrolling students with better understanding and creative thought process.

> But after 2000 the exam pattern was changed and multiple-choice questions were introduced where it was important for a

> student to come up with a correct answer rather than knowing the process of solving the given problem ... IITs are not engineering colleges but are educational institutions where a student is expected to gain skills rather than just information. But present-day students who go to IITs are only going on the basis of the rote knowledge.[15]

Effectively, what Mr Murthy and Mr Ramaiah are highlighting is that in an age where technologies are changing very frequently, the need for creativity and the ability to adapt while also contributing qualitatively towards new developments is crucial. The selection process of India's best universities has been redesigned in such a way that militates against these aspects of intelligence and ability.

A range of engineering graduates who have seen India's Joint Entrance Examination system change over the past 25 years agree that the system stopped working long ago – instead of measuring aptitude, it began measuring the ability to cram.

## Poor Skilling and Training of Graduates

There is growing evidence that with each passing decade, the quality of skilling and training imparted to Indian graduates is deteriorating. Mercer Mettl's report – 'India's Graduate Skill Index 2025' – echoes N.R. Narayana Murthy's concerns about how Indian graduates increasingly lack the creative thinking and problem-solving skills that employers need: 'There was an overall drop in the employability of Indian graduates from 44.3% in 2023 to 42.6% in 2024. The drop is particularly driven by non-technical skills.'[16] The same report says that 60 per cent of Indian graduates in commerce and finance are not employable due to outdated curricula that do not include real-world financial analysis, digital banking or fintech skills.

TeamLease, the recruitment and staffing firm, has published multiple reports highlighting the employability challenge of Indian graduates in the wake of what it calls 'a massive disconnect between academic training and industry training'. The recruitment firm says that 'only 10% of the 15 lakh engineers' expected to graduate this year will find jobs. This is how A.R. Ramesh, the CEO of TeamLease Degree Apprenticeship, breaks down the drivers of unemployability for Indian graduates: 'To break it down, India produces approximately 1.5 million engineering graduates each year. While 60% of them actively seek employment, only 45% meet industry standards in terms of skill readiness.' Now, with the additional demand-supply gap created by the rise of AI and advanced technology skills, this figure drops further to around 10–15%' (Table 2.2).[17]

Ramesh further explains,

> [The] issue isn't necessarily the lack of jobs but rather a mismatch in expectations and skill sets. Essentially, while jobs exist, they aren't accessible to the majority of graduates due to their inability to meet the evolving demands of the tech-driven market … A key challenge is the misalignment between academic curricula and industry expectation … the training these students receive is often outdated …[18]

**Table 2.2**: Breakdown of Employability and Skills Gap Data

| Category | Percentage/Rate |
|---|---|
| Employability rate among graduates | 60% |
| Industry-standard meeting rate | 45% |
| Skills gap in AI and new technology | 25–30% |
| Expected employment rate (2024) | 10–15% |

**Source**: TeamLease survey as quoted in 'Pursuing Engineering Once a Fad, Now a Dilemma: Only 10 Percent of 15 Lakh Graduates Likely to Land Jobs This Year', *The Times of India*, 29 October 2024.

A report by the All-India Council for Technical Education (AICTE) found that only 45 per cent of engineering graduates were employable in 2023, despite India producing nearly 1.5 million engineers annually.[19] Major industries, especially in the IT and manufacturing sectors, report that graduates lack critical problem-solving and technical skills, forcing companies to invest in extensive training programmes before hiring new employees. In 2022, Infosys and TCS – two of India's largest IT firms – had to launch dedicated training programmes for fresh graduates because most lacked fundamental coding and analytical abilities. And yet, in spite of launching dedicated training programmes to teach the basics to graduates, Infosys is having a hard time getting the talent that it needs, as evidenced by this article in *The Ken*, titled 'Infosys: The Job That Millions of India's Engineering Grads Took for Granted Is Now a Tough Sell':

> Picture Infosys during recruitment season [...] Of the 5,000 graduates offered jobs in 2022 – the majority of whose joining was delayed by two years – 755 have been laid off so far for

> failing to clear tests. [...] The latest layoffs were two weeks ago. For the rest, the latest Java test was on 13 May, and the database management systems test will be on 20 May. The assessments this time were tougher than usual, said five trainees and ex-employees The Ken spoke to. The threshold for passing was raised from 50% to 65%. On top of this, new material was added, and the number of questions was increased.[20]

## Skills Mismatch: The Semiconductor Industry as a Case Study

Leaving aside sub-par skilling in India's universities, a separate dimension of the problem is that India's graduates are not acquiring the skills that India's employers are seeking. A socialist education system is not producing what a capitalist economy needs.

According to a Jefferies Report published in March 2025, India has a strong engineering talent pool and houses ~20 per cent of the world's semiconductor design workforce. However, the country still needs to develop the specific skill sets required for chip manufacturing and testing.[21]

To be specific, the semiconductor industry in India is expected to generate approximately 1 million jobs in India by 2026, with significant opportunities in chip fabrication, assembly, testing, marking, packaging and related areas. Some of the key jobs in the semiconductor industry are process integration engineer, semiconductor wafer inspector, technical specialist, preventative maintenance technician, design engineer, process engineer and quality control specialist.[22]

As of 2022, India had about 1,25,000 semiconductor design engineers, accounting for approximately 19 per cent of the global design engineering workforce. By 2027, India is projected to need between 2,50,000 to 3,00,000 skilled professionals in the semiconductor sector, encompassing roles in R&D, design, manufacturing and advanced packaging.[23]

This widening gap between the demand for skilled semiconductor professionals and the current – highly limited – supply is the main stumbling block for India's semiconductor industry. 'To reach the target of having 1 million skilled employees by 2026 for India to become the semiconductor hub, India will need to upskill 5,00,000 people every year,' says NLB Services CEO Sachin Alug.[24]

India produces over 1.5 million engineering graduates annually. However, only a fraction are industry-ready for semiconductor roles, primarily due to gaps in specialized training and practical exposure.[25] One of the reasons for this is that most engineering students in India are focused on data science or AI and machine learning because that's where they think the jobs are. As a result, it is difficult to get Indian engineering students interested in electrical engineering, which is the key underlying educational grounding needed for semiconductor talent.[26]

So, even though semiconductor design engineers command salaries north of ₹1 crore per annum by the time they have five or more years of work experience under their belt – and even though global giants like Qualcomm and Intel have large and growing offices in India – India struggles to train semiconductor engineers even as millions of engineering graduates sit idle.

## The IT Sector Slowdown

With 8 million employees, India's tech sector is the largest recruiter of graduates in the country. [27] In the first two decades of the twenty-first century, as the Indian tech sector grew by around 15 per cent per annum, the sector hired in excess of a million graduates a year. As a result, Indian IT companies enjoyed a dominant position, as the most sought-after employers, in the market for Indian talent. Most of the recruitment drives of Indian firms in the first two decades of the twenty-first century attracted engineering graduates from all streams. This reality, coupled with decades of success (good jobs, good pay, opportunities to work in the Western world) had already persuaded India's youth to forget about actually becoming an engineer and building, say, a factory or a bridge or discovering a new molecule. The apex of the Indian social pyramid was occupied by parents who could say, 'My child is a computer science engineer and works in Silicon Valley.' Beyond social pride and beyond success in the job market, such a, career involving studying engineering but then becoming an IT worker, boosted one's prospects in the marriage market.

As a result, the core engineering jobs took a backseat and those pursuing these jobs as careers did not consider themselves to be part of the elite. Roles that required superior hand-eye-motor coordination, precision engineering or open-ended thinking skills (such as those crucial for semiconductor design or robotics) were deprioritized. Since the engineering students in the universities are interested in little else other than IT jobs, the universities too seem to have given up trying to do much else other than provide credentials. Mercer Mettl's report on India's Graduate Skill Index 2025 says that 70 per cent of the current Indian college students aspire to join IT companies.[28]

However, 2023 onwards, hiring in the Indian tech sector slowed down dramatically. As we discuss in more detail in Chapters 3 and 4, the Fortune 500 clients of the Indian IT Services firms are increasingly using AI to reduce the amount of work they outsource to third-party providers. In turn, the Indian IT Services firms are also using AI to reduce the number of people they hire. Furthermore, in the post Covid-19 era, the

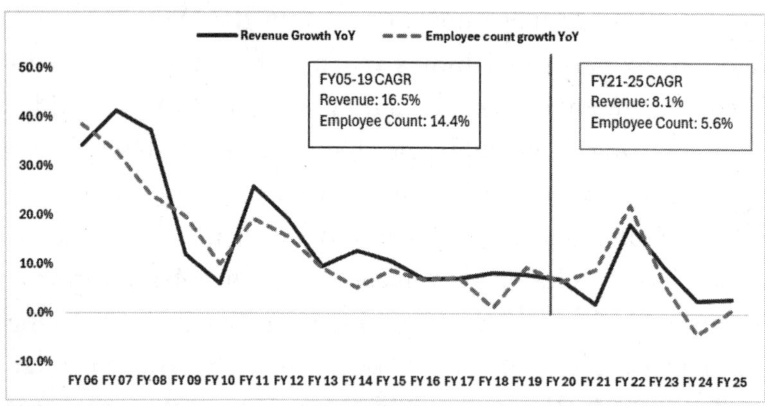


**Figure 2.3**: The IT sector's sluggish revenue growth has translated to weak employee count growth

**Source**: Marcellus Investment Managers using company annual reports from TCS, HCL Tech, Infosys and Wipro

increase in penetration in global IT outsourcing has slowed down. It seems unlikely to accelerate in the current geopolitical climate, where companies in the developed markets do not want to come across as aggressive outsourcers lest that trigger a political backlash in their domestic market. The combined effect is a sharp reduction in hiring by the Indian IT Services firms, as shown in Figure 2.3.

## Automation of Jobs in Offices and Factories

### *Automation in Small Businesses: A Case Study*

It was a stiflingly hot summer morning in Pune, as is the case generally during the month of May. After driving for roughly half an hour from Pune, we reached a small town called Phursungi – officially part of the enormous district that is Pune, yet bearing absolutely no resemblance to the city located half an hour away.

As we entered the local industrial belt, the road started becoming bumpy and the open landscape, with a smattering of a few smaller shops, was transformed into a meticulously planned set of equal-sized and equidistantly placed 'units', or 'galas' as they are called locally. Each gala had the same façade, same grey colour and similar shuttering.

We were visiting a modular furniture manufacturer who operated in Pune and had a manufacturing facility in Phursungi. As we entered the unit that belonged to the furniture manufacturer, we realized that he had combined a couple of them to get a larger premise for manufacturing.

Even more interestingly, mirroring what we saw outside, there was barely any labour within the facility. To our surprise, the machines in this 600 sq. ft unit were whirring away – cutting, drilling and shaping large chunks of plyboards, with just a couple of people to handle the raw plyboard and finished pieces. This unit had machines imported from China and Japan to do precision plywood cutting, laminate pasting and edge bending. When asked about the manufacturer's sales, he replied that his annual revenues were around ₹100 crore ($11 million).

When asked about the lack of labour and ability to scale, he promptly replied (in Hindi) to this effect:

> Why do we need more people to scale? We have the best-in-class machines doing most of the job required to make modular furniture, and the only two places where people are required are for handling the machinery and plyboard pieces and then packing them up. Our sales representative then takes these to the actual site and assembles these by hand without any elaborate toolkit. These pieces are made to measure and therefore have to fit perfectly into the space for which they are made. A whole kitchen is erected within a week's time.

### *Autor, Murnane and Levy's Breakthrough in Labour Market Economics*

What is playing out in this small business in Phursungi is what we see in our factory visits across the country. Even the smallest of manufacturers are now employing high quality machinery to grow their operations, cut costs and run businesses with minimal recruitment. From the factories of SMEs (small and medium enterprises) to the large factories of our investee companies, robots and automated production lines are now ubiquitous in India and factories are designed for minimal labour requirement. In fact, most factory owners prefer to employ as little labour as possible. Just about the only place where labour is required in modern Indian factories is during packing, and from what they tell us, the companies are planning to automate the primary, secondary and tertiary packing procedures as well.

In 2003, three American economists – David Autor, Frank Levy and Richard Murnane – published a paper in the prestigious *Quarterly Journal of Economics*. Little did these economists know at that time that the dynamics described in this paper – 'The Skill Content of Recent Technological Change: An Empirical Exploration' – would reshape the politics of the Western world a decade or so later.[29]

In his award-winning book *A World Without Work*, Daniel Susskind describes their argument:

> Starting in the 1980s, new technologies appeared to help both low-skilled and high-skilled workers at the same time – but workers with middling skills did not appear to benefit at all. In many economies, if you took all the occupations and arranged them in a long line from the lowest-skilled to the highest-skilled, over the last few decades you would have often seen the pay and the share of jobs (as a proportion of total employment) grow for those at either end of the line,

but wither for those near the middle ... This phenomenon is known as 'polarization' or 'hollowing out'.[30]

The chart below, taken from Susskind's book, encapsulates this phenomenon across the developed economies (Figure 2.4).

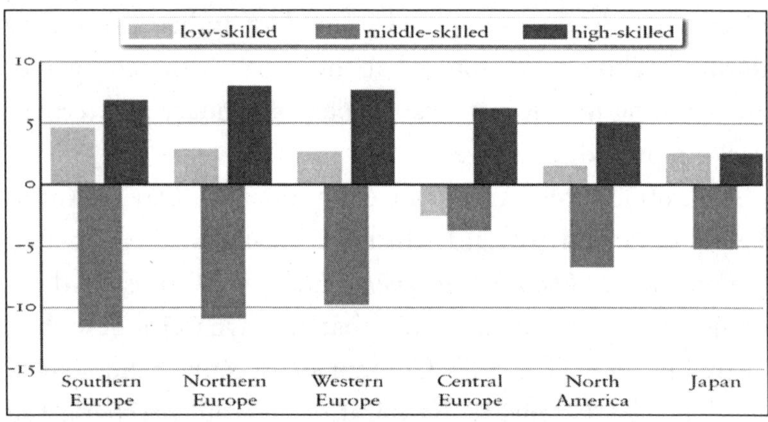


**Figure 2.4**: Percentage point change in share of total employment (1995–2015)

**Source**: Daniel Susskind, *A World Without Work: Technology, Automation, and How We Should Respond*, Metropolitan Books, 2020.

Susskind further explains that in the West, not only is technology gobbling up the jobs of middle-skilled workers like secretaries, administrative clerks, production workers and salespeople, but also the labour markets are becoming increasingly two-tiered. In specific, the wages of high-skilled workers (the top 0.01 per cent as he calls them) are pulling away from those of the middle-class.

## *Applying Autor, Murnane and Levy's Framework to India*

Economist Sudipa Sarkar applied the Autor, Murnane and Levy framework to the Indian labour market in her doctoral thesis. Using detailed data on labour market activities from the household level survey of National Sample Survey Organisation (NSSO) for three subsequent decades starting from 1983–84 to 2011–12, Ms Sarkar (who now teaches at the National Law School of India University) – showed that the Indian urban labour market too has been impacted by 'polarization'.

As shown in Figure 2.5, Ms Sarkar showed that the further we travel in time from the economic reforms of 1991, the more pronounced is the polarization, i.e., the hammering of middle skill and middle-earning jobs, such as clerical and bookkeeping jobs, sales jobs and record keeping related jobs.[31]

The U-shaped profile of the labour market shown in the figure above arises because while the labour market share of high-skill jobs (usually non-routine cognitive work, e.g. managers, business owners) and low-skills jobs (non-routine manual work, e.g., service workers who do non-methodical work using their brains, eyes and limbs) is either rising or holding firm, the middle-skill jobs are disappearing. Ms Sarkar's empirical research showed that the further we move into the era of economic liberalization in India, the deeper the U-shape. More specifically, she noted that 'the large decline in employment shares in both clerical and sales occupations may be an indication that computerization has started replacing some routine tasks in urban India, particularly in the last few years'.[32]

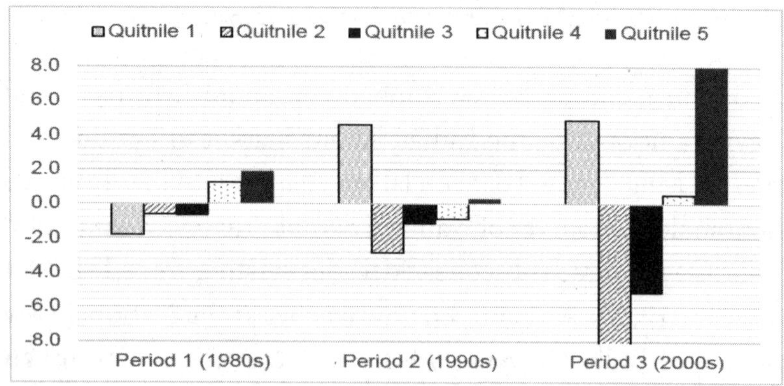


**Figure 2.5**: Changes in employment share (in percentage) across occupational skill quintiles

**Note:** Occupational skill quintile is created by dividing 281 occupations into approximately 20 equally weighted groups in 1983 based on the mean earnings of the same years for the period 1983 to 2004. For Period 3 (2004 to 2011), National Classification for Occupations (NCO) 2005 three-digit occupational codes are matched to NCO 1968 codes at two-digit level, and then the combination of occupation and broad industry has been grouped into quintiles using mean wage of the year 2004.

**Source:** Sudipa Sarkar, 'Employment Change in Occupations in Urban India: Implications for Wage Inequality', University of Warwick, January 2017.

While Ms Sarkar's research shows us that post 1991, the Indian labour market started punishing middle-skill jobs, a more precise timing of when the pounding really began for such jobs emerges from a paper written by Pankaj Vashisth and Jay Dev Dubey in 2018. Titled 'Changing Task Contents of Jobs in India: Implications and Way Forward',[33] their paper shows that while demand for manual labour started conking off from the 1980s itself, demand for routine cognitive skills in the manufacturing sector (the sort of clerical, bookkeeping, record keeping and sales jobs referred to as 'middle skill' in

Ms Sarkar's paper) started falling around the turn of the century – see Figure 2.6 and focus on the line with the triangle icons. Trying to explain why that specific time-period is a watershed, the authors hypothesize that the opening of Indian manufacturing to 100 per cent foreign direct investment might have triggered automation and thus reduced demand for routine cognitive skills.

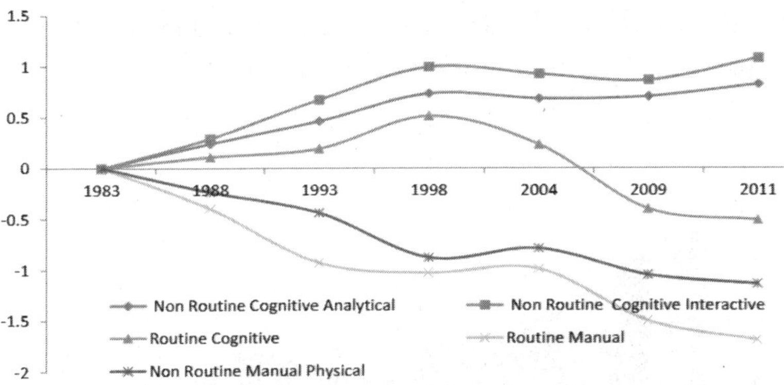


**Figure 2.6**: Changing task content of manufacturing sector jobs

**Source**: Pankaj Vashisht and Jay Dev Dubey, 'Changing Task Contents of Jobs in India: Implications and Way Forward', Indian Council for Research on International Economic Relations, New Delhi, No. 355, March 2018, https://tinyurl.com/jz6fmxta.

What we learn from these two pieces of academic research on the Indian labour market is that while in the early phases of India's modernization (1980s and 1990s), middle-skill jobs were less at risk – thanks to the automation of basic tasks in offices and factories – in the twenty-first century the picture changed. In particular, over the past generation, routine cognitive skills have seen a reduction in demand in the Indian labour market. A generation before AI came into the picture, middle-skill jobs were already losing share in the labour market.

In fact, if we were to look at the recently published data in the Annual Survey of Industries (ASI), the number of supervisors employed in manufacturing units (as a percentage of all employed) in India has gone down significantly (see Figure 2.7) over the past decade or so, suggesting that the hollowing of middle-skill jobs – including managerial and supervisory jobs of a routine nature – which began a generation ago has continued.[34]

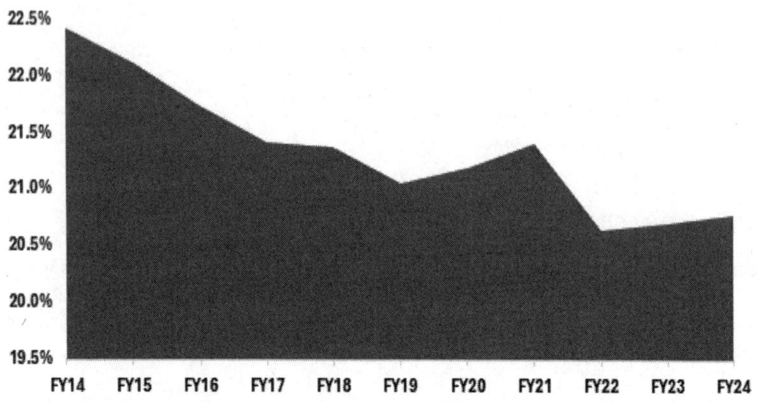


**Figure 2.7**: Share of supervisory/managerial employees in formal manufacturing has been steadily falling over the past decade

**Source**: Marcellus Investment Managers using ASI data

Validating the research published by Ms Sarkar and Messrs Vashishth and Dubey, P.C. Mohanan, former acting chairperson of the National Statistical Commission (NSC), says, 'The decline in administrative job roles has been observed for quite some time now. Besides, the increasing trend of contractualization and outsourcing by producers as a measure to cut input costs implies that many managerial and supervisory roles no longer exist. While workers are needed to produce and operate machinery, supervisors are no longer required for them.'[35]

The implications of this multi-decadal surge in automation in Indian workplaces will become evident when we discuss the jobs and wages situation in India in Chapters 4 and 5.

## Middle Class Disenfranchisement

None of the middle class's vulnerabilities that have been described in this chapter can be called an abrupt change. Rote learning in the Indian education system goes back decades. Saurabh remembers how, as far back as the early 1980s, he was rote learning the 16-times table as if his life depended on it. The erosion in the quality of Indian graduates has also happened, as the entry bar has been lowered to let in less able candidates. Similarly, automation too kicked in gradually in the first two decades of the twenty-first century. All of this begs the question: Why did none of this lead to a national debate on the structural challenges facing the Indian middle class? We reckon the answer lies in the middle class's relationship – or lack thereof – with the Indian political system.

In independent India, the middle class has been notable for its refusal to enter politics on the premise that it is the 'dirty' relative to the cozy confines of corporate life, where the middle class feels safer even though most rational observers would argue that the boardroom of a Nifty company is just as much of a snake pit as the Parliament.

As a result, the core of the Indian political elite now constitutes people either from working-class backgrounds or from deeply entrenched political families (who have ruled Indians for the last three decades, often by switching from one political party to another).

Its aversion to the rough and tumble of active political duty has cost the middle class a seat at the table, and made it by and large a bystander (at best, a commentator) in India's multi-layered democratic political system. In fact, electoral turnout is the lowest in the most prosperous enclaves of India's largest cities, as most middle-class Indians regard voting day as a public holiday. For example, in the 2019 general elections, the voter turnout in Odisha's Bhubaneswar was 46 per cent, of which only 10 per cent were from the middle class.[36]

Therefore, unsurprisingly, politicians rarely feel the need to cater to the middle class's interests or listen to its grievances; the politician thus prioritizes the poor for votes and the elite for their money (which greases the wheels of the electoral machine). Consequently, the 'democracy in India has ceased to be a genteel club where the poor are resigned to subordinate their interests in favour of the entrenched'.[37]

A combination of the above, plus an inability to come together on a pan-India basis with a cohesive set of demands and solutions, has made the middle class almost irrelevant to the political discourse. As mentioned in Manisha Pande's *Middle Class India*, 'Politically, the middle class is divided on the issues of identity and nationalism. Each social group has its own definition of nationalism, which differs from the others.'[38]

Thanks to its multitude of grievances, the middle class finds itself splintered not just on a pan-India basis and in a large metropolis like Mumbai, but even within specific neighbourhoods in India's megacities. This lack of cohesion means that even if a political leader were inclined to listen the middle class's demands, they wouldn't know which of the dozens of demands to cater to in order to garner a significant chunk of votes. The poor, on the other hand, are ready and able to offer their votes to the highest bidder from their own community. That makes them supplicants in the Indian political system and also the beneficiaries of the doles and subsidies dished out by the ambitious political elite, which is happy to use the middle class's tax payments to fund such expenditures. In fact, given that India has 970 million voters and only 40 million middle-class income-tax payers, buying the votes of the former using the tax payments of the latter is a logical strategy that every politician who wants to rise has adopted.

# 3

# AI: The New Disruptive Force in the Job Market

*I visualize a time when we will be to robots what dogs are to humans, and I'm rooting for the machines.*

– CLAUDE SHANNON, Father of information theory

The August 2025 issue of *Vogue* sent shockwaves through the modelling industry by featuring an advertisement with a model. But this flawlessly beautiful blond-haired, blue-eyed model – who was the face of *GUESS*'s summer campaign – did not exist because she was an AI-generated model. In fact, the advertisement was created without any make-up artists, stylists, camera crew or lighting experts, since AI can do all of this inside the graphics processing unit of an Nvidia chip. Not only was creating this advertisement cheaper for *GUESS* (relative to a conventional advertisement), but it was also faster, since there were no schedules to co-ordinate and no locales or studios to book.[1]

While the replacement of models or stylists by AI might not trigger alarm in policy circles in India, given the niche nature of the industry, these are well-paid jobs in the creative community that constitutes the advertising industry in India. The gutting of such jobs by AI (as can be seen in a number of advertisements in India now) is sending tremors through the middle-class professionals in the advertising fraternity that inhabits Mumbai.

Moreover, as we discuss in this chapter, AI is also having a profound impact on industries that are large employers of low-skill Indians, thus triggering alarm bells at the highest levels of the policymaking community in New Delhi. As we highlight in the sub-section that follows, we saw firsthand in Navi Mumbai how AI is gobbling up low-skill jobs in India.

The substitution of human labour by technology is accelerating across sectors. India's 12 million security guards – one of the largest employment categories after construction – now face replacement by cameras, sensors and bots.[2] White-collar workers are equally vulnerable: IT services companies are cutting thousands of jobs as AI handles coding, quality assurance and customer support. Major firms like TCS, HCL Tech and others have announced significant workforce reductions, with studies predicting 2 million job losses in IT and customer experience sectors by 2031.[3]

The evidence is mounting: Monthly job listings for white-collar roles have declined roughly 20 per cent since the rise of generative AI, with the sharpest drops among entry-level and middle-skilled workers. The Naukri JobSpeak Index shows that job creation has stagnated since 2023, particularly in

IT services and BPOs (business process outsourcing). Even sectors like manufacturing, supply chain management and retail – previously insulated from digital disruption – are increasingly deploying AI to reduce human intervention.

While Western countries face labour shortages that make automation beneficial, India confronts the opposite problem: a median age of 29 and millions of young workers seeking employment. For a nation already struggling to generate sufficient jobs, AI's 'substitution effect' threatens to eliminate even last resort employment options before the promised complementarity effects – where technology makes remaining workers more productive – can materialize. India's white-collar job creation engine has comprehensively jammed.

## A Dark Cavern in Navi Mumbai

It is 9.00 a.m. on a weekday morning as we approach the suburban office complex in Navi Mumbai. As we step into the lobby, we see that the lifts are already overcrowded with office workers coming in for the morning shift at the dozens of call centres located in this giant office complex. Figuring that we are not street smart enough to navigate our way through the crowds jostling to enter the lifts, our host has sent us a security guard. He takes us up via the fire escape and soon we enter a cavernous room humming with human activity.

The room is dark and soundproof. As our eyes get accustomed to the lack of light, we can see hundreds of monitors glowing in the dark. As we approach these monitors, we can see the silhouettes of the agents who are talking into their mics while looking at the monitors. At this juncture, our host explains to us that his firm manages a third of India's ATMs – around 70k ATMs. Of these 70k ATMs, around 30k are managed from this control centre in Navi Mumbai. It takes us a few minutes to digest what we just heard: 100 people sitting in a room in suburban Mumbai are monitoring a third of India's ATMs.

'How can just hundred or so agents monitor tens of thousands of ATMs?' we ask our host even as we scan the room and see the agents defuse tricky situations thousands of kilometres away.

'You see, AI-powered bots do most of the work,' says our host. As we stare quizzically at him, he smiles and says,

'Each ATM that we monitor has sensors and cameras placed around it. If something untoward is happening, the bots have been trained to pick it up. For example, if someone is withdrawing cash without removing their motorbike helmet, our bot will immediately flag that to one of the agents in this room. The agent will then speak to the helmet-wearing customer through his mic. If the customer does not heed the message coming from the loudspeaker placed above the ATM, the agent will inform the local police station who will then send in the cops.

'Of course, this is just one of the use cases that our network of sensors, cameras, bots and agents deal with. Jammed ATMs, electricity failure, cash shortage in the ATM, smoke, insects in the ATM, fire ... the list is long, and we have shown India's largest banks that our network can look after their

ATMs without the need for a security guard to be physically present 24x7.'

'But won't it be cheaper for the banks to employ a human security guard to be present on the ground?' we ask.

'Absolutely not,' says our host, who is clearly used to this line of questioning. 'The all-in cost to a bank of using two security guards on 12-hour shifts to guard an ATM is ₹6 lakh per annum. Our cameras, sensors, bots and agents do the same job for half that cost.'

A few metres away we can hear one of the agents telling a customer in faraway Muzaffarpur, a district town in Bihar, in Hindi, 'You cannot insert the card into the ATM more than thrice. This is your fourth attempt.' On the screen we can see the startled customer stare at the CCTV camera and swear in Hindi.

It is at this point that the enormity of the tech transition that India is undergoing hit us. The 100 agents in the cavernous dark room in Navi Mumbai are doing the job that 60k security guards would have done across the 30k ATMs that are being managed from this room! And this is possible because the AI-powered bots have been trained to watch the ATMs via camera and sensors and then flash up on the operators' screens if anything is amiss. The operators are therefore only looking at the ATMs where something has deviated from the norm (which has been 'trained' into the bots).

As shareholders in some of India's best run banks, we take comfort in the millions of dollars of cost savings being generated by replacing the security guards with bots. However, as investors who want to see the Indian economy thrive, we feel fear and remorse. Around 12 million Indians earn a living as security guards.[4] These guards protect us in our homes, our offices, our shopping malls and our hotels. The humble *chowkidar* now constitutes one of the largest sources of employment in India after construction labour. Entrepreneurs who have built flourishing businesses around skilling and providing labour supply in India say that the country has nearly 23k registered private security agencies. 'Security is turning out to be one of the most important sectors for facilitating the transition from farm to non-farm jobs. It is one of the fastest growing segments in the job market,' says Manish Sabharwal, founder of TeamLease. 'China's transition from farm to non-farm employment occurred in factories. India's transition is happening in customer service, sales, logistics, and security.'[5]

Published in 2024, the NSDC (National Skill Development Corporation)–KPMG report describes security guard jobs as 'a last resort' for urban individuals and a stopgap for rural workers during 'poor agricultural seasons'. Given that only around 150 million Indians are in regularly paid non-farm employment, other studies have described the security profession as one of the largest sources of employment in India.[6]

Standing in the cavernous control centre for ATMs, we realized that for many of India's 12 million guards, even this 'last resort' will soon be taken away because offices, housing societies, malls and restaurants will be just as open to the business case of replacing guards with bots as the banks have been.

## AI's Double-Edged Impact on Labour Demand

Such is its ease of use and so potent are its uses cases that Generative AI (GenAI, i.e., applications like ChatGPT, Claude and Gemini) has become one of the most rapidly adopted technologies ever.[7] As proactive consumers of technology, Indians in particular seem to have taken to it like ducks to water. Survey data (Figure 3.1) suggests that Indians have been the most enthusiastic adopters of AI in Asia. In fact, several experts suggest that the vast majority of Indian companies are now proactively working to adopt autonomous robots (or bots) in their operations.[8]

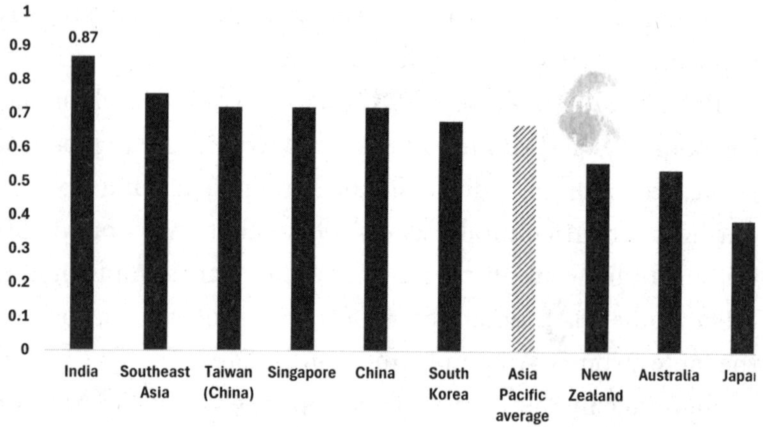


**Figure 3.1**: Developing economies across Asia Pacific have seen higher gen AI adoption

**Source**: Marcellus Investment Managers, Deloitte Gen AI Survey (2024)

Economists studying the impact of technological change on the labour market tend to classify these impacts into two categories. Firstly, the 'substitution effect' is the replacement of labour with machines as technology improves. The replacement of skilled English weavers by the power loom is the most famous example of this effect. For centuries, high school history textbooks have used this case study to highlight the agitation that this effect triggered among the Luddites in eighteenth century England.

The more constructive impact of technology on the labour market is called the 'complementarity effect'. This effect kicks in after new technologies start making the workers who have not been displaced more productive. We will return to the complementarity effects of AI on the Indian job market in Chapter 10. In the remainder of this section, we will focus on the substitution effect that the advent of AI has had on the labour market so far.

## The Impact of AI on Indian Jobs

At least five years before Gen AI entered the global discourse, in 2018 an article by the Centre for Advanced Study of India (CASI) at the University of Pennsylvania said that 'India, which has 65 per cent of global IT off-shore work and 40 per cent of global business processing, will have 69 per cent of its jobs in the formal employment automated by 2030.'[9]

The CASI's estimate – which has been repeatedly referred to by others (including the GoI) seeking to understand the impact of automation and AI on India – was in turn based on a 2013 study by Oxford professors Carl Frey and Michael Osborne titled 'The Future of Employment: How Susceptible Are Jobs to Computerisation?'. Professors Frey and Osborne showed that 'middle-skill' jobs that require routine cognitive and manual applications would be automated in the foreseeable future.[10] This is in-line with Autor, Murnane and Levy's celebrated 2003 paper which we highlighted in the previous chapter. However, our view is that Frey and Osborne's '69 per cent of Indian jobs automated by 2030' estimate does not factor in the impact of Gen AI.

The most authoritative estimate so far of the impact of AI on Indian jobs comes from a study conducted by NITI Aayog – the GoI's primary think tank – in collaboration with NASSCOM (National Association of Software and Service Companies), the tech industry's trade body, and Boston Consulting Group. Published in October 2025, this study says: 'In a business-as-usual case, there will be a downside. In this worst-case scenario, the headcount in the tech services sector could go down from 7.5 to 8 million in 2023 to 6 million by 2031. Similarly, the headcount in the CX sector could go down from 2 to 2.5 million in 2023 to 1.8 million.'[11]

To help us understand its 'worst case' estimate of 1.5 million job losses in the IT services sector and 0.5 million job losses in the CX sector, the NITI Aayog study provides a couple of case studies of white-collar workers whose jobs are disrupted by AI.

We hear about Rekha, a Pune-based junior QA (quality assurance) engineer, whose core job involves designing and executing test cases, data management and regression testing. The advent of AI has significantly disrupted her role, putting her on the path to redundancy. This is because the skill sets that were core and critical for her job role – such as designing test cases, executing test cases, test data management and even regression testing – are easily executable by AI.

Chennai-based Aman, an L1 support agent (the first point of contact for end-users seeking technical assistance, responsible for resolving basic, common issues like password resets, software installations and initial hardware troubleshooting) from the same sector, is in a similar situation to Rekha. His core work revolves around ticket triage and routing, software installation and configuration, account provisioning and deprovisioning, VPN (virtual private network) and connectivity support, file access resolution and basic hardware troubleshooting.

Given that through 2024 and 2025, Google and Microsoft have repeatedly highlighted that a quarter of their coding globally is now done by AI,[12] NITI Aayog's 'worst case' estimate of 2 million jobs lost in IT Services and CX sectors in India – which translates to roughly 20 per cent of the jobs in these sectors disappearing – by 2030 seems realistic.

Another way to assess the impact of AI on tech jobs is to consider the following announcements on AI-related job losses that we have heard in 2024 and 2025:

- India's IT sector employer, Tata Consultancy Services, said in July 2025 that it is planning to reduce its workforce by 2 per cent (~12,000 employees).[13]
- The CEO of HCL Tech, C. Vijayakumar, said in February 2025 that his firm is going to target double the revenue with just half the labour force, thanks to them leveraging AI and technology.[14]
- According to the World Bank's South Asia development update, the rise of GenAI has led to a 'roughly 20 per cent decline in monthly job listing for white collar roles, including moderately educated young workers such as

call centre agents and software developers … the largest slowdowns in job listings have been concentrated among middle-skilled and entry-level workers and in the business services sector'.[15]

- While the years 2023 and 2024 each saw around 25,000 tech sector jobs lost in India due to AI, this figure seems to have doubled in 2025 as per the *Economic Times*.[16]
- The Economic Survey for 2024–25 dedicated a full chapter to AI and noted that as a major services-driven economy, India's workforce in low-value-added IT and BPO sectors is particularly susceptible to automation. It acknowledged fears that AI could lead to large-scale labour displacement, especially in middle- and lower-wage jobs, as AI is expected to surpass human performance in certain tasks across healthcare, finance and education.[17]

In the preceding paragraphs, we have focused on the impact of AI on white-collar jobs because that is the sector where the first round of substitution effects are most visible. However, it seems unlikely that other jobs will be left untouched by AI. In Chapter 2, we highlighted using the Phursungi case study, how our visits to factories – large and small – are increasingly characterized by us walking past mile after mile of highly automated production lines, with hardly any workers visible. Artificial intelligence will come to these factories as well. Specifically, AI seems likely make the control rooms of factories easier to run with fewer people employed.

Similarly, across industries, AI should be able to manage supply-chains smoothly with less human intervention –

loading and dispatching of goods and raw materials can be planned and executed by AI with increasingly little human intervention with each passing year. This would render many of the professionals currently managing supply chains redundant. In fact, both Flipkart and Amazon have deployed smart fulfilment centres in India which use AI.[18]

For example, in an apparel retailing chain, which clothes to stock in which store at what point in the year has long been one of the critical skills of the various professionals running these chains, most notably for the store manager. However, AI is likely to replace a significant part of that judgement call and then automate the ordering, production and dispatch of those items.

All of that being said, when we ask other employers and head-hunters how extensively they think AI will impact middle-class jobs in India, we can see that no one clearly knows as yet what the ultimate impact will be. Even though AI is still finding its footing, as investors in the equity markets we can see that as Indian companies spend money on AI to keep up with the latest technology trends, they need to economize elsewhere to keep their overall expenses in check. The most obvious source of economy for such firms is cutting their people costs. Moreover, the decision to replace people with AI gets easier with each passing year, as Gen AI progressively gets better. Even investment management firms like Marcellus are finding that AI can produce high-quality research, comparable sometimes in quality to what an analyst with a decade of experience would produce.

What is clear however is that the combined and accelerating impact of automation and AI has comprehensively jammed India's white-collar job creation engine. Proof of this comes from the Naukri JobSpeak database of job openings in India. As their website explains, the Naukri Jobspeak Index is a monthly index that represents the state of the Indian job market and hiring activity based on new job listings and recruiter searches on their résumé database. Naukri started publishing this index as far back as 2008 and has been publishing it at an all-India aggregate level as well as for different sectors.

As shown in Table 3.1, since FY2023 the number of jobs available in India has stagnated, with the IT services sector being particularly badly impacted. Unsurprisingly, new jobs in the BPO industry are also not being created. The only ray of hope is the banking and broking sector, where thanks to the unprecedented level of retail trading in India, jobs are still being created.

**Table 3.1**: Job Growth in All Sectors Except Banking, Financial Services and Broking Have Plummeted Post Covid-19

| Naukri JobSpeak (average for months in FY) | FY2010–20 CAGR in Job Listings (A) (in per cent) | FY2023–25 CAGR in Job Listings (B) (in per cent) | Impact of Automation and AI on Job Listings (B – A) (in per cent) |
|---|---|---|---|
| All India | 11 | 1 | -10 |
| IT-Software/software services | 16 | -12 | -28 |
| BPO/ITES/CRM/ transcription | 11 | 0 | -11 |

| Naukri JobSpeak (average for months in FY) | FY2010–20 CAGR in Job Listings (A) (in per cent) | FY2023–25 CAGR in Job Listings (B) (in per cent) | Impact of Automation and AI on Job Listings (B – A) (in per cent) |
|---|---|---|---|
| Banking/financial services/broking | 14 | 15 | +1 |
| Telcom/ISP | -3 | -7 | -4 |
| Retailing | 13 | 2 | -11 |

**Source:** Marcellus Investment Managers using Naukri JobSpeak Index

With 8 million graduates joining the labour market each year in India and with virtually no jobs being available for them due to the tech disruption, the consequences of what we have described above for the Indian middle class are dramatic, both in terms of livelihood and in terms of their standing in India's socio-economic pyramid. That's what we will now turn to in Chapters 4–7.

# 4

# Job Growth Is Stagnating

*[A]s the middle class invests in human capital accumulation and produces a large pool of educated workforce in the near future, there will be further demand for skilled jobs. Quality jobs thus need to be created in education-intensive sectors. The recent employment data released by the NSS however show record levels of unemployment in the country, especially among the educated youth (NSSO, 2019).**

You don't need to be a seasoned recruiter to appreciate that Dheeraj Singh has an impressive CV. He graduated with a BTech from IIT Kanpur and then went on to his MBA from IIM Calcutta. Then, after spending a decade working in large

---

* Sandhya Krishnan and Neeraj Hatekar, 'Understanding the Burgeoning Indian Middle Class through Its Expenditure and Asset-Ownership Pattern', *The Middle Class in World Society*, Christian Suter, S. Madheswaran and B.P. Vani (eds), 2020, Routledge.

consultancy firms and in private equity, he joined the Michael and Susan Dell Foundation where he was a programme director. Then, in 2023, he set up the 'Global IIT–IIM Alumni Support Group' which describes itself as 'research-cum-advocacy think tank and global peer-based network of 1,000 alumni of IITs and IIMs belonging to the socially marginalized communities that aims to advance members' professional growth in the corporate sector and promotes diversity, equity and inclusion in the Indian higher education [sector]'.[1]

In recent years, Dheeraj has consistently brought to the public eye data on mental health problems in India's most elite academic institutions of higher learning, the IITs. To be specific, Dheeraj has pointed out in the national media that according to the data obtained by him through RTI (right-to-information) requests, 115 students across IITs have died by suicide since 2005. Of these, 98 deaths occurred on campus, with 56 students hanging themselves, while 17 suicides took place off-campus.[2] Furthermore, he has highlighted that the suicide rate has accelerated in the 2015–25 period compared to the ten years prior to that. In fact, the suicide rate has *doubled* over this period compared to the ten years prior to that.[3]

While a cocktail of factors seems to be responsible for these suicides – including discrimination among students and of students by faculty based on their caste, gender and religion – a growing source of stress among the IITians is the lack of jobs. Sumit, a graduate of IIT Bombay with a research degree in sociology, reflected on the competitive nature of IIT life and said, 'IIT is like a well-planned game. You have to consider your move at every step; plan everything from the first semester until you graduate. One misstep can derail your ambition of a highly competitive job or opportunity.'[4]

The lack of jobs in turn is interplaying with the divisions associated with identity – divisions which arguably exist in any university campus anywhere in the world. A graduate (who wished anonymity) from IIT Guwahati recounted an incident involving the placement cell at IIT Guwahati: 'The placement cell organizes various rounds of interviews and tests for job placements. However, members of the placement cell often unduly help their friends. There have been instances where students who prepared extensively for interviews struggled during actual tests, only to find that some candidates had access to unfair advantages, such as cheating from their rooms.'[5]

The IIT students have good reason to worry about their employment prospects. In the post Covid-19 world, stories about the lack of jobs for graduates in general and IIT graduates in particular have become commonplace. The job market does not seem to care that of the 13 lakh (1.3 million) students who apply to the IITs, only 20k get admission into these elite institutions.[6] According to the data procured by Dheeraj, approximately 8,000 IIT graduates (amounting to nearly 40 per cent of the graduating class) remained unplaced across India's 23 IIT campuses.[7]

Dheeraj also points out that the employment situation is worsening with each passing year. Between 2022 and 2024, the number of students registered at the older nine IITs increased by 1.2 times. Meanwhile the number of unplaced students rose by 2.1 times. In the 14 newer ones, the number of registered students grew by 1.3 times, but the number of unplaced students went up by 3.8 times. Dheeraj said, 'Unplaced students are dealing with stress, anxiety, and hopelessness due to poor job placement scenarios. [...] The doubling of unplaced students points to a precarious state of affairs in the best engineering colleges of the country. Around 61% of the postgraduates are still unplaced. This is an unprecedented job crisis our premier colleges and our young graduates are facing.'[8]

## The Jobs and Wages Challenge for the Middle Class

From the summer of 2023 onwards, Indian companies' earnings growth has decelerated at a rapid rate (Figure 4.1). Underpinning this deceleration is a sharp conk-off in consumption growth along the mainstay of the Indian

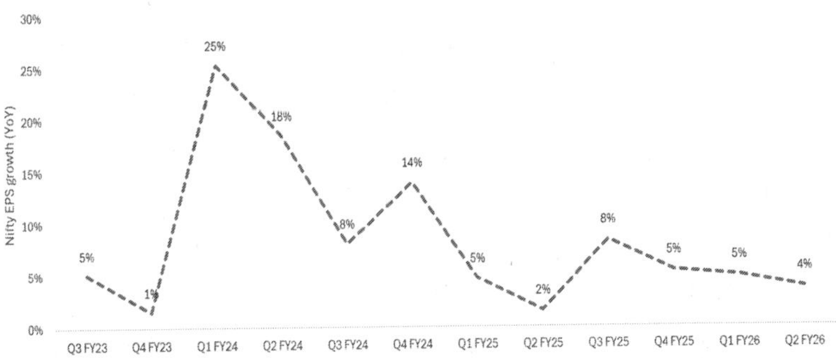


**Figure 4.1**: From FY2023, the Nifty 50 has witnessed arguably its sharpest ever slowdown in earnings growth

**Note:** Data for Nifty earnings per share (EPS) is point in time, using constituents as of each quarter end date whose EPS was calculated using free float adjusted weight as of that quarter end

**Source**: Marcellus Investment Managers using data from Bloomberg BEst EPS

economy. Key drivers of this consumption downturn are a sharp deceleration in white-collar job creation alongside a reduction in real wages for white-collar workers over the past eight years. In this chapter, we delve deeper into the proximate causes of the slowdown in job creation. In the next one, we quantify the extent to which wage growth has slowed down and then present our hypothesis for why this has happened.

## Structural Factors in Play in the Job Market

As we explained in Chapter 1, 40 million middle-class Indians directly or indirectly employ 200 million working class Indians. While there are a variety of metrics available in India to measure employment, most notably the Periodic Labour Force Survey (PLFS), it does not accurately try to capture the issue of white-collar job creation in India, simply because it considers self-employment as legitimate employment. As a result, this sort of survey data makes it difficult to figure out what exactly is happening to middle-class employment in India.

In this regard, we believe, that the Jobspeak Index that Naukri, India's largest employment classifieds website, publishes every month, is a better indicator for measuring white-collar job demand and creation in India. Naukri started publishing this index as far back as 2008 and has been publishing it at an all-India aggregate level as well as for different sectors.

In the decade ending in FY2020, white-collar job openings in India grew at a scorching pace of 11 per cent per annum

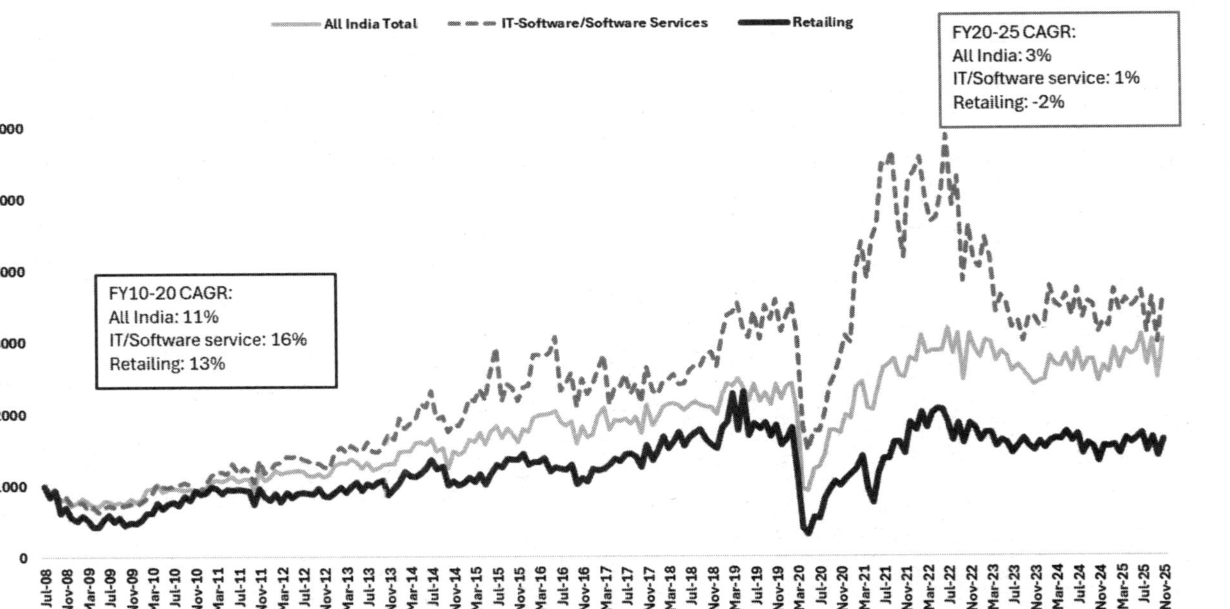


**Figure 4.2**: Even after factoring in the post-Covid-19 spurt in jobs, white-collar job creation has slowed down dramatically in India over the past five years (2020–25)

**Source**: Marcellus Investment Managers using Naukri JobSpeak data; annual numbers are arrived at by averaging the monthly values for each of the years

implying that every six years, the number of white-collar jobs in India was doubling. In sectors like IT/Software Services the growth was even more dramatic – 16 per cent per annum (implying a doubling of jobs every four years).

From FY2020, however, the picture changed dramatically. Job creation growth has slowed down to 3 per cent per annum (implying a doubling of jobs every 24 years). Given that India's population is growing at 1 per cent per annum and the number of students graduating from university is growing faster than that (thanks to rising enrolment rates for university education), on a per capita basis the post FY2020 era has basically seen a stagnation in job availability. In fact, as Figure 4.2 shows, the post-Covid-19 slowdown in jobs has hit some of those very sectors which were considered the backbone of India's middle-class employment dream – the software, IT and retail sectors.[9]

So why is this happening now?

Our research points to five sets of reasons that have, individually and collectively (by interplaying with each other), comprehensively jammed India's white collar job creation engine:

- the reluctance of banks to lend money to companies for new projects;
- the shift in market share from smaller, more labour-intensive businesses to larger, more capital-intensive businesses;
- an overdose of regulations for businesses generally but with particularly adverse impacts on smaller businesses;
- the slowdown of the Indian IT Services sector, India's biggest source of white collar jobs; and

- the use of AI (as discussed in the previous chapter) to replace white-collar office workers with bots.

We will dig deeper into each of these factors in this chapter.

### *How Banks Became Reluctant to Finance New Projects*

In 2015, the then RBI governor, Raghuram Rajan, made Indian banks do something that they had rarely done before. He made them conduct an asset quality review (AQR) so that the RBI could assess the true level of non-performing assets (NPAs) in the banking system as opposed to the fictitious NPAs that many of the banks were then reporting (in order to show higher profits, higher net worth and consequently higher share prices).

While the banks hated the AQR, most observers – including us – believed that the RBI Governor had done the right thing.[10] However, one unfortunate and unintended consequence of AQR was that in the decade that followed, banks became incredibly reluctant to lend to corporates for project finance. Between FY2014 and FY2024, loan sanctions by banks for projects in India (i.e., capex) have grown at a CAGR (compound annual growth rate) of 12 per cent, significantly lower than overall credit growth in the country.[11]

This outcome in turn produced two other unfortunate side-effects: (a) it pushed banks to market loans aggressively to India's middle class, and progressively the middle class sank deeper into debt (a subject we discuss in greater depth in Chapter 6); and (b) the difficulty of accessing capital for projects resulted in the Indian private sector comprehensively throttling off on the capital expenditure required to build new businesses. The result is that private sector job creation has been anaemic over the past five years.

### *'Creative Destruction' Of India's Main Job Growth Driver – The SMEs*

More than 90 per cent of Indians who have employment, work for firms with less than ten workers.[12] Over the last decade, India has seen a slew of reforms, most notably GST. The reforms by themselves are not a cause for concern. However, the impact of these reforms on SMEs has upended the lives of millions of Indians who work for small companies.

Demonetization (2016), the introduction of GST (2017) and then Covid-19 (2020–21) hit India in quick succession. Most importantly, this troika of developments deeply impacted India's large informal sector which is responsible for the majority of the Indian population's livelihood. Why so?

As we had explained in our previous book, *Behold the Leviathan*,

> Imagine a village economy cut off from the rest of the world with no road or telecom connectivity to anywhere. In such a village, a range of smaller business, such as the barber, the greengrocer, the butcher, the blacksmith, the moneylender, etc., will build profitable local monopolies.
>
> Now imagine that one fine day this village gets road and telephone connectivity to the nearest large city, which is ten kilometres away. Here is what is likely to happen now:

1. The most profitable and most enterprising companies in the village will set up branch operations in the large city, and if they prosper there, repatriate some of their profits back to the native village to scale up their village enterprise, thereby grabbing profit share in their native village.
2. Aggressive companies from the large city will enter the village and offer lower prices alongside better products to the villagers. This will lead to many of the village enterprises shutting down as they will not have the technology, the expertise and the scale of the big-city competitors.
3. Over time, the number of companies in the village will shrink, both because of consolidation in each sector of the village as the smaller village enterprises struggle to survive, and also because of imports of many necessities coming from the big city.

In very simple terms, this is what has happened in India over the past decade. The nation has gone from being a village-like economy (with poor connectivity between various regions in the country) to big-city integration with the village (or invasion of the village, depending on your point of view) as connectivity improved. On the bigger, pan-India canvas in the aftermath of this integration, more efficient tech savvy companies have grabbed profits from their less efficient competitors.[13]

It is easy to see the hammering of smaller Indian companies in India's corporate profitability data (Figure 4.3).

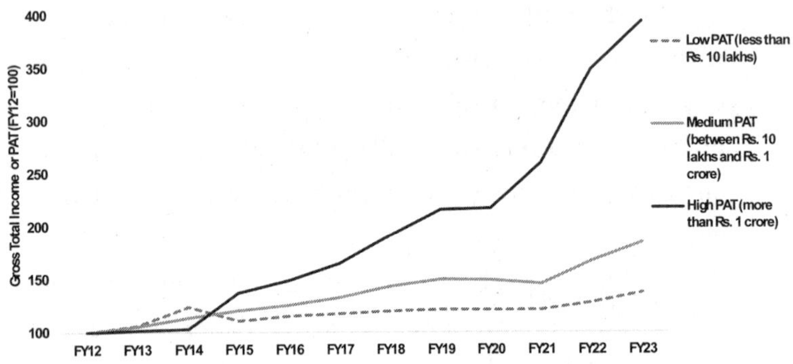


**Figure 4.3**: Smaller Indian companies with PAT (profit after tax) less than ₹1 crore have seen their profits stagnate over the last decade

**Note:** Sum of gross total income or PAT for each category of profits (according to the IT department) was calculated; companies with profits less than ₹10 lakh were considered as low PAT, those between ₹10 lakh and ₹1 crore were considered as medium PAT and those with profits more than ₹1 crore were considered as high PAT. They were indexed to FY2012 and plotted to see the growth in the decade that went by (FY2012–FY2023).

**Source**: Marcellus Investment Managers using data from the Income Tax Department and the Ministry of Finance[14]

This bludgeoning of India's massive informal sector has hit job creation in India. The larger companies tend to be more capital (rather than labour) intensive, and as the share of larger companies in economic activity increases, job creation diminishes in India. This aspect of India's economic development can be seen in Figure 4.4, which shows that the share of factories employing less than 20 people has declined over the last 22 years. In contrast, the MSMEs (micro, small and medium enterprises) employing 100–999 people and large enterprises (employing more than 1,000 people) have grown the fastest. Unfortunately, for India, the largest share of its jobs come from the smallest factories (the 'Less than 20' category in Figure 4.4).

**Table 4.1**: More Than 80 Per Cent of India Inc Account for Less Than 2 Per Cent of India Inc's Profits

| Profit Bucket | Profit Threshold | Average PAT in FY2023 (₹ lakh) | PAT CAGR (FY2012–23) | Percentage of India Inc's Companies (According to Income Tax Filings) | Percentage of India Inc PAT (According to Income Tax Filings) |
|---|---|---|---|---|---|
| Low PAT | 0 to ₹10 lakh | 2.32 | 3 | 54 | 0.3 |
| Medium PAT | ₹10 lakh to ₹1 crore | 36.06 | 6 | 29 | 1 |
| High PAT | ₹1 crore and above | 43.02 | 13 | 17 | 98 |

**Note:** Sum of gross total income or PAT for each category of profits according to data by the IT department was calculated; companies with profits less ₹10 lakh were considered as low PAT, those between ₹10 lakh and ₹1 crore were considered as medium PAT and those with profits more than ₹1 crore were considered as high PAT

**Source:** Marcellus Investment Managers using data from the Income Tax Department and the Ministry of Finance

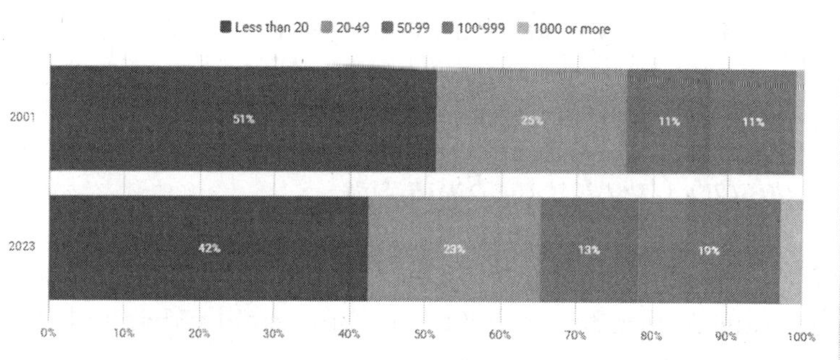


**Figure 4.4**: The majority of India's factories used to employ less than 20 workers

**Source**: Annual Survey of Industries (2001, 2023), Ministry of Statistics and Programme Implementation, GoI; graphic sourced from Data for India

Thankfully, the GoI is alert to the challenges posed by the rapid formalization of the economy. According to the Economic Survey of India released in January 2025, 'Even as large companies invariably tend to prioritise capital-intensive growth over labour-intensive growth, small and medium enterprises are likely to have a better balance between the two, encouraging employment generation. That is a compelling reason to ensure that the state does not hinder their growth.'[15]

The challenge, however, for the government and for the Indian economy in general, is to create an environment in which smaller businesses can flourish. As we highlight in the next sub-section, it does not seem clear to us that – despite its best intentions – the government is being able to strike that balance at present. In the meantime, the inexorable forces of consolidation in a competitive free market economy with good communication infrastructure, much-improved roads and an integrated pan-India indirect tax system is helping large companies consolidate market share with adverse consequences for job creation.

### *Regulatory Overdose for Businesses*

Often, when we speak to owners of small Indian companies, the conversation first turns to just how rapidly many of them are being disintermediated by technology (think of the millions of *kiranas* [stores] in India that are losing their share of their customers' wallet in the wake of Quick Commerce). Then a few minutes later, these conversations – like the conversations Saurabh used to hear in the 1980s, when his relatives would discuss at the dining table how difficult it was for them to deal with the 'licence raj' – turn to the many different layers of red tape that these businesses have to contend with.

In fact, one of the key impediments to their growth, say small business owners, is the inability to expand or start new businesses due to onerous regulatory requirements. For instance, often promoters are unable to secure land to set up a new plant or expand their existing manufacturing footprint in time due to the huge amount of paperwork, and the multiple layers of permissions and licences involved.

In a discussion with a senior political journalist who has been covering India for nearly three decades now, she explained the ludicrousness of many of the 'factories rules', which were decided in the 1950s and subsequently never amended. One such rule still in existence is the mandate for spittoons in factories under the UP Factories Rule Book. As Noida is part of UP, this rule applies to it and all establishments within the city. While perfectly reasonable for manufacturing units, this is also applied to services company premises. Just imagine this – a government officer walks into the office of modern tech firm and says that the company has to pay a fine because there are no spittoons on the premises and, according to the law, a firm employing such a large number of people must have multiple spittoons.

In Marcellus' offices in Mumbai, we don't have a cook stove because having one in the office entails being regulated by the Food Safety and Standards Authority of India (FSSAI). Once you have procured the FSSAI licence to run an office canteen, if you buy a chiller for the canteen then you need another licence. Then, if you decide that you will have storage facility in your canteen, you need a separate licence. To make things more interesting, some of these licences are given by the state and some by the Centre.[16] As a result, tens of thousands of small businesses who could employ a cook and a cleaner to serve hot food make do without such staff and facilities.

Thousands of other such impositions of red tape rob middle-class India of much needed jobs and contribute to the job freeze that we are living through currently. Thankfully, the GoI is cognizant of this. The Economic Survey in January 2025 stated, 'The government has implemented several policies and initiatives over the last decade to support and promote the growth of MSMEs … However, while these initiatives have made significant strides in promoting MSMEs, some challenges in the regulatory environment remain. Regulatory compliance burden holds back formalisation and labour productivity, limits employment growth, chokes innovation and depresses growth.'[17]

The Survey goes on to state that deregulation is more critical for MSME growth than large enterprises because compliance costs, in terms of time and financial resources, are more significant for MSMEs (relative to their larger competitors which 'usually find a way around compliance').

Tellingly, the Survey conceded that extant regulations in India act as 'binding constraints' on the growth of small businesses by increasing the cost of market entry and by force-fitting inefficient models for operations. It then goes on to provide the following examples of how regulations provide perverse incentives to small businesses:

> [F]actory regulations make it cheaper for a business to run two 150-worker factories than one 300-worker factory, discouraging economies of scale. Regulations also hurt workers by discouraging job creation, limiting wages, and encouraging informal employment. For example, Indian workers cannot formally work overtime because the law requires employers to pay at least twice the regular wage.
>
> Regulations increase the cost of all operational decisions in firms. For example, factory owners must dedicate time and resources to obtain the Change of Land Use license and ensure compliance with zoning regulations. Factory owners must also invest in transportation, additional land, construction of rooms for rest and canteens, and paperwork to employ women on night shifts.[18]

Encouragingly, the Survey concludes by mentioning that reforms are required on these fronts in order to lessen the burden on small businesses and give them a greater chance of succeeding: 'Regulations must be rationalised to ensure that the regulation is the minimum necessary to achieve its objectives and the maximum feasible given the limited managerial and other resources at the disposal of small and medium enterprises. The focus of reforms and economic policy must now be on systematic deregulation.'[19]

### *The Slowdown of the IT Services Sector*

As discussed in Chapter 2, with 8 million employees, India's IT Services sector is the country's largest employer.[20] Revenues for the four largest IT Services firms – TCS, Infosys, HCL Tech and Wipro – grew at a CAGR of 15.8 per cent in the 15-year period between FY2005 and FY2020. During this period, employee headcount also grew at around 15 per cent per annum in these firms.[21] Effectively, the IT Services sector was adding in excess of a million jobs each year – jobs which would create further ancillary employment of the sort highlighted in Chapter 1 (cooks, drivers, cleaners, etc.).

Unfortunately, in the post Covid-19 era, as tech adoption by the Fortune 500 companies – the largest clients of the Indian IT services firms – has accelerated, revenue growth for Indian IT services firms has decelerated. In the five-year period ending FY2025, revenue growth for the four largest listed IT services firms has slowed down to a CAGR of 6.8 per cent.[22] Naturally, therefore, employment growth for these four firms has slowed down proportionately, implying that the number of recruits absorbed by the sector is now less than 0.5 million per annum.

Vishnu Gopal, Marcellus' tech analyst, says that Indian IT is no longer the sunrise industry it once was. In the early noughties, global outsourcing penetration was low at mid-single digits; this has since moved a level north to 30 per cent. This rise in the prevalence of outsourcing in the developed markets has been accompanied by market share gains by the large Indian IT players who have utilized the low-cost white-collar labour abundantly available in India. In the post-Covid-19 era, the increase in penetration in global outsourcing has slowed down and seems unlikely to accelerate in the current geopolitical climate, where companies in the developed markets do not want to come across as aggressive outsourcers lest that trigger a political backlash in their domestic market (Figure 4.5). Moreover, further room for market share gains by Indian IT services firms also seem to be very limited, as their developed clients are diversifying their vendor base across geographies to manage risks.

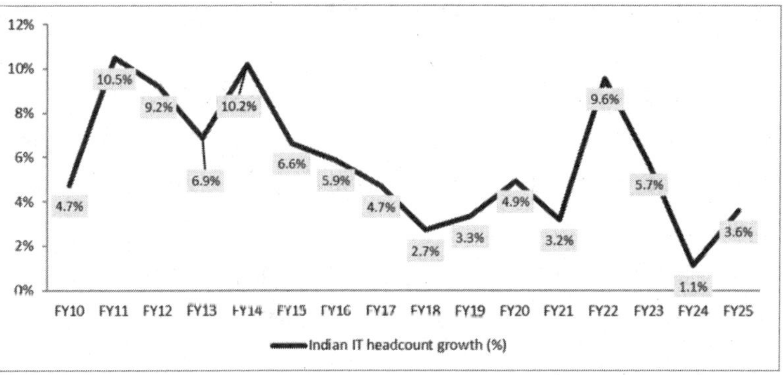


**Figure 4.5**: Indian IT headcount growth has tapered down after Covid-19 led spurt

**Source**: Marcellus Investment Managers, NASSCOM

## *The Replacement of Office Workers with AI*

The disruption of middle-class jobs by AI – as discussed in the previous chapter – is likely to create a challenge for most modern economies. What makes this transition more painful in India is that the AI disruption is coming at a time when Indian SMEs are struggling to cope with both red tape and the modernization of the economy while the country's main job creation engine – tech services – is facing its own problems related to maturity and customer demand. Now, if you combine these factors with India's incredibly youthful demography – a median age of 29 and 8 million graduates emerging from the university system each year (as mentioned previously) – hopefully you can see why India faces an economic breakpoint.

## From Fewer Jobs to Weaker Wage Growth

If employers need fewer workers to get the job done, then given the relentless growth in India's middle-class labour supply, the demand–supply mismatch is likely to push wages downwards.

Is this happening in India? If so to what extent? In the next chapter we seek to answer these questions.

# 5

# Real Wages Are Stagnating

*The more productive capital grows, the more it extends the division of labour and the application of machinery; the more the division of labour and the application of machinery extend, the more does competition extend among the workers, the more do their wages shrink together.**

The middle-class squeeze isn't just about headlines – it's about mathematics. When a Mumbai-based chartered accountant posted data showing that half of India's office workers earn less than skilled construction workers (see Table 5.1), it went viral instantly. A raw nerve had been struck.

**Table 5.1**: Salaries in White-Collar Jobs Lag Salaries in Blue-Collar Jobs

| Worker Type | Typical Monthly Earnings (₹) |
|---|---|
| White collar: office, entry level | Less than 15,000 |
| White collar: average | 11,837–28,460 |

* Karl Marx, *Wage-Labor and Capital*, 1849.

| Worker Type | Typical Monthly Earnings (₹) |
|---|---|
| Construction: unskilled | 10,500–15,000 |
| Construction: skilled | 15,000–21,000+ |
| Construction: with overtime | 30,000+ |

**Note:** Actual earnings vary by region, skill and job market conditions
**Source:** Harshad Shah's post on LinkedIn (July 2025)[1]

This chapter examines the brutal arithmetic behind India's middle-class crisis: how salaries at Nifty 50 companies have failed to keep pace with inflation for eight years, how the average middle-class income has barely budged from ₹10.23 lakh to ₹10.69 lakh over a decade,[2] and how real wage growth for managers has collapsed from 5.1 per cent annually to just 2.2 per cent.[3] Meanwhile, the true cost of middle-class living – food inflation at 11 per cent, medical costs at 14 per cent, school fees spiralling upwards – doubles every eight years. Add to that a government shifting tax burdens from corporations to individuals, and the result is mathematical inevitability: a middle class forced into debt just to maintain the illusion of stability.

## Salaries are Not Keeping Pace with the Cost of Living

If workers are being displaced by technology – in-line with the picture we have painted in the preceding chapters of this book – then economic theory says that two opposing effects will kick-in with respect to wages:

- The demand for workers will drop (as seen in the final figure of the previous chapter) and this in turn should depress wages; and
- The workers who are in employment should get paid more given that they are now using technology to produce more output for their employers (e.g., the agents in the command centre in Navi Mumbai – referenced in Chapter 3 – earn much more than the security guards they have replaced).

Which of these effects will dominate is hard to say on theoretical grounds alone. So, let's turn to data to inform our judgement on this key issue. To be precise, let's use data from India's 50 largest listed companies. If companies in India are using technology to reduce their workforce and drive efficiency gains, it is in the country's largest companies where this effect will show up first.

We looked at the average income earned by employees of the Nifty 50 companies as they stood on 31 March 2025 and then calculated how this average income (for the same set of 50 companies) has increased in the preceding nine years (i.e., from FY2016). We also compared it with average CPI (consumer price index) inflation during this period to understand if salaries kept pace with the cost of living.

As it turns out, average incomes have **not** kept pace with the cost of living as far as the Nifty 50 companies are concerned. In other words, if someone was just relying on their salary increments in the last nine years, far from being able to earn and save money for the future, their salaries wouldn't have been able to keep up even with price of food (see Table 5.2).

**Table 5.2**: In the Past Nine Years, Nifty 50 Companies' Employees' Salaries Have Not Kept Pace with Inflation

| Particulars | FY2016 | FY2025 | CAGR |
|---|---|---|---|
| Cumulative no. of employees | 2,287,469 | 4,928,077 | 10% |
| Cumulative salaries and wages paid (in ₹ billion) | 2,304 | 5,398 | 11% |
| Average salary per employee (in ₹) | 1,007,261 | 1,095,408 | 1% |
| CAGR in CPI inflation | | | 5% |
| CAGR in real salary per employee | | | -4% |

**Note:** Contractual employees were also included wherever data was available in both FY2016 and FY2025

**Source**: Marcellus Investment Managers using data from Bloomberg and annual reports of companies

To see if this had also been the case in the earlier part of the twenty-first century, we did the same analysis for Nifty companies as they stood on 31 March 2016 (FY2016) going back to FY2008 (for the same set of 50 companies). It turns out that employee salaries were keeping pace at least with inflation back then (see Table 5.3). In other words, pre-2016, the employees of the Nifty 50 companies were not losing money in real terms and were able to save (albeit a tiny amount, it was still positive).

**Table 5.3**: Between FY2007 and FY2016, Nifty 50 Companies' Employees' Salaries Grew Faster than Inflation

| Particulars | FY2007 | FY2016 | CAGR |
|---|---|---|---|
| Cumulative no. of employees | 1,424,590 | 2,014,707 | 4% |
| Cumulative salaries and wages paid (in ₹ million) | 596 | 2,480 | 20% |
| Average salary per employee (in ₹) | 418,683 | 1,231,186 | 13% |
| CAGR in CPI inflation | | | 9% |
| CAGR in real salary per employee | | | 4% |

**Note:** Companies forming part of Nifty as of 31 March 2016 were chosen for the analysis; only permanent employees were considered in both FY2007 and FY2016 and disclosures pertaining to contractual employees did not exist for many back in FY2007

**Source**: Marcellus Investment Managers using data from Bloomberg and annual reports of the companies

If you define the middle class as those who are financially equidistant between the rich and the poor, then income tax data shows that the Indian middle class is visibly losing ground relative to not just the rich *but also relative to the poor*. Over the past decade, that **53 per cent of the Indian population that files non-negative tax returns** (as of 2023–24) and earns between ₹5 lakh and ₹1 crore per annum, **has seen its income stagnate** (see the dashed line in Figure 5.1).[4]

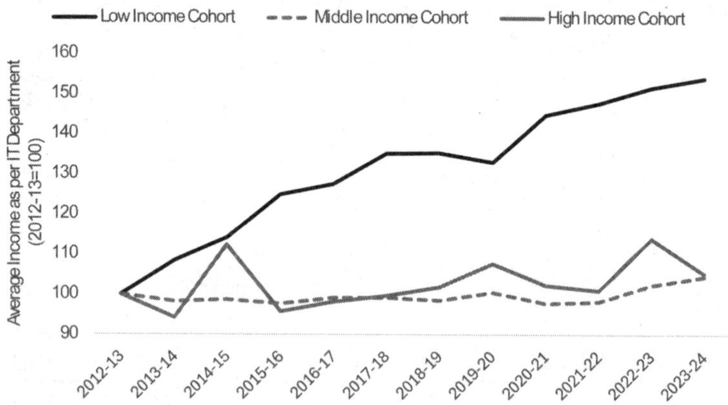


**Figure 5.1**: Middle income cohort (as measured by income tax returns) has seen their incomes stagnate over the last 11 years

**Note:** Sum of gross total income for each cohort was divided by the number of filers in each cohort, which was then indexed to 100 in 2012–13 to see the growth over the years. Buckets from 0 to ₹5 lakh of gross total income were considered as low income, those between ₹5 lakh and ₹1 crore were considered as middle income, and those beyond ₹1 crore of income were classified as high income.

**Source**: Marcellus Investment Managers using data from the Income Tax Department and the Ministry of Finance[5]

As can be seen in Table 5.4 (based on the same data as Figure 5.1), average annual income for this half of the tax-paying population was ₹10.23 lakh a decade ago and rose to ₹10.69 lakh in 2023–24. This has happened at a time when: (a) those earning below ₹5 lakh per annum have seen their income rise appreciably from an average of ₹2.36 lakh to ₹3.63 lakh; and (b) those earning above ₹1 crore per annum have seen their income inch up from ₹2.69 crore to ₹ 2.83 crore on an average.

The last two columns of Table 5.4 show that: (a) a substantial number of filers have moved from low income cohort from

2012–13 to middle income cohort in 2023–24; (b) their incomes, however, have not risen at the same pace as their entry into the cohort; and (c) the movement from the middle income to high income cohort has not been material in the last 10 years (implying that a large chunk of the population is still within the middle income cohort whose incomes on an average haven't grown in this period).

**Table 5.4**: Average Income Growth for the Middle-Income Group Has Fallen behind that of the Low-Income Group in the Last 11 Years

| Income Category | Avg Income in 2012–13 (₹ Lakh) | Avg Income in 2023–24 (₹ Lakh) | 11 yr CAGR of Average Income | % of Filers in 2012–13 | % of Filers in 2023–24 |
|---|---|---|---|---|---|
| Low income (₹ 0 to ₹ 5 lakh) | 2.4 | 3.6 | 4.0% | 80.6% | 46.9% |
| Middle income (₹ 5 lakh to ₹ 1 crore) | 10.2 | 10.7 | 0.4% | 19.3% | 52.8% |
| High income (beyond ₹ 1 crore) | 269.4 | 283.5 | 0.5% | 0.1% | 0.3% |

**Note:** Average income for each income category was arrived at by summing gross total income from IT department's data, divided by the number of filers in that category; percentage of filers in each category arrived at by summing the percentage filers under each bucket according to the IT department data

**Source**: Marcellus Investment Managers using data from the Income Tax Department and the Ministry of Finance

Now, let's move from the Nifty 50 to the broader Indian economy. Using compensation data from *Data for India*, we estimated how much real wages are growing for each segment of the labour force, namely, managers, other employees, directly employed workers and contract workers. As Table 5.5 shows, while real income growth has slowed down over the past decade (compared to the prior decade) for all segments of the workforce (barring directly employed workers), the slowdown is sharpest for the managers. From seeing their real incomes grow annually at 5.1 per cent over 2001–12, managers have had to contend with a mere 2.2 per cent annual salary growth over 2012–23. You can see in the table that no other segment of the workforce has seen this sort of 50 per cent+ slowdown in its real wage growth. To our mind, this data validates what the income tax data is telling us in terms of the slowdown in the middle class's income growth.

Anandorup Ghose, partner at Deloitte India and one of India's leading experts on professional compensation, says, 'The Economic Survey showed decline in real wages since 2017–18 for salaried employees.' He added that the 'International Labour Organisation (ILO) data places India in the bottom quartile among 130 countries in terms of real wage growth.'[6]

**Table 5.5**: Among All Categories, Managerial Incomes Have Slowed Down More in the Last Decade vs the Previous One

| | Salary (₹) and Growth (in per cent) | | | | | Inflation (in per cent) | | Real Income Growth (in per cent) | |
|---|---|---|---|---|---|---|---|---|---|
| **Categories** | **2001** | **2012** | **2023** | **2001–12** | **2012–23** | **2001–12** | **2012–23** | **2001–12** | **2012–23** |
| Managers | 1,62,913 | 5,55,357 | 13,00,000 | 12 | 8 | 7 | 6 | 5.1 | 2.2 |
| Other employees | 71,873 | 1,89,505 | 4,12,412 | 9 | 7 | 7 | 6 | 2.5 | 1.4 |
| Directly employed workers | 49,838 | 1,06,841 | 2,25,151 | 7 | 7 | 7 | 6 | 0.5 | 1.1 |
| Contract workers | 26,668 | 74,509 | 1,76,091 | 10 | 8 | 7 | 6 | 3.1 | 2.3 |

**Source:** Data for India, Bloomberg

## Rapidly Rising Cost of Living

So far in this chapter, we have used the government's CPI inflation data as a proxy for how much the cost of living of the middle class has risen. This indicator suggests that over the past decade, cost of living has risen at around 5–6 per cent per annum. However, the official CPI estimation process uses a basket of goods that have little or no resemblance with the middle class's consumption basket. For example, 50 per cent of the CPI basket is food; thankfully, one will be hard pressed to find a middle-class family in India that spends half of its income on food.

Based on the price inflation we can see in many of the items that the middle class purchases, we reckon that the cost of living for urban middle-class families is doubling roughly every eight years implying around 9 per cent per annum inflation as opposed to the 5–6 per cent per annum inflation number used so far in this chapter. For example,

- Cost of a typical vegetarian thali rose at 11 per cent per annum in the last five years while salaries of employees rose by just 6 per cent per annum.[7]
- Cost of an Alto (small car) rose by 8 per cent per annum from ₹2.83 lakh in FY2019 to ₹4.23 lakh in FY2025. On the other hand, the price of Hero Splendor (entry level motorcycle) rose by 7 per cent per annum from ₹56,000 in FY2019 to ₹77,000 in FY2025.[8]
- The cost of medical treatment in private hospitals is rising at 14 per cent per annum.[9]

- Transport and communication CPI has risen by ~5 per cent per annum over the last six years.[10]
- A good proxy for the cost of secondary education is the rise in education loans outstanding as per RBI's data. Outstanding education loans rose from ₹65.3k crore (US $7.3 billion) in 2020 to ₹1.29 lakh crore (US $14.3 billion) in 2024, registering a CAGR of nearly 19 per cent per annum.[11]

Unfortunately for the middle class, even as its income stagnated over the past decade, the cost of living has risen sharply, especially in the post Covid-19 era. School fees, rents (or EMIs on home loans), medical insurance premiums and food and FMCG inflation drove a big jump in the middle class's expenses and squeezed household savings.

An important driver of the slowdown in urban demand is the rising cost of food. Dabur India's CEO Mohit Malhotra says, 'The growing food inflation is impacting demand in urban India, particularly for discretionary products.'[12] Firms like HUL, Marico, Dabur and Tata Consumer Products have either raised prices of certain products by 3–5 per cent or resorted to 'shrinkflation' – reducing the weight of products per package – with the increase in prices of key raw materials, such as palm oil, coffee, cocoa and wheat. Palm oil – a key input for personal care and snack brands – has seen a duty hike of 20 per cent; tea, of 30 per cent. The CEOs of India's FMCG firms are saying that the increase in commodity prices has affected sales of their tea brands like 3 Roses, Taaza and Red Label, which cater to the price-sensitive middle class.[13] In Chapter 7 we will return to the subject of how the middle class's consumption is being compressed by the job and wage slowdown.

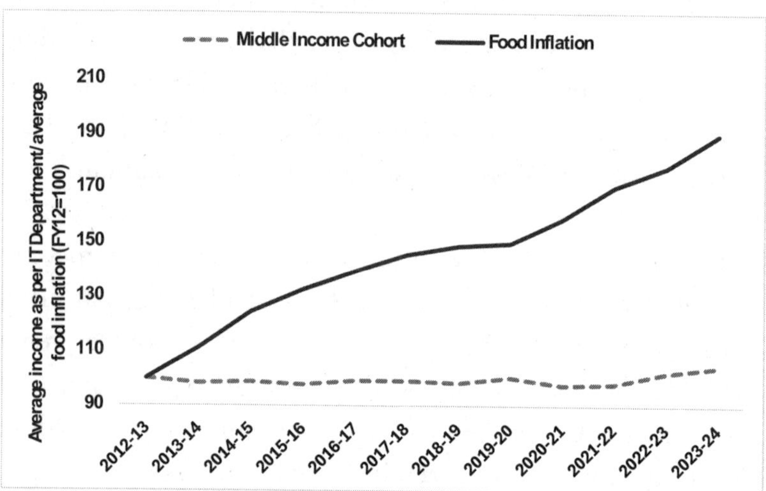


**Figure 5.2**: Food inflation has been eating into Indian middle class's stagnating incomes over the past decade

**Source**: Marcellus Investment Managers using data from the Income Tax Department and the Ministry of Finance

## The Rising Tax Burden of the Middle Class

As if stagnant income and rising cost of living were not enough, since FY2021, the government has had to rely on the middle class to finance its revenue growth. As shown in Figure 5.3, in the post Covid-19 world, income taxes as a percentage of GDP in FY2025 are significantly higher than they were before Covid-19 (3.6 per cent now vs 2.5 per cent before Covid-19). In contrast, the government's collections from corporate taxes have fallen significantly (as a percentage of GDP): 3 per cent now vs 3.5 per cent before Covid-19.[14]

Effectively, the government has shifted a significant part of its tax load away from corporates (through a big cut in the corporate tax rate which the Finance Minister announced in September 2019) and towards the middle class.

Given that individual income taxes as a per cent of GDP have risen by 1.1 per cent of GDP between FY2019 to FY2025, that translates into an incremental load of ₹1.5 trillion (US $17 billion) on the middle class which (as described in Chapter 1) bears the majority of the income tax burden. Combining this factoid with what we can see in the preceding figures of this chapter suggests that, on a post-tax basis, the decline in the middle class's real income is even sharper.

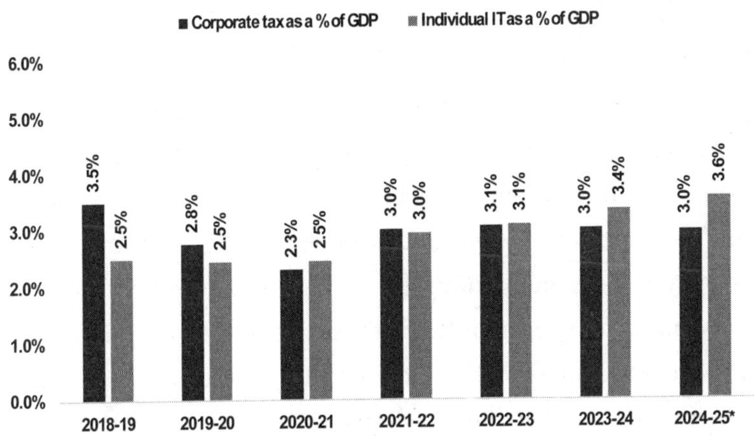


**Figure 5.3:** Income tax continues to drive direct tax collections; data for 2024–25 is provisional

**Source**: Marcellus Investment Managers using data from the Income Tax Department and the Ministry of Finance

To see how all these forces impact the life of an urban middle-class family, consider the life of Prakash Bhasi, a 54-year-old technician with a packaging company in Mumbai. Until a few years ago, he used to believe that a household income of ₹22 lakh per annum would be enough for his three-member family even after paying the ₹45,000 monthly instalment for his one-bedroom flat in Navi Mumbai. Now, however, he's feeling the pinch due to a 30 per cent rise in his cost of living in recent years. Food prices have risen sharply, as have the prices of cars. In fact, unable to afford a new car, Mr Bhasi has purchased a used car. In a similar vein, he now buys unbranded FMCG goods; he feels the branded ones are out of his reach.[15]

While we will discuss in Chapter 9 how the government – after five years of watching the situation deteriorate for the middle class – has finally begun cutting taxes, all of this begs the question as to why they chose to increase the income tax load on the middle class at a time when this segment of the economy is under obvious pressure. The answer, we believe, goes back to the structural vulnerabilities of the middle class, as explained in the closing pages of Chapter 2. To be specific, the middle class's relative insignificance at the ballot box makes this constituency the most obvious target for the government when it comes to boosting tax revenues. While the elite and the masses have political leverage (in different ways), the middle class doesn't.

## From Jobs and Wages to Debt

If middle-class India is operating in a punishing job market where jobs are hard to come by and wage growth is elusive while cost of living doubles every eight years or so, what is the most likely coping mechanism for them? The answer, in one-word, is 'debt'. In the next chapter we explain how the Indian middle class became one of the most indebted groups of people in the world.

# 6

# Debt Is Skyrocketing

> *The [petty bourgeoise] sink[s] gradually into the proletariat, partly because their diminutive capital does not suffice for the scale on which Modern Industry is carried on, and is swamped in the competition with the large capitalists, partly because their specialized skill is rendered worthless by new methods of production.**

Over the past decade, a silent crisis has been unfolding in middle-class India. While incomes have stagnated and job opportunities have dwindled, borrowing has surged at an unprecedented rate. The result is a paradox that would have seemed unthinkable just ten years ago: Indians now carry one of the highest debt burdens in the world, excluding mortgages – surpassing even consumption-heavy economies like the US and debt-fuelled growth stories like China.

This transformation has been swift and dramatic. Until 2019, India's non-housing household debt remained broadly

* Karl Marx, *Communist Manifesto*, 1848.

aligned with international peers. The Covid-19 pandemic marked an inflection point, and unlike other nations, where borrowing subsequently moderated, India's trajectory continued its steep ascent. Today, non-housing household debt as a percentage of GDP stands at 32 per cent in FY2025, up from 23 per cent in FY2017. For borrowers caught in this cycle, the mathematics are brutal: Nearly 40 per cent of annual income is now consumed by debt servicing alone.[1]

What makes this borrowing binge particularly alarming is its composition. These are not loans funding productive assets or wealth-creating ventures. Instead, much of this debt finances non-essential consumption – vacations rank as the most common reason for taking personal loans, with over a quarter of such borrowing dedicated to holidays. Social media, discussed in Chapter 8, plays a significant role in these consumption-fuelled debts. The affluent segments of the middle class are borrowing for aspirational purchases like premium smartphones and lifestyle upgrades, while less affluent households turn to debt for essential needs like healthcare and education. The RBI's December 2024 Financial Stability Report reveals that 45 per cent of all borrowers are classified as sub-prime, and nearly half of their loan requirements are directed towards consumption rather than investment.[2]

The consequence is a debt trap of staggering proportions. Nearly half of all Indians taking personal loans have multiple live loans outstanding, often juggling borrowings from three or more lenders simultaneously. With effective interest rates above 10 per cent and incomes growing at best in the high single digits, the mathematics is unforgiving: debt burdens are growing faster than the ability to repay them. This chapter examines how a convergence of changing social attitudes towards debt, the financialization of essential needs and aggressive lending practices has ensnared between 5 and 10 per cent of India's retail borrowers in a vicious cycle where new loans are taken simply to service old ones.

In light of the scarcity of jobs and wage compression discussed in the previous chapters, it is not surprising that the RBI has highlighted that net household savings in India (i.e., household savings less household borrowings) as a percentage of income hit a 50-year low in FY2023 and despite rising to 6 per cent in FY2025, is still much lower than what it has been historically (Figure 6.1). The reason for this figure plunging is

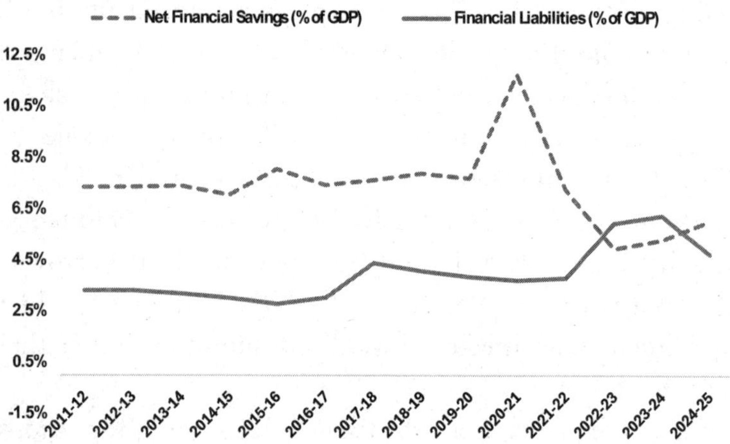


**Figure 6.1**: Net financial savings as a percentage of GDP are down because of rising liabilities; underlying figures are in ₹ billion

**Note:** If the figures are updated for a particular year in the subsequent years, those updated figures were used in the charts

**Source**: Marcellus Investment Managers, data for each of the years pulled out from multiple published documents by the RBI.

not so much falling savings; it is the soaring financial liabilities that are to blame. Indian households have become world champions in borrowing money – lots of it, non-stop and at high cost.

## One of the Most Indebted People in the World

Over the past decade, not only have Indians borrowed at an increasing rate while their incomes have stagnated, but now they are also one of the most indebted people across the world whose debt (excluding mortgages) as a percentage of GDP now surpasses that of the US and China, as mentioned earlier.

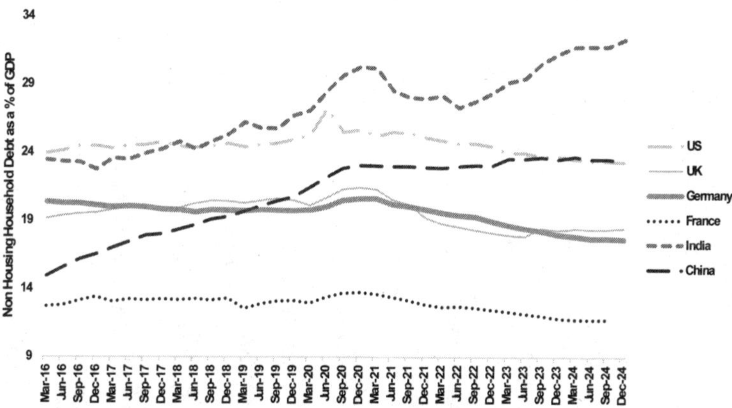


**Figure 6.2**: Their borrowings make Indians today one of the most indebted people in the world (excluding mortgages)

**Source**: Marcellus Investment Managers, CEIC, several sources collated by Motilal Oswal Financial Services Ltd.

What Figure 6.2 shows is that until 2019, India's non-housing household debt was broadly in line with other countries. In 2020, reeling under the impact of Covid-19, India witnessed a steep fall in GDP, and resultantly the line spiked up during this period. After this shock, India's non-housing household debt has surged at a rate faster than any of the countries shown in the chart. As a result, India has now surpassed developed countries that are traditionally considered to be consumption heavy (like the US) as well as developing countries that have typically relied heavily on bank credit for development (like China).

As Figure 6.3 shows, non-housing household debt as a percentage of households' gross domestic product now stands

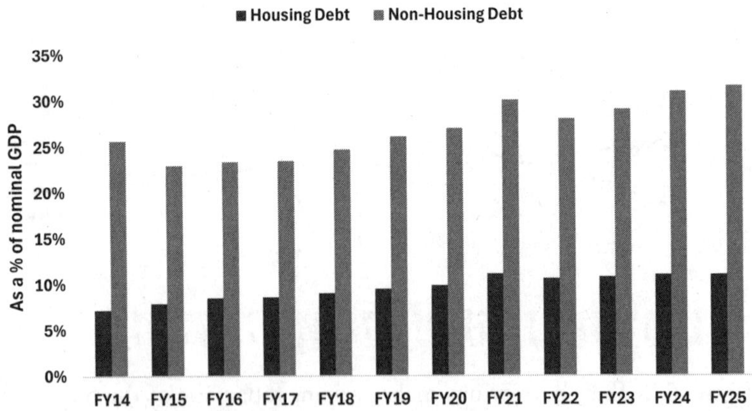


**Figure 6.3**: Excluding mortgages, household debt as a percentage of gross domestic product has been rising

**Source**: Marcellus Investment Managers, RBI and National Housing Board (collated by Motilal Oswal Financial Services Ltd.), Ministry of Statistical Programming and Implementation (collated by Ambit Capital)

at 32 per cent, up from 23 per cent in FY2017. The result of such high levels of debt is that for borrowers, nearly 40 per cent of their annual income is being used to service debt.[3]

Most worryingly, most of these retail loans are not for creating productive assets but for satisfying consumption needs. More specifically, this borrowing is financing aspirational consumption (such as phones and holidays) for the more affluent members of the middle class and essential consumption (such as healthcare and education) for the less affluent members of the middle class. We discuss both aspects of Indians' borrowing binge further on in this chapter.

This surge in borrowing to finance consumption is also evident in data published by the RBI. Specifically, if we were to look at the RBI's Financial Stability Report from December 2024,[4] it shows that not only have consumption related loans risen in the past several years, but also that 45

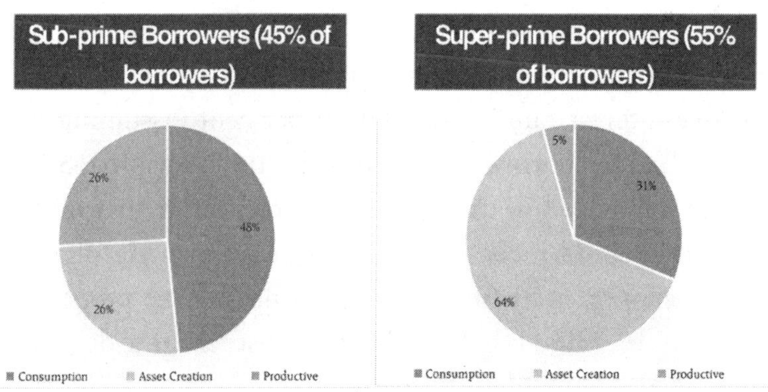


**Figure 6.4**: Growing use of loans to finance consumption rather than productive asset creation

**Source**: RBI, Financial Stability Report (December 2024)

per cent of all borrowers are sub-prime and nearly half of their loan requirement is towards consumption (see Figure 6.4 on p. 103).

## The Middle Class Debt Trap

Nearly 50 per cent of Indians are open to using personal loans to improve their current lifestyle. A third are willing to take a personal loan to buy consumer durables like mobile phones, television, washing machine, etc. Interestingly, productive assets like two-wheelers (23 per cent), car (12.5 per cent), house (12 per cent) and gold (10.5 per cent) come further down the pecking order.[5]

The RBI's June 2025 Financial Stability review states that 68 per cent of those taking a personal loan less than ₹50k have more than three live loans during origination and 12 per cent of all borrowers have loans from three or more lenders.[6] Taking a weighted average of the interest rates that these households are paying on their various loans would show that their effective interest rate is north of 10 per cent (assuming that this is a 'prime' borrower catered to by India's banks). Salary surveys referenced in the previous chapter show that middle class's household incomes are rising at high single digits at best. Therefore, mathematically speaking, a large proportion of India's middle-class households are stuck in a debt trap where their annual debt burden is likely to grow faster than their income.

The massive increase in the middle class's borrowing seen over the past decade has exposed these households to a debt trap – a circumstance where borrowers, having borrowed more than they can possibly repay, given their modest incomes, are forced to take out fresh loans to repay the already outstanding loans.[7] The classic signs of a debt trap are borrowers with modest incomes having multiple debts outstanding. This is exactly what the RBI's Financial Stability Reviews are pointing towards.

The December 2024 Financial Stability Review says that **nearly half** of the borrowers (the top two lines in Figure 6.5) availing credit card and personal loans have another live retail loan outstanding, which are often high-ticket loans (i.e., housing and/or vehicle loan).[8]

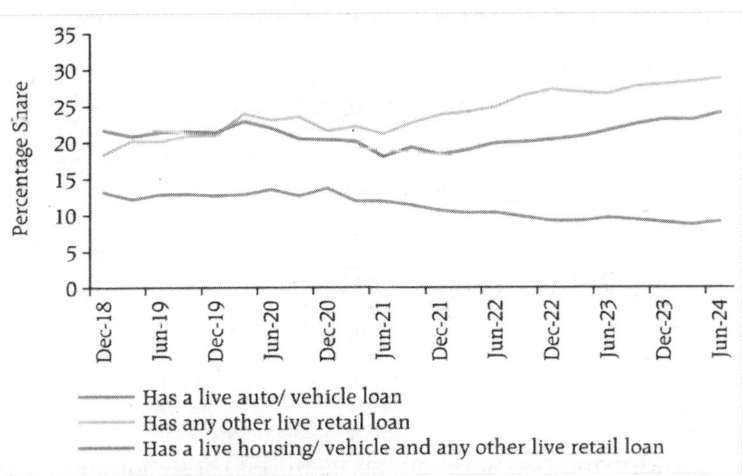


**Figure 6.5**: Personal loan/credit card customers at risk of default

**Source**: RBI, Financial Stability Report (December 2024)

Now, while we hope that these borrowers with credit card loan and personal loans plus another high-ticket loan outstanding (basically, the middle line in Figure 6.5) do not default, our scope for optimism is limited when we look at another broad swathe of middle-class borrowers.

Around 45 per cent of India's retail borrowers have lower credit scores.[9] Let's define this segment of borrowers as 'subprime'. According to the RBI, subprime borrowers spend 48 per cent of their loans on consumption, compared to super-prime borrowers – those with excellent credit scores – who only use 31 per cent of their debt that way.[10] Joining the dots between these pieces of data suggests that between 5 and 10 per cent of India's retail borrowers are caught in a debt trap. Here is how we join the dots:

- About 67 per cent of Indian families have availed of personal loans.[11]
- Around 25 per cent of these borrowers have credit card loan and personal loans plus another high-ticket loan outstanding (line in the middle in Figure 6.5).
- At least 45 per cent of these borrowers are likely to be subprime,[12] and according to the RBI, subprime borrowers spend 48 per cent of their loans on consumption (as mentioned earlier).[13]

Multiplying the numbers given in the three bullets shown above suggests that between 5 and 10 per cent of India's retail borrowers are caught in a debt trap where they are using multiple loans to finance day-to-day consumption.

In the remainder of this chapter, we point to three factors other than joblessness and stagnating wages that are pushing a growing number of middle-class households towards a debt trap: a) greater social acceptance of indebtedness to live the good life; b) extensive use of debt to finance the essentials of life such as education and transport; and c) greater willingness on the part of lenders to finance retail borrowers.

## Social Acceptance of Borrowing to Live the Good Life

### Changing Attitudes to Debt

Dr Godse, a psychologist who works with young business owners says,

> A lot of people are today under far more financial stress than what is visible, mostly because credit card and UPI usage is rampant. With physical currency, one was aware and mentally calculating how much s/he has spent versus what is left. With cards and UPI, the action of making a payment is so automated and game like, it makes them keep doing it over and over again without realizing that they are draining their own money.[14]

Data also shows the rising trend of people using credit cards and EMI-ing their way through even small ticket transactions. If we were to look at the data for credit card spends per card, these have gone down over time, while the number of transactions per card have actually risen (see Figure 6.6).

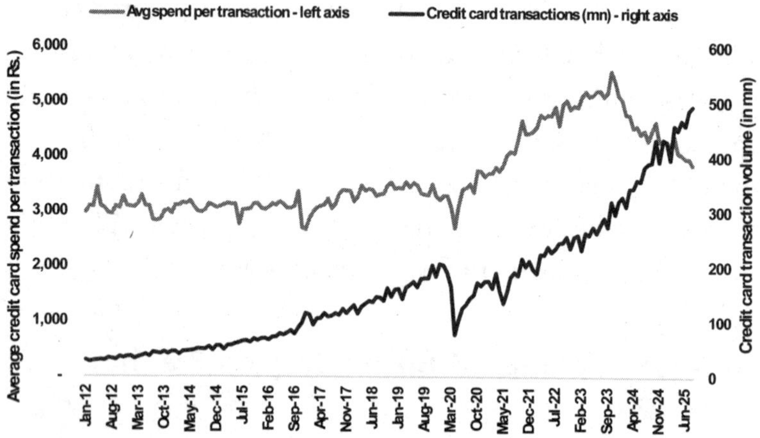


**Figure 6.6**: Average credit card spends have fallen even as the number of credit card transactions have soared

**Source**: Marcellus Investment Managers, Avendus Spark Institutional Equities

This behaviour in spending is also visible beyond the credit card ecosystem. According to Dr Sharmila Banwat,

> People have got out of the habit of making monthly budgets and adhering to them. With the advent of quick commerce and e-commerce and the option to get everything within minutes, the need for instant gratification manifests through low self-control financially and reinforces consumption leading to repetition of the action. Increased financial insecurity and instability also leads to psychological disorders like anxiety and depression, leading to an endless spiral to the bottom.[15]

In the face of stagnant incomes and rising cost of living, the middle class has chosen to upgrade its lifestyle using the only route open to it – namely, more borrowing. During our trips to small town India, we increasingly hear from the branch managers of India's leading banks that borrowing money to finance a holiday or a high-end smartphone purchase, or borrowing money to speculate in the F&O market are increasingly commonplace behaviours. Branch managers of these banks inform us that such loans are often 'pre-approved' by the banks' lending algorithms, which operate on the basis of the historical credit scores of these borrowers.

There is a simpler way to understand the scale of the household borrowing explosion unfolding in front of us. As Figure 6.7 shows, personal loans balances (i.e., loans other than housing, vehicle, education loans) have nearly trebled in the past six years.

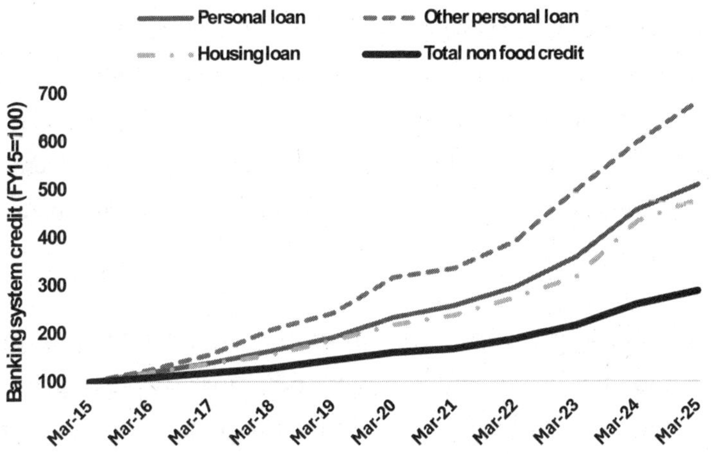


**Figure 6.7**: Near trebling of other personal loans has come at a time when overall credit growth has nearly doubled

**Note**: Other personal loan category includes personal loans beyond housing, advances against fixed deposit, credit cards, education and vehicle loans

**Source**: Marcellus Investment Managers, RBI data collated by Ambit Capital

## Borrowing to Go on Holiday

India's financial media now routinely carries stories – usually of a celebratory nature – which describe how middle-class workers are upgrading their lifestyles by borrowing. In one such newspaper article, we read about Vikas, an autorickshaw driver, who had borrowed to purchase a smartphone. His quote points to a dynamic of ever-increasing debt, fuelled by rising aspirations:

> My borrowing behaviour has shifted significantly when it comes to mobile phones. Initially, I borrowed to purchase basic phone models that met my essential communication needs, was affordable and functional. However, as I gained access to more flexible credit options over time, I borrowed to purchase a smartphone not just out of necessity, but as part of my aspirations to improve my income. [...] For example, my new smartphone helps me to use apps to get customers for a ride and also captures beautiful memories of time spent with my family.[16]

Vacationing is the most common reason for availing of a personal loan. As shown by Figure 6.8, more than a quarter of personal loans in India are taken for the purposes of going on holiday. In fact, two-thirds of such borrowers (who borrow to holiday) are salaried professionals.[17]

This celebratory and aspirational nature of borrowing has helped us understand something that used to puzzle us in the

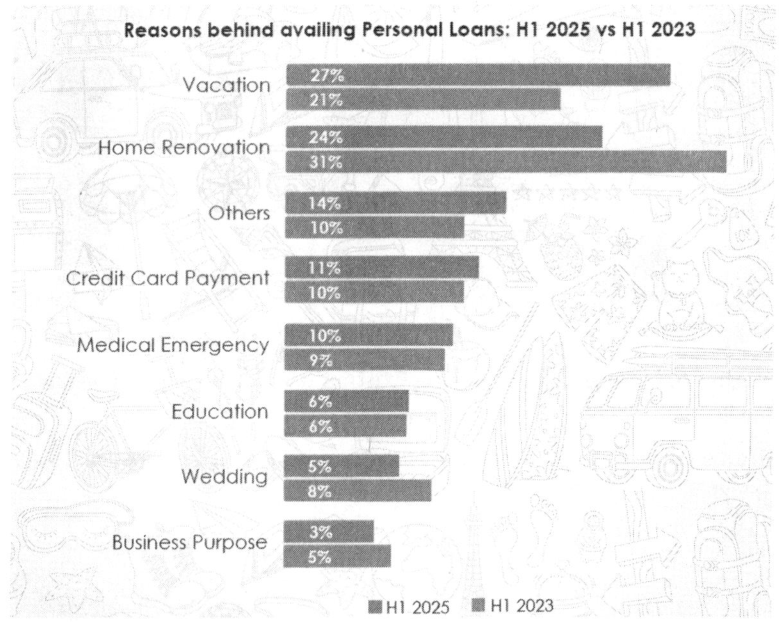


**Figure 6.8**: Most of the retail loans have been availed for non-economic, one-time use

**Source**: 'How India Travels Using Holiday Loans: A Consumer Insights Report by Paisabazaar', *Paisabazaar*, July 2025.

initial years of the post Covid-19 lending boom – the more affluent the Indian professional:

- the higher the likelihood that they will be a borrower (see Figure 6.9), and
- the higher the proportion of their annual income going towards debt servicing (see Figure 6.10).

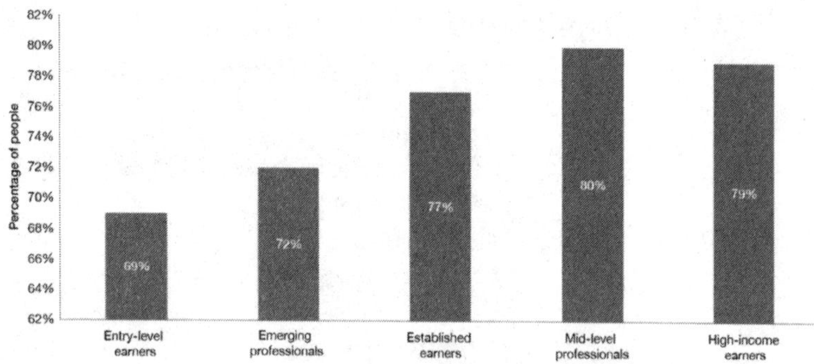


**Figure 6.9**: Percentage of paying existing loan EMIs across income levels

**Source**: *How India Spends: A Deep Dive into Consumer Spending Behaviour*, PwC and Perfios, 2024, https://tinyurl.com/3ca763s3.

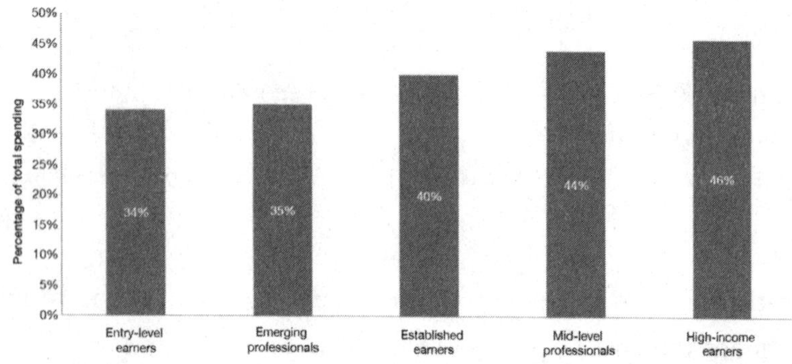


**Figure 6.10**: Distribution of loan EMI payments as a percentage of total spending across income levels

**Source**: *How India Spends: A Deep Dive into Consumer Spending Behaviour*, PwC and Perfios, 2024, https://tinyurl.com/3ca763s3.

Unfortunately for the Indian middle class, UPI, the India Stack (digital public goods meant to digitize and ease identity, data and payments in India) and India's sophisticated digital ecosystem have made it very easy for them to fulfil their aspirations to live the good life by quickly and easily borrowing large sums of money using their smartphones. Ashish Tiwari, chief marketing officer, Home Credit India, says that lower-middle-class borrowers are showing an increasing preference for borrowing for 'consumer durables and small business ventures'. As digital literacy proliferates, these borrowings are being conducted via banking apps, chatbots and WhatsApp payments rather than the traditional process of going to a bank branch, filling a form and then patiently waiting for several days for the bank to extend a loan.[18]

Tech innovations aside, there is a powerful financial innovation that is wreaking havoc on their finances. That innovation is the EMI. For example, ~40 per cent of smartphones in India are purchased using EMIs.[19] Let's take the example of a ₹1 lakh smartphone. On an EMI basis, it feels very affordable – ₹4,166 a month, no upfront payment. In fact, we have often seen taxi drivers in Mumbai now use iPhones worth more than ₹1 lakh.

But the EMI is not the full story. You have to add the processing fee for the loan, the inflated MRP and insurance on the phone. The result is that the buyer of the iPhone (i.e., the borrower) is actually paying an amount around 20–25 per cent higher than the initial estimate of ₹1 lakh.

Then comes the next layer of pain for the unsuspecting borrower. The zero-interest period is usually for the first three to six months. After that, the interest rate comes into play, sometimes at rates upwards of 20 per cent. At an interest rate of 20 per cent on the inflated principal amount of ₹1.25

lakh, the EMI after the initial six-month zero-interest rate period will be north of ₹6,500 a month, more than 50 per cent higher than the EMI payment for the first six months. This is how affluent professionals like the CFO profiled in the introductory section of this book get trapped in a cycle of high interest rates, high EMIs and dwindling cashflows to pay these EMIs. This cycle is the 'debt trap' that has ensnared 5–10 per cent of middle-class households.

## Use of Debt to Finance the Essentials of Life

A separate – less affluent – strata of the middle class is borrowing to finance the essentials of life. In fact, data suggests that borrowing has become the default behaviour for this strata of society. A staggering 67 per cent of Indian families have taken personal loans. In fact, majority of Indians (53 per cent) have taken personal loans before reaching the age of 30.[20]

In absolute terms, these translate into indebtedness on a massive scale. 'In 2024, an estimated 15 to 20 million middle-class Indians, earning between Rs 5 lakh and Rs 30 lakh annually, are relying on instant loans.'[21] Much of this borrowing is being driven by young professionals, students and micro-entrepreneurs who face rising living costs, while their wages or earnings are stagnant. Given that India has only 40 million income-tax payers, the fact that 15 to 20 million Indians are relying on instant loans suggests that around half of middle-class India has borrowed money to be able to sustain their day-to-day consumption. Given that borrowers in general are using nearly 40 per cent of their annual income to service debt, for this (more needy) segment of the middle class, it is likely that upwards of half of their annual income is being used for debt servicing.

Take the example of Rahul Singh, a delivery agent with a food delivery app. Rahul says that he borrowed money not just to finance his home renovation but also for '[...] covering essential expenses, such as rent, medical bills and any other unforeseen expenses, which were critical for survival'.[22]

## Education Loans

As highlighted in Chapter 2, a range of data show that university education in the context of the Indian job market neither improves pay nor increases the likelihood of employment.[23] Given the limited commercial viability of education, it is worrying that Indian students have borrowed in excess of $8 billion to fund their education.

Not only is the outstanding education loan figure a very large figure, but it is also growing rapidly. 'After a robust growth of over 80 per cent and 70 per cent in fiscals 2023 and 2024, respectively, education loan assets under management (AUM) of non-banking finance companies (NBFCs) is expected to grow at a healthy clip of 40-45 per cent to cross Rs 60,000 crore in the current fiscal from Rs 43,000 crore in FY2023–24, according to a Crisil report.'[24]

Given that the commercial viability of becoming a graduate in India is questionable, it is not surprising that non-performing assets (NPA) on student loans in India are running at 4 per cent of loans outstanding.[25] (A loan is classified by a lender as NPA when repayments are overdue for more than 90 days, thus indicating that the borrower is struggling to repay the loan.)

In addition to the challenges discussed around graduate employment in Chapter 2, there is an additional adverse dynamic that is making it difficult for Indian students to repay education loans. Many of these loans are taken for pursuing overseas degrees. Often these 1–2-year postgraduate degrees cost Indian students upwards of ₹50 lakh. They pay out these large sums of money in the hope of landing a job in a developed economy and then repaying their education loan back home in India. Unfortunately, however, developed economies like the US are increasingly keen on tightening their labour market laws to make it difficult for Indians to work in their country. This leaves the Indian students in a financial no-man's land – they have incurred the cost of a Western education without having access to the underlying cashflows of a Western graduate.

## Willingness of Lenders to Finance Retail Borrowers

As highlighted in Chapter 4, the erstwhile RBI Governor Raghuram Rajan's AQR of 2015 put the fear of god in banks when it came to lending to corporates. As a result, banks focused their lending efforts on retail borrowers. In the space of a decade, retail loans doubled from 15 per cent of the banking system's loans outstanding to 30 per cent. As shown in Figure 6.11, at the vanguard of this surge in retail lending were the loans with the highest interest rates – the personal loans.

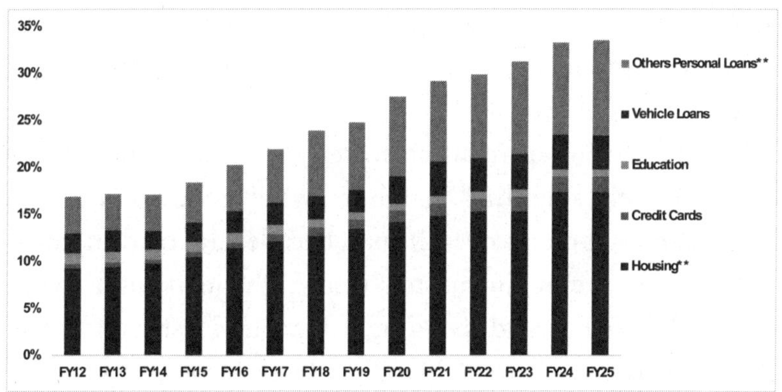


**Figure 6.11**: The percentage of retail loans in total loans outstanding in India has risen materially

**Note**: Loans outstanding data adjusted for the effect of merger of HDFC and HDFC bank; total non-food bank credit used as the denominator for percentage calculated above

**Source**: Marcellus Investment Managers, Reserve Bank of India, sourced by Ambit Capital

Facilitating this surge in bank lending to retail borrowers was not just modern technology (such as UPI and smartphones) and financial innovations (such as the EMI), but also the availability of increasingly high-quality credit scoring on retail borrowers to the banks.

Credit scoring for retail borrowers is a statistical method used by lenders to assess the creditworthiness of individuals, based on factors like payment history, credit utilization and length of credit history. This process generates a credit score, which lenders use to make decisions on loan eligibility, interest rates and other loan terms – with higher scores indicating lower risk. Key entities involved are credit bureaus in India, such as *CIBIL*, Experian, Equifax and CRIF High Mark, that collect and analyse borrower data to produce these scores.

These credit bureaus then earn their money by selling the credit scores to lenders who in turn utilize the scores for their lending decisions.

Credit scoring of retail borrowers relies upon underlying data on their spending and borrowing behaviour. Three distinct developments over the past decade have made it much easier for the credit bureaus to collect high quality underlying data on borrowing and spending behaviour. Firstly, under the Jan Dhan Yojana, nearly 600 million bank accounts have been opened in India over the past decade – more than doubling the number of bank accounts in the country.[26] Secondly, the rise of UPI has meant that almost every Indian now creates a digital payment trail (which was not created when cash was the main mode of payment), and this payment trail creates copious data for the algorithms used by the credit bureaus. Thirdly, the ubiquity of smartphones allied with UPI means that nearly 700 million Indians are creating digital payment trails that can be fed into the algorithms used by the credit bureaus.[27]

These three factors have allowed Indian lenders to democratize access to credit dramatically over the past decade. Unfortunately, for the Indian middle class, this period has coincided with a dip in their personal cashflows. Thus, supply has met demand to create a massive surge in retail borrowing in the post-Covid-19 era.

At 60 per cent of India's GDP, consumption is the mainstay of the Indian economy. Despite the massive surge in retail borrowing, the Indian middle class's consumption growth has slowed down over the past decade. Such is the intensity of the jobs and wages slowdown that a surge in borrowing has not been able to offset those two adverse factors. In the next chapter we examine the extent of the consumption slowdown.

# 7

# Job, Wages, Debt … How All of this Impacts Consumption

*For most people, the most critical problem faced by the middle class remains financial, especially after the Covid-19 pandemic. Given the aspirations and lifestyle it has, the middle class has been struggling with the financial strain in the wake of job cuts and lay-offs following the pandemic. Rising inflation has made matters worse, and it has increased the economic insecurity of the middle-income groups. Increasing costs of housing, healthcare, education, and other essential goods and services has put significant financial strain on the middle class.**

The cascading effects of job scarcity, wage compression and mounting household debt have converged into a consumption crisis that threatens the foundations of India's economic

* Manisha Pande, *Middle Class India: Driving Change in the 21st Century*, Aleph Book Company, 2024, pp. 303–04.

growth. In FY2023, net household savings as a percentage of income plummeted to their lowest level since 1977 – not because Indians have stopped saving, but because their borrowings have exploded.

The most visible manifestation of this crisis appears in the FMCG sector, India's fourth-largest industry and a reliable barometer of urban demand. Over 15 years, FMCG volume growth has collapsed from around 10 per cent annually to a mere 3 per cent. This is not a temporary blip – it represents a fundamental shift in consumption patterns. In October 2024, Nestlé India's managing director captured the severity when he observed that 'the middle segment which used to be the segment most of us FMCG companies used to operate in, which is the middle class of the country ... seems to be shrinking'.[1]

The automobile sector tells an even grimmer story. In the post Covid-19 era, car sales in India aren't growing slowly – they're actually declining year after year. This mirrors the FMCG slowdown with eerie precision, both having begun their descent approximately 15 years ago.

Contributing to this perfect storm is relentless food price inflation, averaging 6 per cent annually over the past decade and a half, implying a doubling of prices every ten years.[2] As FMCG companies pass these costs to consumers, Indian households respond by throttling off consumption: buying less frequently, switching to smaller pack sizes and trading down to cheaper alternatives. The middle-class consumer – fatigued by debt, joblessness and real wage declines – is sending an unmistakable signal: 'I don't have the capacity to buy anymore.' This consumption crisis now threatens to derail the very economic growth engine that has powered India since the 1991 reforms.

## The Project Manager Exits

A week prior to Diwali in October 2025, Saurabh was waiting for a flight at Lucknow Airport when a white-collar professional approached him and introduced himself as a project manager at one of India's largest IT Services firms. After mentioning that he had read Saurabh's previous books he launched into a monologue:

> You have to write about people like us. I have worked in Indian IT services for 20 years including seven years in USA and two years in the UK. Currently, I am earning ₹70 lakh per year and I live in Kolkata. I don't have an extravagant lifestyle and yet at the end of each month, I find that I have no savings. When I lived in America for seven years, I was paid around US $150k per annum and yet at the end of each year, I used to be able to save some money. Ex-colleagues of mine who visit me from America can't believe how much it costs to live in cities like Gurgaon, Pune, Bangalore or Mumbai. House rents are higher in India's metros than what they are in America's smaller cities. Eating out at decent restaurant now costs as much in Gurgaon as it does in a place like, say, Buffalo, New York. Unless I watch every penny that I spend, I don't have any savings at the end of the year. I don't understand why this is happening. After tightening my belt for the past couple of

years, I have thrown in the towel. I have quit my job and am leaving India for an IT job in the Middle East in a couple of months.

At the time Saurabh heard this IT worker's monologue at Lucknow Airport, we had spent two years researching this book. We knew that a combination of fewer jobs, falling real wages and rising debt was suffocating consumption for millions of middle-class families living in similar circumstances to the frustrated and bewildered project manager from one of India's largest IT services firms.

## Middle Class India's Consumption Growth Has Slowed

From the ashes of the Second World War and from the ravages of Hiroshima and Nagasaki, Japan rebuilt its economy at such speed and vigour that by 1990 it was the world's second largest economy. Central to this rebuilding was Japan's export orientation: exports of goods and services as a percentage of Japanese GDP rose from almost nothing at the end of the Second World War to 14 per cent in 1984 and well over 20 per cent as we write this book in 2025.[3] The world learnt to enjoy music on Sony's Walkman, do calculations on Casio's computers, drive Toyota's dependable cars and use Honda's powerful gensets. In India, we fell in love with Suzuki's cars, Honda's motorcycles and Panasonic's VCRs.

Deng Xiaoping's China studied Japan's export-oriented success and, through the 1980s and 1990s, proceeded to transform China into an export powerhouse. China's exports of goods and services as a percentage of GDP rose from 2.5 per cent in 1970 to 20 per cent as we write this book in 2025.[4] South Korea, Taiwan and the cities of Hong Kong and Singapore too adopted export-oriented economic policies in the last three decades of the twentieth century to generate employment for their citizens and wealth for their entrepreneurs.

India's policymakers saw all of this play out in front of them. They saw East Asia become the factory of the world, but they couldn't adopt the same export-oriented policies because they hadn't put in place the policies and infrastructure to provide adequate education, healthcare, sanitation or law enforcement for their people. In the initial decades after Independence, the middle class's grip on the levers of power meant that the government in India largely delivered on the priorities of the middle class: high-quality university education, good urban infrastructure, and reliable law and order in the big cities. To this day, the productivity of India's factory workers is a fraction of that of East Asian workers.[5]

Without an adequately educated and nourished workforce, India proceeded to build a very different economic dynamic to drive its economic growth. Rather than exporting goods manufactured by the masses, India exported services. Specifically, India exported IT Services and knowledge intensive products like pharmaceuticals, thus allowing its university educated middle class to monetize their hard-earned degrees. For India too, exports of goods and services as a percentage of GDP rose from 6 per cent in 1980 to 21 per cent in 2024. However, the fact that India primarily exported services rather the goods meant that the structure of its economy evolved very differently compared to the East Asian Tigers.

In the decades since the economic reforms of 1991, consumption – and specifically, the middle class's consumption – has been the main engine of India's economic growth. Manisha Pande summarizes the origins of this growth engine nicely in her book on middle class India. She says that following the economic liberalization of 1991, the construct of the Indian economy was far more conducive to the growth of the services sector, as opposed to the manufacturing sector. This was because manufacturing required many permissions and licences, apart from huge capital and plentiful availability of land. In contrast, the challenges for the service sector were more modest. A software licence, some hardware and brainpower were enough to start a business. This created an economy where a middle-class person, who had intellectual prowess and business instincts, could become an entrepreneur. 'It was a marriage between intellectual prowess and global requirements.'[6]

As a result, the reforms of 1991 acted as a catalyst and 'led to the emergence of a new middle class'. This middle class was largely based in India's large cities and was 'guided by the diktats of a free market economy, which made it highly competitive by nature, consumerist in behaviour, and aspirational in outlook'.[7]

As the incomes of this class of consumers grew through the 1990s and noughties, the middle class's spending grew proportionately. That in turn created more demand and more middle-class jobs, and thus a virtuous cycle was triggered which powered the Indian economy for the best part of two decades. This explains why, in stark contrast to China and the East Asian Tiger economies, India's economic renaissance was led by domestic consumption (rather than by exports), so much so that consumption accounted for 60 per cent of India's GDP.

Unfortunately, in the post-Covid-19 world of scarce jobs, falling real wages and exploding household debt, it is this virtuous cycle that has broken down as can be seen in Figure 7.1. In the remainder of this chapter, we look at the slowdown in consumption growth in three key categories that account for

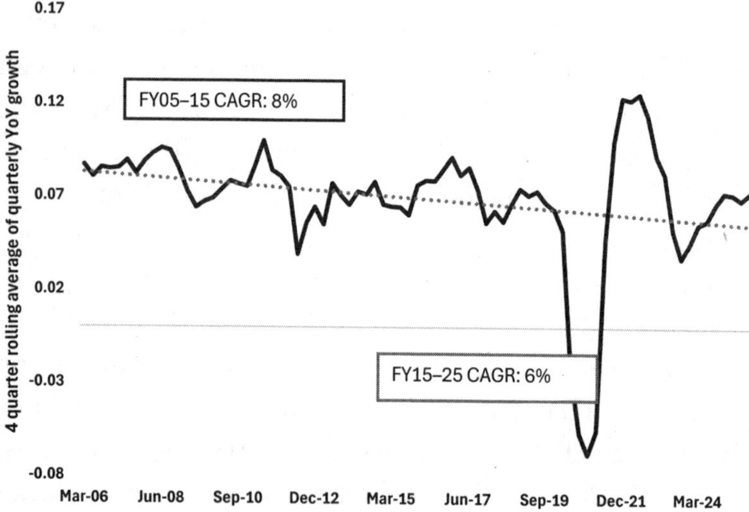


**Figure 7.1**: Private final consumption expenditure has trended downwards over the last 20 years

**Note:** Year-on-year growth was calculated for quarterly datapoints whose four-quarter rolling average was then calculated and plotted

**Source**: Marcellus Investment Managers, Ministry of Statistics and Programme Implementation (collated by Kotak Institutional Equities)

the majority of consumption spend on goods in most middle-class households – FMCG, auto and consumer durables – and highlight sector-specific factors that might have contributed to the ongoing slowdown. As you read the sector-specific narratives below, it is worth keeping in mind that despite a broad swathe of middle-class India pushing themselves towards a debt trap, we are living through an extended slowdown in consumption growth.

## FMCG

As can be seen in Figure 7.2, over the past 15 years (from FY2011 to FY2025), FMCG volume growth has slowed down steadily – from around 10 per cent per annum 15 years ago to around 3 per cent per annum now. This slowdown is a big deal, not least because this sector is one of the most important parts of India's economy. It is India's fourth-largest sector and includes many daily-use products making the sector a good barometer for the overall level of demand in urban India. Most of the FMCG sales (about 65 per cent) come from India's cities and towns. The key segments within this sector are:

- food and beverages (19 per cent of the sector);
- healthcare items like medicines and supplements (31 per cent); and
- household and personal care products like soaps, shampoos and cleaning supplies (50 per cent).

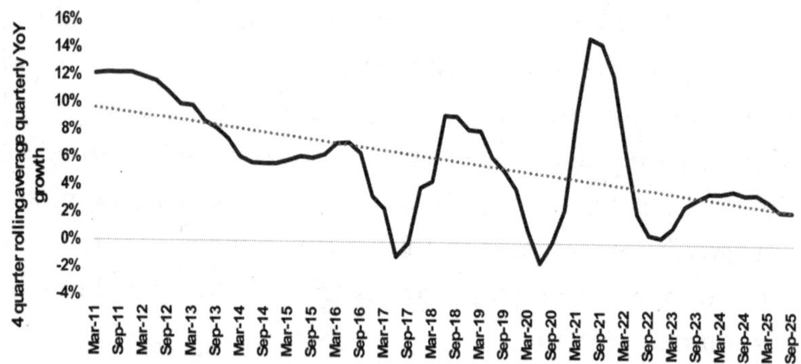


**Figure 7.2**: The FMCG volume growth has trended downwards over the last 14 years (FY2011 to FY2025)

**Note:** Companies used in the FMCG sector for this chart are: Bajaj Corp, Britannia, Colgate, Dabur, Emami, Godrej Consumer Products Limited, GSK Consumer, Hindustan Unilever, Jyothi Labs, Marico, Nestle India and Tata Consumer Products Limited; YoY volume growth was calculated for these companies, and their four-quarter rolling average was plotted

**Source**: Marcellus Investment Managers, Company results, aggregated by Kotak Institutional Equities

Just the food and beverage segment alone makes up around 3 per cent of India's GDP.[8]

In October 2024, Nestle India's then MD, Mr Suresh Narayanan, said after the firm's Q2 FY2025 results that 'there used to be a middle segment which used to be the segment most of us FMCG companies used to operate in, which is the middle class of the country. That seems to be shrinking'.[9] As longstanding investors in this sector, we can see that the slowdown in FMCG volume growth is widespread and long-lasting. Almost every company we have researched in this sector has flagged weak urban consumption as a major challenge.

Beyond the factors discussed in the previous chapters, an additional factor that is impacting the FMCG sector is commodity price inflation for key inputs like wheat, rice, oilseeds and milk. This surge in agro-commodity prices in turn has been driven by global factors – see Figure 7.3, for example. The international price of wheat in US $ were flat for decades until the turn of the century. Since then, they have risen relentlessly.

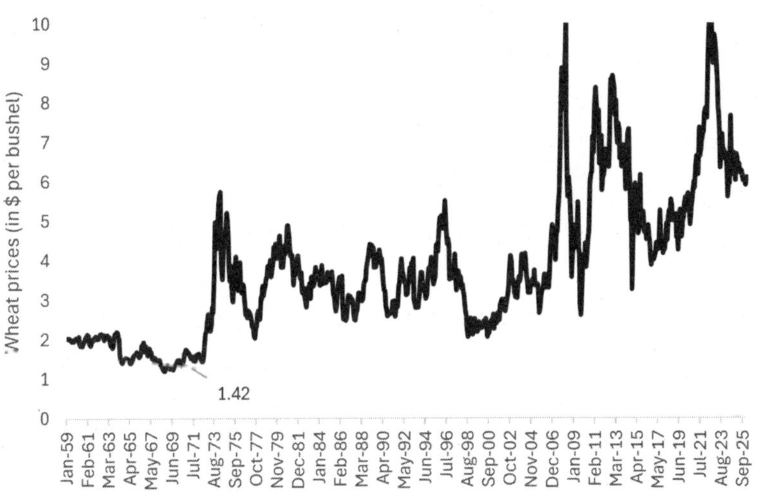


**Figure 7.3**: International prices of wheat have risen sharply in the twenty-first century

**Source**: Marcellus Investment Managers, 'Wheat Prices (1959–2025)', *Macrotrends*, https://tinyurl.com/yvywdjz2.

The result is that food prices in India have grown at around 6 per cent per annum on average over the past decade and a half (implying a doubling in food prices every decade, as mentioned).[10] Given the extended surge in raw material prices, the FMCG companies have obviously passed much of this on to their consumers, who in turn have responded by throttling off on consumption. Multiple consumer surveys over the past decade have pointed to this link, namely, as the FMCG companies hike their product prices, the overwhelming majority of Indian consumers buy less either by reducing the frequency of their purchases or by migrating to smaller pack sizes.[11] For example, Dabur, for instance, reported that customers are switching from 1 litre juice packs to smaller 200 ml ones. Nestlé noted a similar trend, with its ₹14 Maggi packs growing faster than larger ones.[12]

## Auto

In the post-Covid-19 era, the conk off in car demand has mirrored the slowdown in FMCG demand – see Figure 7.4. In fact, in the post-Covid-19 era the number of cars sold in India is shrinking each year! Even more interestingly, as shown in Figure 7.5, the slowdown in car demand began around 15 years ago, mirroring an identical trend in FMCG demand.

So, what has driven this dramatic slowdown in car demand? One clue lies in a statement made by Mr R.C. Bhargava, chairperson of Maruti Suzuki. He said, 'In FY18-19, 82% of the cars that were sold were below ₹10 lakh. Now that segment is not growing anymore. It is declining actually. So, you can judge for yourself if that large segment does not grow and

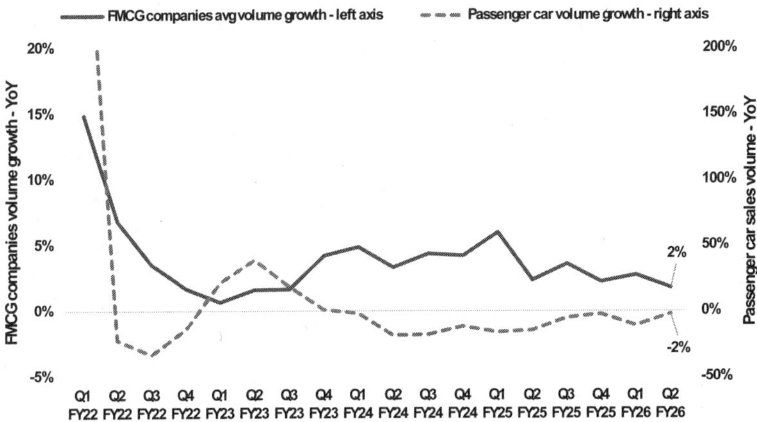


**Figure 7.4**: Both FMCG and passenger car volumes have taken a beating

**Note:** Companies used in the FMCG sector for this chart are: Bajaj Corp, Britannia, Colgate, Dabur, Emami, Godrej Consumer Products Limited, GSK Consumer, Hindustan Unilever, Jyothi Labs, Marico, Nestle India and Tata Consumer Products Limited; YoY volume growth was calculated for these companies and their average was plotted across the quarters; YoY growth for passenger car volume was averaged across quarters and plotted

**Source**: Marcellus Investment Managers, Society for Indian Automobile Manufacturers, company results, aggregated by Kotak Institutional Equities

actually declines how much can the other segment grow and make up for this 80% segment.'[13]

Between FY2019 and FY2024, the average selling price (ASP) of cars rose by 50 per cent. According to data from the industry, the ASP has gone up from ₹7.65 lakh in FY2019 to ₹11.5 lakh in FY2024.[14] This rise in prices in turn has been driven partly by the rise in the cost of components that go into a car (these have risen by 20 per cent over the past three years alone) and changes in regulatory norms for Indian cars.[15]

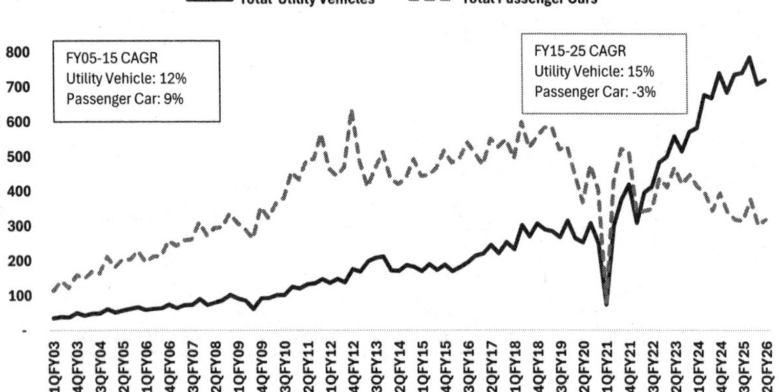


**Figure 7.5**: Passenger-car volume growth has been trailing utility vehicle volume growth post Covid-19 (in thousands)

**Note:** Volume in thousands has been plotted for both categories

**Source**: Marcellus Investment Managers, Society for Indian Automobile Manufacturers, collated by Kotak Institutional Equities

The implementation of stricter emission norms in India, such as the transition from BS IV to BS VI in 2020 and subsequent real driving emission (RDE) norms, has required manufacturers to incorporate expensive, advanced technology and components (e.g., onboard diagnostic devices and sophisticated sensors). The car manufacturers have largely passed on these costs to the consumer.[16]

Interestingly, the 50 per cent rise in the average price of a car between FY2019 and FY2024 has resulted in a sharp acceleration in the demand for utility vehicles (UVs) – see Figure 7.5. Given that a typical UV costs at least a third more than a typical car, this peculiar trend has been labelled as 'premiumization' by auto experts. As the price of the standard family car has risen steadily to cross ₹11 lakh, more affluent customers are saying 'we might as well pay a third more and get a roomier UV with better road clearance which makes for more a comfortable ride through the mountainous speed breakers in Mumbai, Delhi or Bangalore'.[17] By units of vehicles sold, the UV market in India is only half as big as the cars market, but the buoyancy in UV demand among shrinking car sales points to a future where the sub-₹ 10 lakh car segment might entirely die out in India. This would be a remarkable development for a country where median household income is ₹1.5 lakh per annum.[18]

## Consumer Durables

Mirroring the situation in cars and FMCG is the consumer durables volume growth. Here too volume growth has trended down from around 11 per cent 15 years ago to around 1–2 per cent in 2024. However, in contrast to the FMCG and car sectors, consumer durables prices in India have risen at a lower rate than overall CPI inflation in India. Thanks to China's willingness to supply critical components at ever lower prices and thanks to technological advancements in the wider world (notably, more processing power packed on to ever smaller chips), key consumer durables like TVs and microwaves cost no more today than they did a decade ago. So, in spite of this and in spite of the widespread availability of EMI financing, why has demand growth fallen so sharply over the last 15 years (Figure 7.6)? The short answer is 'no one seems to know'.

When we meet the promoters who own India's largest consumer durables manufacturers or their C-Suite executives, the image rabbits caught in headlights flashes through our head. The metaphorical headlights in play are the jobs, wages and debt crisis outlined in the preceding chapters. So powerful and so sustained are these 'headlights' that the consumer durables industry leaders do not seem to be able to comprehend what is going on. The 'experts' who write on this subject in the financial media appear to be equally perplexed; almost every

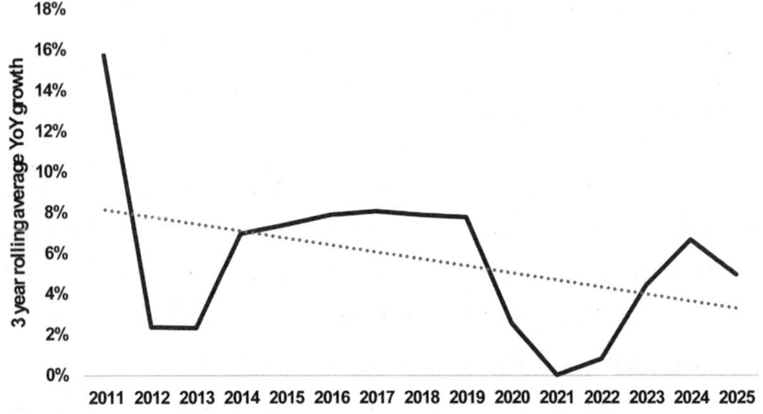


**Figure 7.6**: Consumer durable volume growth has also witnessed a sequential decline over the last decade)

**Note:** Items whose volume growth was considered are: home laundry appliances, large cooking appliances, microwaves, refrigeration appliances, air treatment products, food preparation appliances, heating appliances, irons, small cooking appliances and vacuum cleaners

**Source**: Marcellus Investment Managers, Euromonitor, collated by Kotak Institutional Equities

year they write about 'expected recovery in demand next year' but none fructifies. And every year, the brief flurry in demand around Diwali is written about as if this is the first time ever that Diwali has triggered a brief bout of buying.

Since the slowdown in demand growth for durables cannot be attributed to supply-side factors (that have been benign for this sector), this appears to be a pure demand-side slowdown. Fatigued by debt, joblessness and wage hikes below the rate of overall CPI inflation, the Indian consumer is implicitly saying, 'I don't have the capacity to buy anymore.'

## The Tide Changes in 2025

The good news is that the finance ministry, the RBI and the Prime Minister's Office appear to be awake and alive to dangers posed by the jobs and wages slowdown. In the next section of the book we describe, how after a five-year flirtation with boosting capex, India's policymakers are responding to the consumption crisis that threatens to derail the economic growth engine that has powered India's growth in the decades following the reforms of 1991. But before we get to the policy response, we have one more disruption to deal with, namely, the catastrophic impact of social media on the Indian middle class.

# 8

# The Side Effects of Social Media

*At the electronics trade show, CES 2025 in Las Vegas, Nvidia CEO, Jensen Huang, showed a glimpse of what's coming. Next up is Agentic AI, which can perceive, reason, plan and act. The one after that is Physical AI, which could drive vehicles and make general robotics functional ... Goldman Sachs CEO David Solomon described to the Financial Times how AI is commoditising 95% of documentation work that now takes an army of skilled executives at his bank weeks ... Countries such as India will struggle to lift people out of poverty as traditional paths for individual economic prosperity would vanish.**

As explained before, courtesy Jio's launch in 2016, almost free mobile data was available to virtually everyone in the country and sure enough, within a few months of launch, millions of young Indians found themselves with unlimited access

* Dinesh Narayanan, 'Opinion | Move over Middle Class, "Replicants" Are Coming', *NDTV*, 10 February 2025, https://tinyurl.com/32kkkfwe.

to the internet. What followed wasn't just a technological revolution. It was a psychological and financial catastrophe in the making.

This chapter examines how cheap smartphones and free data combined with social media to create a perfect storm for India's middle class. The same generation that couldn't find graduate jobs despite their degrees now spends hours daily on social media, bombarded by curated images of wealth and success they cannot attain. The psychological toll is measurable: anxiety and depression medications are growing twice as fast as other pharmaceutical categories.

But the damage isn't just psychological. Egged on by influencers promising easy money, 9 million Indians – mostly young men – have plunged into F&O trading. Over three years, they've collectively lost ₹3 lakh crore (US $33 billion) to institutional investors and brokers. Meanwhile, the same AI tools that glamourize trading on social media are eliminating the very jobs these traders need to fund their losses. From call centres to coding jobs, automation is gutting India's white-collar employment even as 8 million new graduates enter the job market annually.

## Social Media and the Illusion of Prosperity

Social media has changed the world but its impact on India, and on Indian men in particular, appears to be more profound than it has been in developed economies. There are three reasons for this: (a) mobile data is almost free in India and thus the use of social media is greater here than elsewhere in the world; (b) India has a young population whose formative years have been spent immersed in social media; and (c) the income gap between the rich and the poor in India amplifies the impact that social media has on the spending habits of the poor. The combination of these factors is emotionally and financially impacting the Indian middle class.

## India's Low-Cost Internet Access

As we write this book in 2025, the median Indian is 29 years old.[1] When she was 20 years old, something remarkable happened in her life. Courtesy Jio, in 2016, India got access to almost free cellular Internet connectivity on handheld devices, as mentioned earlier. As a result, not only did the demand for smartphones boom (see Figure 8.1), but more importantly a large proportion of India's population spent the most formative years of their life locked into the Internet via low-cost smartphones and almost-free mobile data (Figure 8.2).

As India has become more prosperous, the time lag between technology adoption between the West and India has reduced dramatically over the years. Those who grew up in the 1990s and 2000s will tell you that while in the West laptops and cellular phones had become ubiquitous by the end of the twentieth century, it was only in the mid noughties that Indians got widespread access to it.

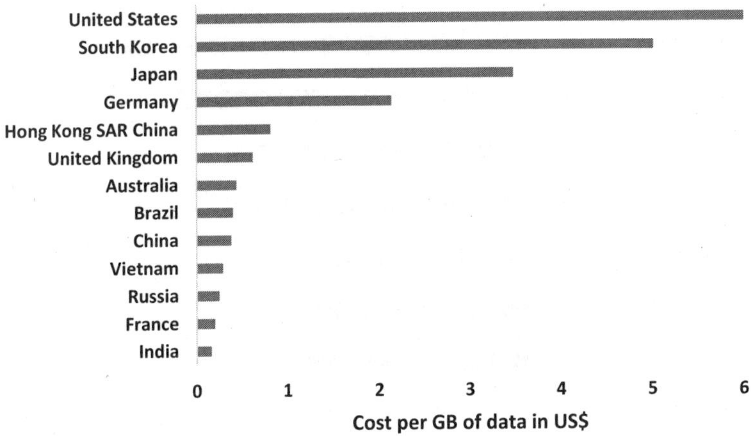


**Figure 8.1**: Cost of 1 GB worth of data in India is 1/40th that in the US

**Source**: Marcellus Investment Managers, Global Relocate; data as of 2025[2]

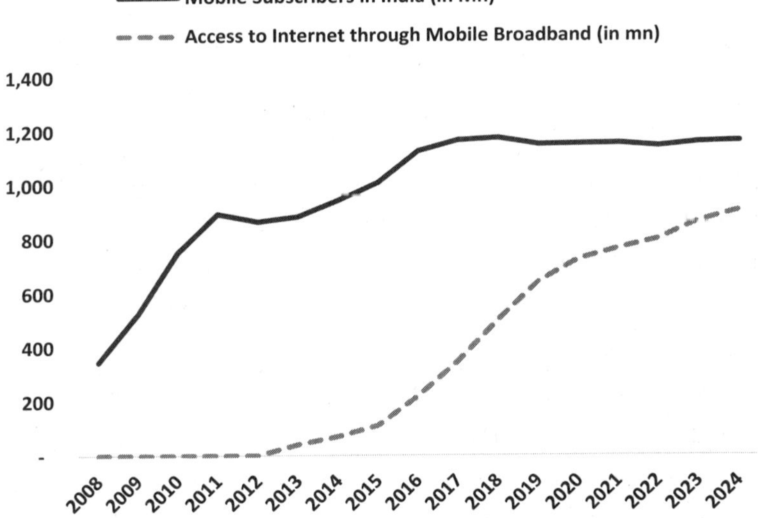


**Figure 8.2**: Nearly 80 per cent of people owning mobiles are using them to access the Internet

**Source**: Marcellus Investment Managers, Comprehensive Annual Modular Survey, Round 79, National Sample Survey Office, accessed through Data for India

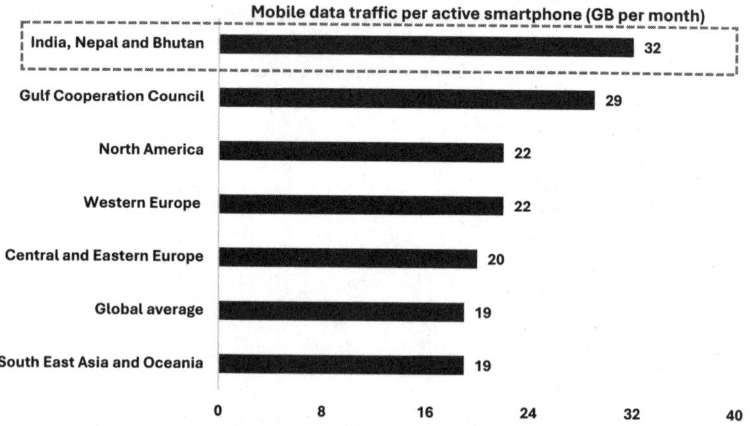


**Figure 8.3**: Indians' Internet usage per smartphone is higher than the US and European nations

**Source**: Marcellus Investment Managers, Ericsson Mobility Report, June 2025; data as of 2024

Case in point for the reduction in time of technology adoption lag is the launch of newer models of iPhones in the US and in India. Earlier, when the newest version of the iPhone was first launched in the US, it would then be launched in India a few months later. However, now the newest version is launched almost simultaneously. In fact, now the latest version is usually first made in India before it is made anywhere else in the world.

What this also means is that whatever practices now emerge in the Western world, with respect to technology, get copied in India almost in real time. In fact, Indian users of mobile phones possess an advantage over their counterparts in the West: the cost of mobile data in India is 1/40th that of the West.

As one would expect, in the wake of mobile data and smartphones proliferating, access to social media was democratized. The introduction of low-cost and fast cellular Internet in 2016 coupled with widespread smartphone penetration, meant that every Indian now had a legal identity (via Aadhaar), an economic identity (via a Jan Dhan bank account) and a digital identity (via smartphones and the Internet – see Figure 8.4 to understand the rapid growth of Internet access in India). This trinity of **J**an Dhan, **A**adhaar and **m**obile phone usage has been dubbed as 'JAM'.

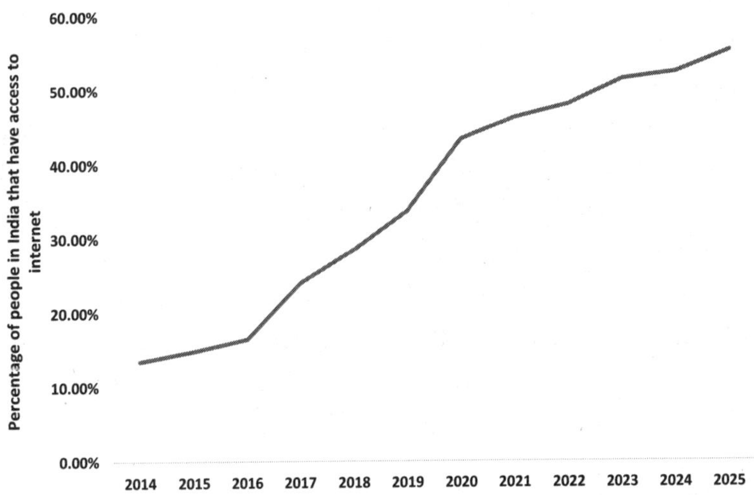


**Figure 8.4**: The majority of India's population (i.e., ~800 million people) now has access to the Internet

**Note:** The figure indicates percentage of population that has access to any kind of Internet connection (cellular/broadband etc.)

**Source**: Marcellus Investment Managers, Statista[3]

While the JAM trinity has enabled millions of Indians to lead better lives, with women in particular leveraging JAM effectively to generate income, it also has adverse side effects – both psychological and financial.

## The Side Effects of Social Media

### Psychological Distress

Indians spend an average of five hours a day on their smartphones, with nearly 70 per cent of that time devoted to social media, gaming and video streaming. This amounts to a collective 1.1 trillion hours spent online.[4]

As people spend more time online with bigger, better devices, their physical interactions in the real world have decreased. Younger Indians today struggle with extended verbal conversations, although they can easily 'chat' online for hours at a stretch through messaging or texting.

According to Dr Anand Godse, a consulting psychologist on the panel of deAsra, a not-for-profit that helps entrepreneurs in their journey to set up and scale their businesses (see Chapter 11),

> Our digital identity has become a very large aspect of who we are today. And because it is very well curated and controlled, only a certain side of our personality is reflected on social media, which most mistake for the whole personality a person has. Because of this perceived importance of the digital personality and the effort it takes to maintain it, most people try to suppress or internalize other aspects of their being which may or may not sit well with their digital or virtual personality. What this effectively leads to then is mental

issues related to internalization of problems, like anxiety and depression issues. This is currently rampant, especially in the younger generation. With ever more digital or virtual presence which creates a personality illusion basis what is shown, it is likely that incidence of delusion, schizophrenia and manic episodes will rise in the future.[5]

Indeed, rise in mental health disorders, specifically anxiety and depression, is a grim reality today, which is also reflected in data. If we look at the consumption of psychiatric drugs used to treat these two disorders versus psychiatric drugs used to treat other neurological and psychological disorders, the former has grown roughly at twice the pace as latter (see Figure 8.5). To contextualize, the Indian pharmaceutical market grew at 11

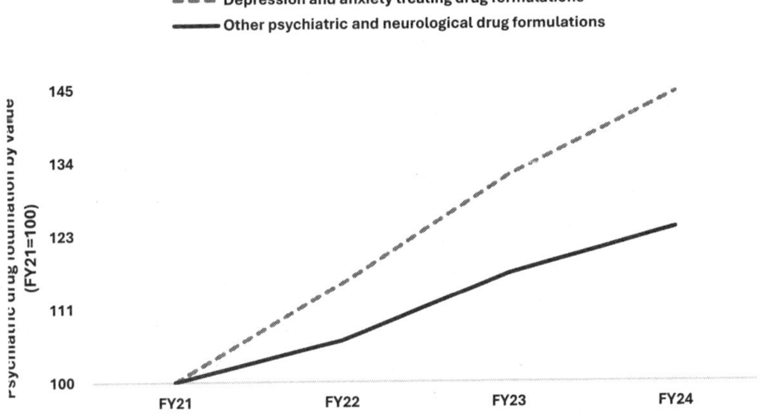


**Figure 8.5**: Anxiety and depression treating drug formulations have outpaced both other neurological drugs and Indian pharmaceutical market

**Note:** Top formulations for neurological and psychiatric disorders were selected for this analysis

**Source**: Marcellus Investment Managers, IQVIA

per cent per annum in FY2021 to FY2024, versus anxiety and depression treating drugs growing at 13 per cent per annum during the same time period.

Echoing Dr Godse's observation, Dr Sharmila Banwat, a practising psychologist based in Mumbai, told us,

> The generation that has come of age surrounded in the digital era, i.e., generation Z (or those born between 1997 and 2012) can be considered as the lost generation. These are the people who find it more convenient to be online than be present in real situations. They generally showcase indicators of neurodivergence such as low frustration tolerance, impatience, low attention span, lower problem-solving abilities and low memory span. Because they have received whatever they wanted and instantly, they have a tendency for instant gratification, which has led them to seek things they would be better not looking at – like access to pornography and gambling.

Data validates what Dr Banwat is saying. Most porn websites are banned in India. Clearly, this has not stopped people from watching it. We used Google Trends to assess Indians' interest in porn. While the interest peaked somewhere around 2016, the growth had already started coming off post 2011. Then something changed. Post 2023, one can see Indians' interest in porn growing at an accelerating rate (see Figure 8.6).

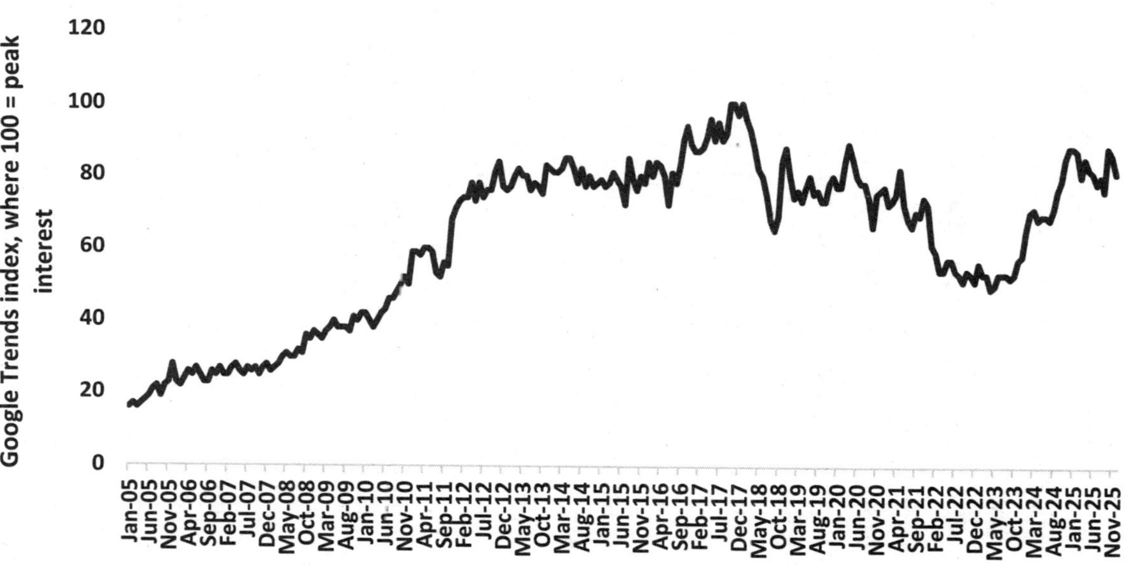


**Figure 8.6**: Interest in the term 'porn' has started rising again after falling post 2017

**Source**: Marcellus Investment Managers, Google Trends

## Borrowing to Trade in the Stock Market

Warren Buffet famously said, 'I view derivatives as time bombs, both for the parties that deal in them and the economic system ... In our view, however, derivatives are financial weapons of mass destruction, carrying dangers that, while now latent, are potentially lethal.'[6]

Access to social media has not only affected India's anxiety levels, but it has also had another startling side effect that we see in our business of tracking financial markets.

In the last five years since Covid-19, we have seen an explosion of F&O trading in India. A retail investor, as per Securities and Exchange Board of India's (SEBI's) guidelines, is an individual investor whose investment in securities does not exceed ₹2 lakh.[7] On 25 January 2023, India's financial markets regulator did something which had rarely been done before. Using data sourced from India's ten largest stockbrokers, the SEBI published a detailed study of retail investors in the Indian F&O market. The study spanned the period from FY2019 to FY2022, which meant that it included the entire period during which Indians were locked down due to Covid-19. Many of us in Marcellus are not accustomed to F&O trading as we operate primarily in the 'cash equities' market (i.e., we buy shares outright for cash and hold on to them for long periods of time). Hence, we were surprised to read in SEBI's report that:

- unique individual traders increased from 7.1 lakh in FY2019 to 45.2 lakh in FY2022, a growth of over 500 per cent (in subsequent years, this number has risen to 90 lakh);

- 88 per cent of traders were active in FY2022, with the highest participation being from the 30–40 age group (39 per cent);
- 89 per cent of individual traders incurred losses in FY2022, with an average loss of ₹1.1 lakh; and
- only 11 per cent of traders made profits, averaging ₹1.5 lakh, with the top 1 per cent accounting for 51 per cent of total profits.[8]

Even more surprising was the geographic location of these traders. India's largest cities were accounting for an increasingly smaller proportion of F&O trading volumes; the growth in such trading, SEBI said, was coming from Tier 2, 3 and 4 cities. Furthermore, as bulleted above, traders aged 30–40 years had the highest participation. Unsurprisingly, men accounted for 80 per cent of the trading volumes. Based on SEBI's report we formed a picture in our head of 30–40-year-old small town Indian men who are routinely losing a lakh or more every year on F&O trading (in a country where the per capita income is just over ₹2 lakh). In July 2025, SEBI, announced that in FY2025, retail traders lost a record ₹1.06 lakh crore in F&O trading, a 41 per cent jump from ₹75,000 crore the previous year.[9]

Naturally, ₹1.06 lakh crore or ₹1.1 trillion (US $12 billion) is a lot of money to lose for any investor, let alone for retail investors who are the smallest fish swimming in the sea that is the Indian stock market. Just to put this loss into context, in FY2026, the GoI's education budget is ₹1.3 trillion.[10] This loss in investments plays into the debt trap we have discussed in Chapter 6, where consumers are taking loans even for basic necessities.

The transfer of wealth from retail investors to brokers and institutional investors via the F&O market does not stop there.

Based on SEBI's research, we know that the typical F&O trader is a 30–40-year-old small town male who routinely loses a lakh every year on F&O trading. While only about a quarter of these F&O traders have an annual income above ₹5 lakh (which is our lower bound for the middle class), many of the sub-₹5 lakh earners are speculating with their middle class parents' painstakingly accumulated savings (as was the case with V.S., the trader who we met in the introductory section of this book).

Over the course of FY2022–25, the cumulative losses of retail investors in the Indian F&O market amounted to ₹3 lakh crore or ₹3 trillion ($33 billion). The even worse news is that these losses – which are effectively wealth transfers from the middle-class retail investors to the elite – are rising with each passing year. Here are the retail investors' escalating losses (in ₹ thousand crore) for the past few years – FY2022: 41, FY2023: 66, FY2024: 75 and FY2025: 106.[11]

To put the ₹3 trillion cumulative loss figure for retail investors into context, in FY2023, the GoI's social welfare payments amounted to ₹2.3 trillion. That means that every three years, India's retail investors are losing as much money in the F&O market as the GoI spends on social welfare payments in a single year.

While retail traders are struggling, proprietary traders (prop traders or trading members of India's stock exchanges who themselves trade on their own account) and foreign institutional investors (FPIs) are reaping the benefits. In FY2024, prop traders made ₹33,000 crore ($4 billion) in gross profits, while FPIs earned ₹28,000 crore ($3 billion).[12]

## How F&O Trading, Courtesy Social Media, Boomed in India

Futures and options trading has always had two attractions, namely, the opportunity to earn spectacular returns and investment of very little money upfront. However, five other factors gradually came together over the preceding decade to create the tsunami of retail F&O trading which we are seeing today.

Around 2010 cheap smartphones began to be widely available in India thanks to Chinese handset makers like Xiaomi, Oppo and OnePlus. Then in September 2016, Jio launched ultra-low-cost mobile broadband. This meant that Indians could now use their phones to use the Internet nonstop without having to worry about the cost. In the same year, something else happened that has great significance for the F&O story.

The National Stock Exchange began its derivatives journey on 12 June 2000, with the launch of Nifty index futures. These contracts followed a monthly expiry cycle, always ending on the last Thursday of the month. Over time, this Thursday rule applied to most derivatives, including the popular Bank Nifty. Then, in May 2016, weekly options were introduced for Bank Nifty, also expiring on Thursdays. This introduction of weekly

F&O contracts – the third factor – meant that every week there would be an expiry date and therefore every week there was an 'event' that F&O investors could look forward to.

By the time the fourth factor – Covid-19 – struck India in February 2020, almost every Indian had the means to surf the net, and the F&O market provided a venue with the promise of weekly excitement. The lockdown through 2020 and through much of 2021 meant that most of us were stuck in our homes. Those of us who had jobs would use the Internet to work from home but for those who did not have jobs, trading on the F&O market became one of the few means of earning money and giving themselves dopamine hits through the day.

The fifth and final factor that has played a key role in sucking millions of middle-class Indians into F&O trading is the glamourization of F&O trading through the use of influencers. As all of India sat at home in 2020, brokers realized that they no longer had to advertise to get business. Instead, the brokers would pay an 'influencer', who would usually be an attractive and articulate young professional. The influencer's main job was to tell the retail investor 24x7 that making money in stock markets is not only easy, but it is also what smart, successful people do and here is how you can do it by trading in F&O. By 2021, social media in India was full of reels and tips highlighting this easy money.[13]

While SEBI cracked down on influencers in 2024, by that time the genie was out of the bottle. Nonstop exposure to online marketing meant that by then a generation of young Indians – 80 per cent of whom were men – were hooked to F&O trading.

## The Consequences of Addiction to Trading

In 2024, when in a ride-share taxi doing our usual rounds of client meetings in the suburbs of Mumbai, we saw that our taxi driver had a laptop open and placed on the passenger seat next to him. The screen of the laptop faced the driver and he kept taking furtive glances at it. When we stopped at a traffic light, the driver took the laptop and typed a few things in. Intrigued, we asked him what he was doing. His reply stunned us.

The 20-something Mumbai taxi driver told us, '*Taxi chalanay mein kya mazaa hai? Asli mazaa to trading karnay mein aata hai* (What fun is there in riding the taxi? The real fun is in trading).' As we probed deeper, we learnt that while he earnt a couple of lakh a year from his taxi driving, over the prior year he had earnt twice as much from trading in the F&O market. He had thus concluded that taxi driving was for losers and that the real money was in trading in the stock market.

Egged on by social media influencers, by countless TV channels and by stories of legendary investors who have triumphed in the stock market, middle-class India has thrown itself headlong into the stock market trading. Retail trading now makes up 35 per cent of India's total derivatives volume. As Figure 8.7 shows, our Mumbai taxi driver is not alone. Millions of other Indians – 9 million of them to be precise – have reached the same conclusion. And that is bad news – for most of them and for the rest of the Indian economy.[14]

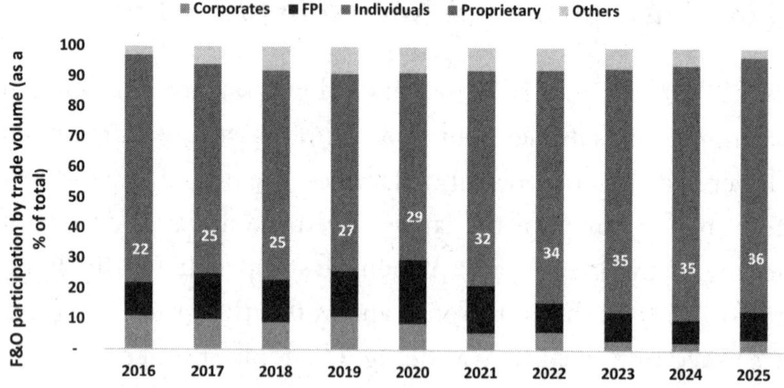


**Figure 8.7**: Retail participation in F&O has surged by 14 per cent points in the last nine years

**Source**: Marcellus Investment Managers, National Stock Exchange, collated by Kotak Institutional Equities

When we meet first time traders, we realize that nobody has ever explained to them the risks embedded even in the most straightforward F&O trades. For example, many first-time traders think that the option premiums they are paying are the only risk they're carrying. This mental framing creates a false sense of security that often becomes a deadly trap for many traders. In fact, buying options is among the riskiest trades in the stock market as Nithin Kamath, the founder of Zerodha, India's largest brokerage, explains using this real-life incident he witnessed as a broker:

> Back in 2009 when I was a sub-broker with Reliance Money, one of our customers went all in before the Indian general election results in May 2009 by buying … call options with all the money he had. He got super lucky as Nifty went up

over 40% in 2 days and this Rs 2L turned into more than Rs 2 crore. But the story didn't end there, he continued trading super aggressively and ended up losing not just the entire Rs 2 crore but more than his initial capital over the next 6 months.[15]

What Mr Kamath's real life incident highlights is the need for investors to focus not on the option premium paid but the underlying contract value that the call option entails. 'To be cognizant of the risk, an important part of the checklist for anyone buying options should be to look at the exposure in terms of contract value and not the premium.'[16] However, this mental framing is not easy and that's why over 98 per cent of retail investors' exposure to derivatives is through options – they appear seductively easy to make money off – and over 90 per cent of those option trades result in retail investors losing money.

In fact, for those of us who have studied both cash equities trading and options trading, the latter is far more demanding because – as Mr Kamath puts it – to make money in options, not only do you have to be right to make money, you also have to be right in a big way just to cover the cost of the option premium you have paid, *and* – this is what makes successful option trading really difficult to succeed at – you have to be right within a short period of time.

## Who Is Winning in the F&O Market?

While it is clear from SEBI's data that middle-class retail investors have lost ₹3 trillion over FY2022–25 in the Indian

F&O market, to understand how the F&O market transfers wealth from the middle class to the elite, it is worth identifying who benefits from the retail investors' losses.

India's largest brokers have profited mightily from the F&O boom. For India's largest exchange, the NSE, 75 per cent of its revenue comes from F&O trading.[17] In FY2025, the NSE's revenues were ₹17,141 crore implying that it was generating revenues of nearly ₹13,000 crore ($1.4 billion) per annum from F&O trading.[18]

These numbers suggest that of the $10 billion that retail investors are losing annually to F&O trading, around a couple of billion are being garnered by the intermediaries in the system. So, who is garnering the remaining $8 billion per annum? The answer: institutional investors.

An institutional investor is a large, professional organization that pools money to invest on behalf of others, such as clients, members or policyholders. Common examples include mutual funds, pension funds, insurance companies and hedge funds. These entities manage vast sums of money and can significantly influence market prices due to the large 'blocks' of securities they trade.

Historically, the Indian F&O market was too small to attract the institutional investors from the developed world. Such investors would buy shares in the Indian cash equities market but were not interested in the Indian F&O market, which remained the preserve of Indian HNWs (high net worth individuals/families) and local fund houses in India. Then came the post Covid-19 surge in F&O volumes. By 2023, average daily transaction value in the Indian F&O

market was exceeding $500 billion and nearly 80 per cent of the world's options contracts by daily turnover were trading in India.[19] Even the average daily transaction value of options trades in a single stock like HDFC Bank were in excess of $300 million per day. Given the colossal amounts being traded in the Indian F&O market by retail investors, the developed market investors realized that there were big bucks to be made in this market.[20]

While the basic mechanics of how F&O contracts work is straightforward, the more advanced mechanics are actually sophisticated enough for those who have figured it out to win Nobel Prizes. In fact, the maths – the calculus to be more precise – is so sophisticated that for several decades now, institutional investors in developed markets have hired super premium academic talent to staff their F&O trading desks. These professional investors often have PhDs in maths, physics, statistics or computer science. They are then given state-of-the-art powerful computers and the latest machine-learning technology so that they can create algorithms (or trading rules) that can identify investment opportunities in the world's F&O markets. In other words, these investors are the inverse of the 30-year-old small town retail investor who is betting the few lakh that he has saved on the F&O market. Therefore, in April 2024, when one of the world's largest trading firms, Jane Street, claimed in a court case in New York (against one its largest rivals, Millenium) that it was generating profits of $1 billion per annum from the Indian F&O market, it did not surprise us.[21]

However, Jane Street's claim led SEBI to dig deeper into the matter. After a year-long investigation, on 3 July 2025, SEBI barred Jane Street from the securities market for allegedly manipulating stock indices using large derivative positions, mainly in the Bank Nifty, which caused losses to retail investors caught on the other side of the trades. In simple English, SEBI is alleging that Jane Street manipulated the share prices of stocks like HDFC Bank, so as to profit from the F&O contracts that are based on HDFC Bank's share price.[22]

While it remains to be seen whether SEBI's allegations against Jane Street are justified or not, what is plainly visible is that the Indian F&O market has become a giant hunting ground where the world's most powerful institutional investors can prey upon hapless retail investors. We now describe the life of one such retail investor.

## Ritesh from Aminabad, Lucknow

Ritesh is a 52-year-old man from Lucknow who, for 35 years, 'sat behind a wooden counter at his readymade garment shop in Lucknow's busy Aminabad market, sandwiched between paan and samosa shops'.[23] The shop – which had been founded by Ritesh's parents – unfortunately shut down during the Covid-19 pandemic and that's when Ritesh – like millions of other Indians – turned to the stock market to make money.

To be fair to Ritesh, his turning to the stock market was not because of a sudden flight of fancy. For many years before he jumped into trading, Ritesh used to get frequent calls from unknown numbers asking, 'Do you want to become a crorepati?'

Once he began trading, it did not take Ritesh very long to find sources of knowledge and trading ideas. Ritesh claims that he followed at least 15 social media influencers but tracked only five on YouTube. He found them by using the keywords 'best trading accounts to follow'. Sometimes logic mattered, and sometimes brand value.[24]

A couple of years into his trading stint, Ritesh was convinced that he had cracked the code for trading on India's two most liquid options – the Nifty (which tracks the 50 largest companies across sectors by market capitalization) and the Bank Nifty (which tracks the biggest banks like HDFC and ICICI). That's when Ritesh made his big move – one that played straight into the hands of clever traders sitting on Wall Street with the world's best technology at their fingertips.

Sitting in his Janakipuram residence in Lucknow, Ritesh bought 10 Bank Nifty stocks, assuming if the stocks went up, the index would rise too. Initially, things worked out well for him, i.e., the index did rise in line with his expectations. As the index rose, he sold index call options, expecting to profit from a correction in the price of the index. However, this time the market went against him – the index kept rising. Ritesh traded ₹2–3 lakh in index options on the Nifty and the Bank Nifty.

After these trades started going against him, Ritesh realized that he was out of his depth. Like many others who lost much of their life's savings, he 'couldn't explain how, but it seemed as if someone always knew what was coming'.[25]

Out of money and out of luck, Ritesh now had to face up to his wife. Thankfully, he seems to have told her how much money he has lost in trading. Ritesh's wife is now driving him hard to recoup the lost money by building a bakery business with her. While she does the baking, Ritesh's job is to pack the orders and deliver them around Lucknow in his car. As he does his daily delivery rounds through Lucknow's bustling streets, he's been unsubscribing from the trading channels he once followed religiously. Ritesh claims that having understood how the stock market really operates, he's a changed man: 'I lost money, but I have clarity now. I know who makes profit, and it's not small traders like me.'[26]

# Section II

---

# The Future of Work

# 9

# The Policy Response

*More than 100 countries – including China, India, Brazil, and South Africa—face serious obstacles that could hinder their efforts to become high-income countries in the next few decades, according to a new World Bank study that provides the first comprehensive roadmap to enable developing countries to escape the 'middle-income trap.'*

*Drawing on lessons of the past 50 years, the World Development Report 2024: The Middle-Income Trap finds that as countries grow wealthier, they usually hit a 'trap' at about 10% of annual U.S. GDP per person—the equivalent of $8,000 today. That's in the middle of the range of what the World Bank classifies as 'middle-income' countries. Since 1990, only 34 middle-income economies have managed to shift to high-income status—and more than a third of them were either beneficiaries of integration into the European Union, or of previously undiscovered oil.**

* '"Middle-Income Trap" Hinders Progress in 108 Developing Countries', *World Bank Group*, 1 August 2024, https://tinyurl.com/2f2kz398.

The employment, wages and consumption slowdown that has played out in India post-Covid-19 is now being recognized by India's policymakers. While their policy response has been substantive (especially with regards to boosting consumption, the mainstay of India's economic growth), the structural issue of helping middle-class India deal with a massive labour market transition – away from salaried jobs to a gig economy – still remains. The economic model that has worked for India since the economic liberalization of 1991 is breaking down under the strain of technological advances. India has to build a new economic model and the journey to a new normal will take at least two–three years and is likely to be painful.

## Retail Sales Light up Diwali 2025

Dhanteras is the day on which millions of Indian households believe it is auspicious to buy jewellery. On Dhanteras 2025, across India's big cities, traffic almost came to a standstill as shoppers spilled out of their homes and offices and into the streets and shopping malls of India. Such was India's demand for silver leading up to Dhanteras in 2025 that the bullion markets in Mumbai, London and New York ran out of silver. The worldwide shortage of silver in turn created a price spike which took silver prices to levels never seen before.

MMTC–PAMP – a joint venture between Switzerland based bullion specialist Pamp SA, and MMTC Ltd, a GoI Undertaking – runs the only London Bullion Market accredited silver and gold refinery in India. Silver and gold bars from MMTC–PAMP are usually in high demand because of their reputation for purity. However, Dhanteras 2025 was unusual even for MMTC–PAMP. Vipin Raina, the head of trading at MMTC–PAMP said, 'Most people who are dealing silver and silver coins, they're literally out of stock because silver is not there ... This kind of crazy market – where people are buying at these levels – I have not seen in my 27-year career.'[1]

As the Indian market ran out of silver on the back of record demand, Indian jewellers turned to the London Bullion Market – via global banks like JP Morgan Chase – for supplies. Around a fortnight prior to Dhanteras, JP Morgan Chase and Co. – the largest precious metals trader and an important bullion supplier to the Indian market – told at least one of its clients that it had no more silver available to deliver to India for the month of October, and the soonest it could offer supplies was in November.[2]

By 9 October – a week prior to Dhanteras – 'the London silver market would be gripped by the biggest squeeze that any of the multiple traders Bloomberg spoke to had seen in their careers'.[3] As banks like JP Morgan and Co. stepped back from the frenzied market, bid-asks spread (the price gap between what sellers want to be paid versus what buyers are willing to pay) soared. As a result, trading became impossible. Effectively, India's insatiable demand for silver had broken the world silver market.

Interestingly, it wasn't just silver. Even car sales skyrocketed in the pre-Diwali and post-Navratri festive shopping season in 2025. Major automakers in India – including Maruti Suzuki, Hyundai Motor and Tata Motors – saw record Dhanteras sales.[4] In fact, on Dhanteras (18 October 2025) India's car showrooms sold over 1,00,000 passenger vehicles, a single day record for India.[5]

So, given the backdrop of stagnant wages, weak job creation and record levels of household indebtedness, what triggered this boom in spending on the eve of Diwali 2025? And how sustainable was this upsurge in spending?

## Unwinding the Fiscal Transfers from the Middle Class to the Elite

Income tax collections from individuals rose from 2.5 per cent of GDP in FY2019 to 3.6 per cent in FY2025. The GST collections as a percentage of GDP rose from 2.5 per cent in FY2019 to 2.8 per cent in FY2025. Effectively, by FY2025 Indian households were paying 1.4 per cent of GDP more to the exchequer each year (than they did in FY2018). In absolute terms, the amount that Indians were paying as income tax went from ₹4.73 trillion in FY2019 to ₹10.10 trillion in FY2024, a CAGR of 16 per cent.[6]

Unfortunately for the Indian consumer, this increased fiscal load that she was bearing coincided with a conk-off in white-collar job creation (as explained in Chapter 4).

This hike in income taxes was used to pay for an ambitious government capex programme that was in part necessitated by the collapse in the Indian economy, in the wake of the first wave of Covid-19 in 2020. However, the government capex wave continued through 2022, 2023 and 2024 – long after Covid-19 had abated. As a percentage of the GoI's total spending government capex went from 13 per cent in FY2019 to 21 per cent in FY2024. In absolute terms, government spending on capex went from ₹3.1 trillion in FY2019 to ₹9.5 trillion in FY2024, a CAGR of 25 per cent.[7]

The biggest areas on which the government expended its capex were roads, railways and defence. Between FY2020 and FY2024, India grew its National Highways from 132k km to 146k km, a CAGR of 2.5 per cent. The number of passenger trains ferrying Indians across India rose from 70k to 79k, a CAGR of 3 per cent. The Indian Navy commissioned its second aircraft carrier, INS Vikrant in September 2022. In March 2025, contracts worth ₹62,700 crore were signed by the Air Force for 156 Prachand Light Combat Helicopters.[8] In 2024, the Army began taking delivery of the T-90S Bhishma tanks, which were out licenced from the Russians and manufactured at the Heavy Vehicles Factory in Chennai.[9]

However, for all the impressive strides made on the back of this record surge in government capex, spillover benefits for the broader economy were hard to spot. Specifically, much of the government capex went into capital intensive activities, such as rail and defence manufacturing. Even road construction in India has steadily become more capital intensive over the past decade; if you see a highway construction team in India today, it has only one-fifth the number of people it had a decade ago thanks to the use of advanced road construction machines that facilitate road construction at a rapid rate.

The capital-intensive nature of government capex meant that middle-class job creation was not meaningfully boosted by the record surge in government capex. Instead, the extra taxes that were being taken from the middle classes to pay for

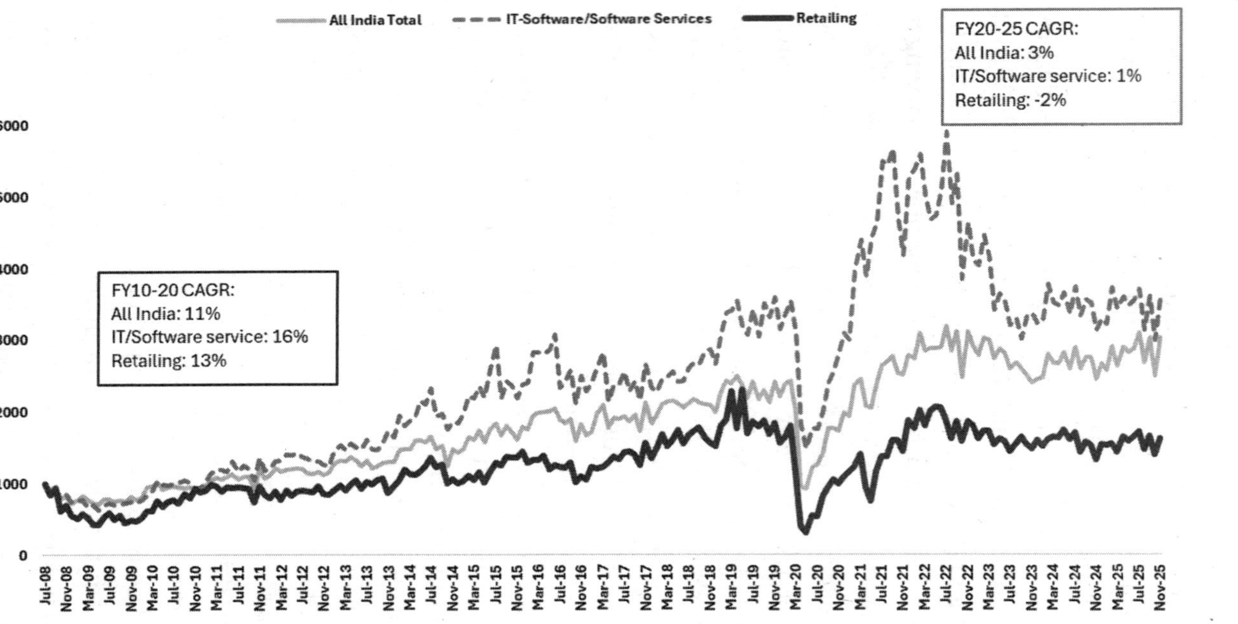


**Figure 9.1**: Even after factoring in the post-Covid-19 spurt in jobs, white-collar job creation has slowed down dramatically in India over the past five years (FY2020–25)

**Note:** Annual numbers are arrived at by averaging the monthly values for each of the years

**Source**: Marcellus Investment Managers, using data from Naukri JobSpeak

this government capex, jammed consumption growth in India. As a result, the rise in income taxes and the rise in government capex neatly offset each other (at around 1.6 per cent of GDP) without really moving the overall economy forward. In simple terms, the middle class's income taxes were used to fund public capex that might, in the long run, help the economy.

Beginning with the Union Budget on 1 February 2025, the GoI began unwinding these transfers and in so doing began stimulating consumption. The Union Budget for FY2026 said that those earning less than ₹12 lakh per annum no longer have to pay income tax. This amounts to a ₹1 trillion per annum stimulus.[10]

Secondly, the RBI also took notice of the conk-off in jobs and consumption and began playing its part in reviving the economy. The four repo rate cuts that the RBI expedited in 2025 are likely to reduce Indian households' annual outgo on interest payments by ₹1.6 trillion (~₹150 trillion household debt outstanding [household debt as a percentage of GDP is ~42 per cent][11] multiplied by 1 per cent cut in interest rate).

Thirdly, in a policy measure billed as GST 2.0, the GoI cut GST on certain items on 22 September 2025. This amounted to a ₹2 trillion per annum stimulus according to our calculations.[12,13]

These three stimuli – adding up to ₹4.6 trillion (US $50 billion or 1.5 per cent of GDP) – played a significant role in creating the consumer spending upsurge between Navratri and Diwali in 2025. To sustain this upsurge, those who manage India's economy are most likely to have to use more interest rate cuts and tax cuts. However, it will greatly help the consumption recovery if the government also tries to plug other sources of leakages in Indian consumer spending such as gambling on games and in the stock market.

## Unwinding the Gambling Disaster

In August 2025, India's IT Minister, Ashwini Vaishnaw, said that online money games had harmed 450 million Indians, causing losses of over ₹ 200 billion (US $2.2 billion) and triggering 'depression and suicides' among many.[14] Our estimates suggest that Indians were spending ₹70k crore (US $8 billion) per annum on online money games.[15] On 1 October 2025, the GoI banned online money games, thus pushing the ₹0.7 trillion (US $8 billion) per annum back into consumption and away from gambling.[16]

As highlighted in Chapter 8, SEBI's research shows that F&O trading facilitates transfer of wealth from middle-class men in India's smaller towns and cities to well-capitalized and well-informed traders and stockbrokers. In light of the government's newly discovered zeal to crackdown on gambling activities that redirect monies away from productive consumption into transfers from the middle class to the elite (which, in totality, reduces consumption while enriching the elite), we are hopeful that SEBI might announce regulatory changes that reduces the amount of F&O trading in India. While stockbrokers and the exchanges are unlikely to welcome such moves, basis the research being made public by SEBI, it appears that India's retail F&O trader were being impoverished to the tune of ₹1 trillion per annum in the F&O

market. If these transfers of wealth from the middle class to the elite (both in India and on Wall Street in New York) can be reduced then those monies could be channelled into productive consumption in India.

Adding the ₹1.7 trillion consumption boost from the potential redirection of spending related to gambling and speculation into productive consumption boosts the overall consumption stimulus to ₹6.3 trillion or nearly 1.8 per cent of GDP from the second half of FY2026 onwards. Note that our 1.8 per cent of GDP estimate (of the stimuli being imparted) broadly offsets the 1.6 per cent extra tax load that the exchequer had imposed on the Indian consumer since FY2019.

## Politics versus Economics in India's Democracy

While the stimuli highlighted above will give a sugar rush to the Indian economy, the odds are high that without further measures to stoke consumption (e.g., further interest rate cuts and more income tax cuts), a couple of quarters out, consumption and therefore profit growth will once again slowdown in India. There are three reasons for this.

Firstly, we are in the early stages of the AI-related job losses in India. While Western tech giants (such as Google and Microsoft) and Western IT services firms (such as Accenture) have been candid that AI will lead to large-scale job losses in their firms,[17] Indian IT firms, financial services firms and media companies have been more coy on the subject, knowing that is a politically touchy issue in India.

While it is hard to gauge exactly how fast AI will destroy India's middle-class jobs, the relatively lean workforces of leading AI companies like OpenAI (~3,500 employees) and DeepSeek (~200 employees) compared to the vast number of employees in established tech giants like Microsoft (2,28,000 employees) suggests that the day of reckoning is going to arrive sooner rather than later, especially for those Indians who are in jobs involving relatively repetitive tasks.[18]

More specifically, in-line with the estimates from NITI Aayog that we cited in Chapter 3 (of around 20 per cent of tech and customer experience jobs disappearing by 2031), the CEOs of listed Indian firms tell us that anywhere between a fifth to a third of their workforce will gradually be eased out as they replace call centres, underwriting teams, HR professionals, coders, research analysts and even marketing professionals with AI. These IT firms, financial services firms and retailers are some of India's most profitable companies and their profits are growing in double digits. However, given that the cost of capital is low for them, it makes sense for them to replace labour with capital. In other words, it makes sense for them to invest in AI today to reduce their headcount costs for the next few years. In fact, if the CEOs of these listed Indian firms are not driving down their headcount cost, they are likely to be asked by investors in the Indian stock market: 'If Google and Microsoft say that a third of their coding is done by AI, how much of your tech team are you planning to retrench?'

Not only is it difficult for the GoI to stop Indian employers from laying of tens of thousands of workers year after year, but arguably it is not appropriate for the government to interfere in this area. After all, if Indian companies do not use the latest technology to reduce costs and boost profit margins, they will be left behind by hungrier, leaner competitors operating in more efficient economies.

A second, more complex challenge is a conflict of interest at the heart of Indian policymaking. The issues discussed in this book impact 40 million income-tax payers in a country with 970 million voters. Politically, these tax payers are not particularly meaningful. Yes, the middle class's taxes finance 53 per cent of the GoI's income tax collections and 30 per cent of the countries' GST collections. And yes, the middle class creates jobs for another 200 million workers in their support ecosystem (e.g., cooks, drivers, cleaners, etc.) but the polity has never been designed to give a lot of time and attention to this stratum of society. After all, even if the middle class's needs were catered to, the lack of coherence in their demands (see Chapter 2) are such that no politician can build a career or win an election solely on the back of middle-class votes.

The third challenge is knowhow. India's governance apparatus is designed to address the problems of low-income voters, not middle-income office workers. The average annual earnings of India's income-tax payers whose salary ranges from ₹5 lakh–₹1 crore is ₹22 lakh ($25k). That makes middle-class India a second-world country like Chile ($17k per capita income) or Portugal ($29k per capita income) or South Korea ($33k per capita income). Neither India's polity nor its policymakers have experience of dealing with the challenges that second world countries face – challenges such as creating a high-quality university education system (at a time when not a single Indian university makes it into the rankings of the Top 50 universities in the world[19]), creating incentives for companies to spend on R&D and generate new knowledge. The result is that in the foundational technologies that characterize our era – AI, electric vehicles, biotech and renewable power – India has little or no intellectual property to offer. Instead, Indian companies have to buy these technologies from the rest of the world, which in turn means that to keep their expenses under control they need to shed workers.

No country is able to grow decade after decade using the same economic model. An economic model that works well for a low-income country (e.g., labour-intensive exports manufactured in sweatshops and exported to the West) does not work for the same country as it gets richer (e.g., the Asian crisis of 1997 that was triggered by a currency crisis for Southeast Asian economies like Thailand, Malaysia and Indonesia). Once an emerging economy hits such a speedbump – also known as the 'middle income trap' that often hits emerging economies as their GDP per capita starts approaching $8k – retooling the economic model becomes essential as reviving growth tends to be a multi-year repair job.

India is not the first emerging economy to hit such a speedbump. As the World Bank's Chief Economist Indermit Gill says,

> Too many of these countries rely on outmoded strategies to become advanced economies. They depend just on investment for too long—or they switch prematurely to innovation. A fresh approach is needed: first focus on investment; then

> add an emphasis on infusion of new technologies from abroad; and, finally, adopt a three-pronged strategy that balances investment, infusion, and innovation. With growing demographic, ecological and geopolitical pressures, there is no room for error.[20]

As explained in Chapter 7, the consumption-oriented economic model that has served India well since 1991 is breaking down, as the middle class finds itself caught in the maws of tech-driven economic change. Transitioning the Indian economy from a salary-driven consumption model to a gig economy driven model will take a few years. While the free market is likely to facilitate such a transition, as discussed in Chapter 4, the government needs to get out of the way by reducing the many layers of red tape that hold down small businesses. It is not clear to us that those who run this vast nation have much to gain from cutting red tape and getting out of the way.

# 10

# AI: New Opportunities in the Brave New World

*In the story of AI and humans, if we get the dance between artificial intelligence and human society right, it would unquestionably be the single greatest achievement in human history.**

## Instruction from the Mahabharata

One of the Mahabharata's warriors, Karna, who was denied education because of his caste, disguised himself as a Brahmin to learn from the great sage Parshuram. His hunger to master skills that the society denied him reveals an eternal truth: when systems resist change, individuals must evolve to thrive. India's workforce faces a similar inflection point today. While AI threatens to automate millions of jobs – from coders to call centre agents, underwriters to warehouse workers – history

* Chen Qiufan and Kai-Fu Lee, *AI 2041: Ten Visions for Our Future*, Crown, 2021.

suggests a more complex story. Recent research shows that over 60 per cent of American jobs in 2018 didn't exist in 1940.[1] India's own NASSCOM data reveals that 65 per cent of tech employees now work in roles that didn't exist a decade ago.[2]

This chapter explores both sides of AI's impact: the painful substitution effects already destroying middle-class employment, and the harder-to-foresee complementarity effects that could create millions of new opportunities in the gig economy, content creation, bot training and entirely novel professions we can barely imagine today.

## India's Workforce Stands at an Inflection Point

India, home to the world's largest youth population, stands on the brink of a historic labour market transformation. In boardrooms and campuses alike, the anxiety and optimism around AI-induced change are palpable. Will jobs vanish? Will we be replaced? Or will new opportunities arise in unexpected corners? In this chapter, we confront these questions.

In 1880, when Thomas Edison patented the incandescent light bulb in Menlo Park, California, it was immediately obvious that candle manufacturers were going to be in trouble. Economists call this the 'substitution effect'. When disruptive technologies arrive, the substitution effect kicks in quickly and is relatively easy to fathom. In Chapter 3, we discussed the substitution effect currently playing out in India in the wake of AI.

However, what is more important – and far harder to fathom – is the 'complementarity effects'. So going back to the late nineteenth century, no one could have predicted that the same electricity that powered the light bulb would 30 years later power the gramophone and lead to the creation first of star singers, and then ultimately result in the birth of Hollywood.

In fact, more recent research from the US suggests that workers in large free market economies possess the legendary warrior Karna's skills to a far greater degree than many thought. In a research paper published in 2021, the economist David Autor showed that over 60 per cent of employment in 2018 was under job titles that did not exist in 1940.[3] In other words, over the course of ~80 relatively prosperous years (in which the US became the world's pre-eminent economic power), the vast majority of jobs in the US were disrupted and then replaced by totally new professions. Job titles like 'web developer', 'chat room host' and 'radio pharmacist' did not exist in the 1940s.

Similarly, in modern day India, it is relatively obvious that AI will, in substantial measure, replace human beings in jobs involving repetitive tasks, e.g., credit underwriting, insurance underwriting, coding, routine financial analysis, clerical and secretarial work in offices and call centres, HR administration tasks, security guards, cashiers and tellers, etc. (see Chapter 3 for more details). What we will try to do in this chapter is to peek into the future and figure out where technology, AI, demographic and social change will create new opportunities in India.

Given how misty the looking glass into the future is and how imperfect this sort of forecasting is, it is easy to see that the professionals who will thrive over the next decade will be those who have the ability to learn, unlearn and relearn – again and again. Work will be plentiful, but jobs are likely to be increasingly scarce in India. Therefore, as discussed in more detail in the next chapter, an entrepreneurial mindset will be essential for survival in the new Indian job market.

And by the way, this scale of change is not new in India. According to a 2024 NASSCOM report, 65 per cent of Indian tech employees are in roles that didn't exist a decade ago. Indians have adapted successfully to disruptive changes before.[4] We are confident that they will be able do so again.

## A Mental Model for AI Will Impact Jobs

In Chapter 3, we highlighted that while AI seems likely to replace humans in repetitive tasks, there are certain things AI cannot do. Chen Qiufan and Kai-Fu Lee explain what AI cannot do today and is unlikely to be able to do in the coming years.[5] They identify three key areas where humans can lead AI:

- **Creativity**: At its simplest, AI cannot apply common sense or think across domains. More specifically, while AI can optimize a narrow objective, it is unable to think creatively. Taking this construct to its logical limit, AI cannot think strategically.

- **Empathy**: While AI can be trained to pretend that it has emotions, since it cannot really *feel*, it cannot make another person feel understood or cared for. It is possible that AI may improve in this area, but it is difficult to see how AI can provide 'human-touch services'.

- **Dexterity**: While AI-trained robots are becoming increasingly dextrous, by definition, AI can't deal with unknown and unstructured spaces, especially ones that it hasn't observed.

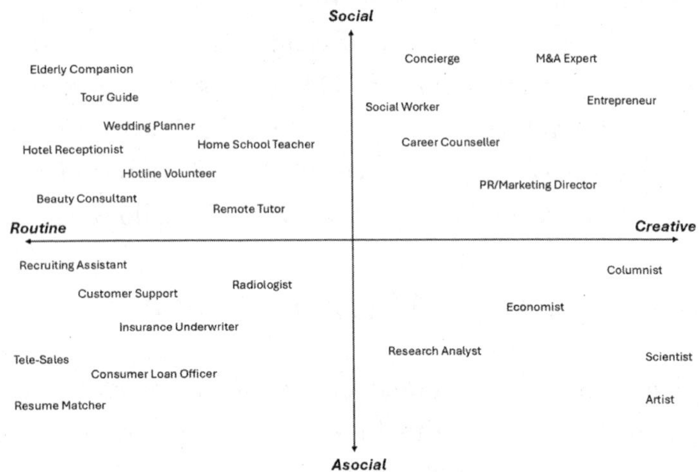


**Figure 10.1**: What sort of jobs AI will create and what it will destroy

**Note**: Cognitive jobs on a two-dimensional chart. Upper right favours humans and lower left favours AI.

**Source**: Chen Qiufan and Kai-Fu Lee, *AI 2041: Ten Visions for Our Future*, Crown, 2021.

Jobs that involve the skills highlighted in the top right-hand quadrant of Figure 10.1 should not only survive, but there is also good reason to believe that they will become even more lucrative. For example, while AI can take over the job of a fund manager operating in India's stock market, it is unlikely to be able to persuade a multi-millionaire in Hyderabad to invest $1million in the same fund manager's newest fund. That job of persuading the millionaire is likely to continue being done by an articulate, empathetic and trustworthy salesperson. As human beings increasingly become irrelevant for manufacturing funds but remain invaluable for selling these funds, rewards are likely to migrate from the fund managers towards the salespeople.

In fact, Chen Qiufan and Kai-Fu Lee's mental model has a further nuance embedded in it. For jobs such as sales – jobs that are highly social but routine – they see AI and humans working collaboratively. For example, in the classrooms of the future, AI could do the job of grading routine homework and exams, and even offer individualized lessons, while the human teacher would focus on being an empathetic mentor who teaches learning by doing, supervises group projects that develop emotional intelligence and provides personalized coaching.[6]

For jobs that are creative but asocial, Chen and Lee have an even more positive view. They say that in such jobs – e.g., a scientist using AI tools to accelerate drug discovery – human creativity can be enhanced by AI.[7]

This is the mental model we will try to apply to understand the professions that will flourish in the age of disruptive tech change. We will look for jobs and professions involving non-repetitive tasks, creativity, empathy and dexterity, and those that marry social skills with tech.

## Professions that Will Benefit From AI

As explained by Kai-Fu Lee's mental model for how AI will impact jobs, in professions where the task is not repetitive and/

or where social skills are central to success in that role, AI will arguably make workers more productive and thus enhance their relevance (and thus their compensation).

The most obvious way that the complementing force helps human beings is that new technologies, even if they displace some workers, often make other workers more productive at their tasks. For example, a taxi driver who uses GPS to follow unfamiliar roads, an architect who uses computer-assisted design software to craft more complex buildings or an accountant who uses tax calculation software to handle harder, more intractable calculations. All of these professionals are likely to become more productive at their tasks due to the use of technology.[8] Teachers, lawyers, engineers, filmmakers and scriptwriters too fall in this category. The roles which require context, emotion or cultural nuances will benefit from using AI.

Thankfully for India, AI's ascendancy is triggering the rise of global capability centres (GCCs) in India. As explained in our preceding book *Behold the Leviathan*, GCCs are large offices – employing several thousand white-collar workers – set up by companies headquartered in the developed economies. Inside these vast offices – typically located in cities like Hyderabad, Bengaluru (previously Bangalore), Pune, Gurugram (previously Gurgaon) or Chandigarh – sit not just IT workers but also HR, finance and accounts, marketing and compliance professionals. The shortage of such staff in the developed economies mean that thousands of Western firms find it easier and cheaper to employ Indians to remotely perform these roles. Presently, India has around 2,500 GCCs, with each one typically employing 10,000 people. Almost every day a new GCC is being set up in India.

Many of the GCCs being set up in India are in fact AI centres of excellence (COEs). Examples include McDonald's, Siemens, Walmart and JP Morgan. Inside these AI COEs, the jobs that have been created include bot trainers, AI prompt engineers, AI solutions architects, AI quality assurance engineers and model explainability officers. A case in point is Walmart Global Tech India adding over 2,000 roles in FY2024. Over half of these roles pertained to AI-related functions.

## New Professions that AI Will Create

Now we come to the most exciting aspect of the interplay between AI and jobs, the complementarity effect or creation of new jobs.

To be precise, the complementarity force works in three different ways.

- **Technology creates new jobs where none existed previously**: For example, the rise of smartphones and low-cost broadband has been central to the creation of the gig economy. And while some might say that the rise of ride share is simply a 'substitution' of a traditional taxi driver with an Ola/Uber, it is relatively clear that many segments of the gig economy – hairdressers, therapists, plumbers, electricians, domestic helpers, etc. – have resulted in the creation of net new jobs (rather than simply substituting a conventional profession with its gig economy counterpart).

Already, firms like Zomato, Swiggy, Ola and Urban Company employ millions of gig workers. Uber India has over 1 million drivers, while Zomato employs 3,50,000+ delivery agents.[9] The rise of AI-led platforms like Zepto and Blinkit is also expanding logistics-related gig roles. Already 12 million Indians are employed in the gig economy, with these gigs being their primary source of income.[10] These are new jobs that didn't exist 15 years ago. According to India Brand Equity Foundation, the gig economy will employ nearly 23.5 million workers in India by 2030.[11]

- **Technology lowers the cost of production and, therefore, boosts demand and creates jobs**: Let's consider the example of a lawyer to explain this dynamic. Think of a lawyer who is replaced from the task of looking through stacks of papers by an automated document review system. This a piece of software that can scan legal material far more swiftly – and, in many cases, more precisely too. The lawyer can now turn their attention to other tasks involved in providing legal advice. For example, she can do more face-to-face meetings with clients or apply problem-solving skills to a particularly prickly legal conundrum. In all these use cases, if the productivity increases are passed on to the lawyer's customers via lower prices or better-quality services, then the demand for whatever goods and services are being provided is likely to rise. The demand for human workers should rise along with it.[12]

- **Technology fosters growth and prosperity by improving overall efficiency**: Improved efficiency generates demand for goods and services, which in turn creates jobs (albeit in sectors very different from the ones where jobs are being lost). This is perhaps the most powerful impact of technology, and it is the one that is hardest to detect in the short run. In most industrial economies, technological progress has expanded the economic pie manifold. Daniel Susskind highlights that the UK, for instance, has seen its economy grow 113-fold from 1700 to 2000. Over the same 300 years, the Japanese economy grew 171-fold and the US economy 15,241-fold. Intuitively, growth at this scale is likely to have helped workers.[13]

So how come technological progress that appears to destroy jobs end up expanding the economic pie dramatically? Susskind explains that as an economy grows, and people become more prosperous and spend more money, the opportunities for work tend to improve. 'While some tasks get automated and are lost to machines, as the overall level of demand for goods and services rises, demand also increases for all the tasks that are needed to produce these goods and services.'[14]

So how exactly can the exponential economic growth referred to by Susskind in the previous paragraph take place in India? The first clue lies in India's relatively youthful population. As R. Jagannathan says:

> Unlike the advanced nations, where automation is killing jobs, but an older and aging population is unable to upskill,

> in India our population is young and teachable. They are also quick adapters to technology, as we have seen with the mobile penetration we have achieved and in the massive expansion in smartphones as data tariffs were slashed throughout late 2016 and 2017 after the entry of Reliance Jio.[15]

The second clue lies in professions in which new jobs are being created on a large scale in India. We have already highlighted in the preceding paragraphs how the gig economy has created 8 million new jobs in India. New job creation on a similar scale is also taking place elsewhere.

## YouTubers and Influencers

A staggering 80 million Indians are making videos on YouTube. The top 1 per cent of them – around 200k YouTubers – earn on average ₹12 lakh per annum. However, this average figure is misleading because the most successful YouTubers in India earn much more. Less than 1 per cent of creators (those with over 1 million followers) have the potential to earn around ₹53 lakh per month.[16] In fact, thanks to the people we meet during Saurabh's podcasts, we know several influencers who are making tens of millions of rupees each year in India and their success is pulling in millions of more creators to YouTube.

## Data Cleaning, Bot Training and Tech R&D in Indian GCCs

As explained earlier, the GCC boom is in full flight in India with a new GCC opening almost every day. This is creating new tech-related jobs in two different ways. Firstly, India is the second-largest global hub in the training and hiring of AI talent (the first being the US). Multi-national corporations (MNCs) have been driving R&D in AI via various initiatives, ranging from strategic innovation management in the ecosystem to research labs and large-scale R&D centres in India. Secondly, the GCC boom has in turn helped foster a broader SME (small and medium enterprise) ecosystem in India, which acts as suppliers to the GCCs. In this ecosystem, smaller firms specialize in data cleaning, structuring and vectorization as a service to support MNCs in their AI operations. India has also been fast emerging as an AI R&D centre.[17]

'In 2024, an estimated 50,000 Indian (freelance) annotators were present on international digital platforms.'[18] Furthermore, there are another 20,000 full-time annotators (i.e., professionals who label, tag and categorize data to train machine learning models) within India working in salaried roles. The global market for data annotations is valued at an estimated US $8 billion, and is expected to grow swiftly at nearly 26 per cent annually by 2028. From US $250 million in 2020–21, India is expected to service over US $7 billion of the global annotation market by 2030.[19] Bot training is the process of teaching a bot (like an AI chatbot) to understand and respond to user inputs by analysing data, identifying patterns and refining its answers. While we could not find a precise count of how many bot training jobs exist in India, we can see on online employment classifieds sites that there are tens of thousands of job openings in India in this field. For example, on India's largest employment classifieds site, Naukri, alone there are 50,000 vacancies for bot trainers on any given day.[20]

As the cost of training bots falls, it is highly likely that bots will be used for increasingly niche use cases. For example, the celebrated corporate coach Marshall Goldsmith recently launched his corporate bot. So, those executives who can't pay the several thousand dollars required to hire Marshall, can now speak with his bot (for a lower fee).[21]

Similarly, as R. Jagannathan explains,

> Industries in which the increasing use of robots will actually expand jobs include automobiles, electronics, renewable energy sources, skilled systems, robotics, and food and beverages. A Sloan School of Management study notes that automation will need more human input since robots using AI will first need to humanize themselves. Robots have to be taught how humans speak, react, empathize, and react when dealing with customers. Hence, this means automation needs human trainers, not just programmers.[22]

## Blockchain

An expert in the blockchain industry can expect an average salary between ₹5 lakh and ₹20 lakh per annum. Depending on several parameters like skills, experience and industry type, the salary may go as high as ₹80 lakh. The types of jobs available in blockchain tech are developer, architect, security engineer, product manager, UX designer, quality engineer and cloud computing, among others.[23]

## Jobs on the Dark Web

There is good reason to believe that Indian techies are finding jobs on the dark web. These jobs often involve cybercrime such as hacking, creation of content on prohibited subjects, trading cryptocurrency and intermediating in trades in prohibited substances.[24] Payment of these tech services are in bitcoin and our discussions with law enforcement officers suggests that this industry is thriving in India, as it is very difficult for conventional law enforcement efforts to identify the perpetrators of cybercrime. In fact, having been subjected to several cybercrime attacks ourselves, we in Marcellus can testify to just how much the law enforcement system struggles to deal with this menace. For obvious reasons it is hard to estimate how many Indians are involved in such activities, but our friends in the law enforcement ecosystem unhesitatingly say that post Covid-19 there has been explosion in cybercrime and dark web activity in India. Hence, it seems more likely than not that several hundred thousand Indians are already working on the dark web and getting paid in cryptocurrency.

## What Is the Net Employment Impact in India 2024–25?

It seems increasingly clear that India faces a period of transition as AI and automation reduce the demand for labour in sectors that have historically underpinned middle-class income – such as IT services, financial services, media and manufacturing. As highlighted in Chapter 3, the two most authoritative estimates on this seem to be from:

- the Oxford professors, Carl Frey and Michael Osborne, who estimate that 69 per cent of Indian jobs are likely to be automated by 2030; and
- NITI Aayog whose 'worst case' estimate of 2 million jobs lost in IT Services and CX sectors in India – translating to roughly 20 per cent of the jobs in these sectors disappearing by 2030.

Counter-balancing this is the 'complementarity effects' of AI. According to reports:

- AI-related job postings rose by 41 per cent year on year in India in July 2025.[25]
- Over 1,20,000 new tech jobs were posted, largely AI-centric (analytics, ML, data ops) for GCCs alone in FY2025.[26]
- In the next three to five years, AI and GenAI can create close to 100 million jobs in bot training, data validation and real-time handling of data. The underlying intellectual property pertaining to AI might belong to American firms, but it seems more likely than not that the support work related to feeding these AI models will be done by Indians.[27]

Technology is spawning new avenues for employment, many of which are novel, unconventional and hard to quantify – from YouTubers to bot trainers, gig economy workers to data labellers. This ambiguity makes it difficult to grasp the full scope of job creation currently underway. However, if India's free-market can function relatively unshackled by regulatory intervention (something which hasn't happened to date as explained in Chapter 4), then technology is more likely to enable than inhibit India's march towards prosperity. It appears to us that within a few years, the complementarity effects of AI might overtake the painful substitution effects, which are currently playing out. As Nandan Nilekani, the chairperson of Infosys and architect of Aadhaar has explained, life-time employment in any industry will be a thing of the past, and jobs will not be created in big units, but in small enterprises. In Mr Nilekani's words: 'The important thing is job creation is going to happen at millions of small units. Twenty thousand jobs are not going to be created by Maruti in Manesar; 20,000 jobs will happen when 20,000 small units hire 1 extra person. That is the way things will happen.'[28]

The implication of what Mr Nilekani is saying in the context of the growing gig economy in India is that while organized jobs will become scarce for the middle class, there will still be plenty of work for the middle class to do. So, for example, a financial advisor, rather than being an employee of a large high street bank in India, will do the same work as a self-employed advisor. In fact, hundreds of such self-employed advisors are the feet-on-street who sell Marcellus' investment products to Indian families. So large is this community of professionals now that clever entrepreneurs are turning these advisors into loosely affiliated groups of gig workers, each of whom is self-employed but all of whom benefit from the shared services – such as technology, marketing and client support – provided by these entrepreneurs.

In the next chapter, we turn to a case study of a firm founded in Surat 30 years ago by two freshly minted graduates who pioneered this organizational model and in so doing ended up creating economic opportunities for several hundred thousand people. It is business models like these – hybrid between the fading world of large, classically organized corporations and the emerging world of freelance gigs – that, we believe, will become increasingly common in India. To successfully help the Indian labour market transition from the world of office jobs to the world of gig jobs, such models of entrepreneurship in India will not only have to proliferate but will also have to become lucrative.

# 11

# Entrepreneurship in India

*Don't get fooled into thinking you have a lifelong career. At any moment, you need to be prepared to be independent and stand on your own two feet. If you prepare yourself for that, I think you are going to have a much better sort of ride along the way. So think about yourself as self-employed.**

As conventional white-collar jobs continue their post-Covid-19 decline, India is witnessing an entrepreneurial revolution that might offer a lifeline to educated professionals. The numbers tell a remarkable story: nearly a million meaningful enterprises are being created in India each year, driven by three distinct models of entrepreneurship. The first is the 'solopreneur model' – individuals building businesses through grit and creativity. The second is the 'Bollywood model', where talented freelancers collaborate on specific projects before dispersing to

---

* Pankaj Mishra, *Against the Grain: Lessons from the Outliers*, Penguin Random House India, 2024, p. 256.

work on other gigs, a template now spreading from film sets to infrastructure projects, management consulting and AI-related work. The third is the 'network model', perfected by companies like Uber but pioneered decades earlier in FMCG distribution, where hundreds of thousands of independent operators function as spokes in vast national networks.

This entrepreneurial boom isn't happening in a vacuum. Government reforms since 2016 have made starting a business easier, while angel investors and venture capitalists now pour over $50 billion annually into Indian startups. Popular television shows like *Shark Tank India* have transformed entrepreneurship from a risky outlier career into an aspirational mainstream choice.[1] The data confirms this shift: in urban India, 39 per cent of households now depend on self-employment compared to 47 per cent earning regular salaries – a gap that's closing rapidly.[2] For a generation facing job scarcity and wage stagnation, entrepreneurship increasingly appears not as a choice but as necessity rebranded as opportunity.

## Scarce Jobs versus Abundant Entrepreneurial Opportunities

Nestled in the crowded bazaar of Jail Road Market in New Delhi is a tiny shop selling colourful kurtas and pants for women, a common business in this neighbourhood and in hundreds of similar markets across northern India. However, the owner of this shop and her story are anything but common. The owner is Jasmeen Kaur, creator of the now famous words, 'So beautiful, so elegant, just looking like a wow!'

**Figure 11.1**: Two years (2023 to 2025) since she shot to fame, Jasmeen Kaur continues to expand her online presence

**Source**: Instagram.[3] The images are for illustrative purpose only and the copyright remains with the original creator.

Kaur shot to fame with this catchy phrase when Bollywood star Deepika Padukone recited it on social media and made it famous. The rise of Instagram and social media, as well as their accessibility to millions of Indians, ensured that the phrase 'looking like a wow' became viral and made Kaur a celebrity, potentially creating a pan-India (as opposed to local) market for her wares (Figure 11.1). She signifies the rise of a new India – an India where polished English and high-profile university degrees and MBAs are no longer a prerequisite for success.[4]

While 'solopreneurs' like Jasmeen Kaur are the most ubiquitous construct in the Indian MSME universe, there are two other tried and tested templates for entrepreneurship in India that are increasingly getting popular, as mentioned in brief earlier.

The 'Bollywood model' of entrepreneurship has been around for decades, wherein groups of talented freelancers come together to work on a specific project and coordinate within the group to achieve a common goal. The collaborative process is managed by the director and the producer, who in turn oversee numerous specialized departments. Each of the group participants might be working on multiple gigs (movies, TV programmes, commercials) simultaneously, and in doing so combining and coordinating their activities with other group members.

As the Indian economy gradually becomes more complex and more developed, the Bollywood model is being used in a broader range of industries, such as infrastructure projects, capital raising for companies, management consultancy and even political campaigns. Looking ahead, the model would work well in the world of AI-related gig jobs, insofar as fluid teams of data cleaners, annotators and bot trainers could work simultaneously on multiple projects for multiple clients around the world from the comfort of their own homes.

Over the past 20 years, as communication and transport networks have improved dramatically in India, and as GST has unified the country into a single market – the 'network model' has become an increasingly effective template that solopreneurs can use to group together and operate as a national enterprise. While the best-known example of this model is Uber, at least three decades before Uber came to India, this model was in use in a variety of B2C industries – such as FMCG and building materials, where the manufacturer sells their product to a national network of thousands of wholesalers who in turn sell to a local network of hundreds of 'dealers' who are usually shopkeepers operating on the high street. The hub-and-spoke nature of these networks mean that each network can easily and sustainably support multiple layers of 'spokes'. This, in turn, means that hundreds of thousands of solopreneurs can operate inside each of these vast networks.

The rising popularity of equity investing in the opening decades of the twenty-first century then created the grounds for bringing this 'network model' to mutual fund investing, with Surat-based NJ playing a pioneering role. The case study on NJ at the end of this chapter gives more colour on how such networks of over 1,00,000 financial distributors can combine the strengths of a large business (e.g., economies of scale, clever use of technology to drive efficiency and better decision-making, alongside structured industrial strength business processes) with the advantages of being a solopreneur (e.g., strong local contacts, ground-level knowledge of local realities, quick decision-making).

Even as conventional white-collar jobs continue to dwindle in the post Covid-19 world, these three very different templates for building successful businesses show that that there is no shortage of work (as opposed to jobs) for enterprising professionals in India. This is further evidenced by the boom in new company creation in India (see Figure 11.2).

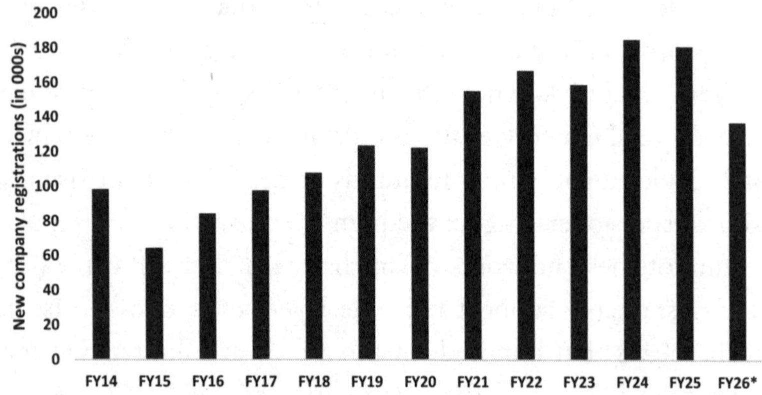


**Figure 11.2**: New company registration has been rising over the last decade

**Note**: * Data for FY2026 taken year to date (until October 2025)

**Source**: Ministry of Corporate Affairs and Centre for Monitoring Indian Economy, collated by IIFL Capital, Business IANS

Note that Figure 11.2 excludes the creation of micro-enterprises in India each year for which there is no formal registration process and hence no official data. Given that India is estimated to have over 60 million micro-enterprises and less than 2 million formally registered active companies, it would not be unrealistic to say that a million meaningful enterprises are being created in India each year.[5]

In fact, surveys repeatedly show that a majority of Indians[6] and more than a third of Indian graduates aspire to be entrepreneurs[7]. Validating this aspiration are immensely popular mainstream TV programmes like *Shark Tank India*, as mentioned earlier. First aired in December 2021, *Shark Tank* swiftly became a focal point of conversation at dinner tables and social gatherings across India. The 'sharks' – who were reasonably well-known in business circles even before the show was aired – became national celebrities, and following the fortunes of the entrepreneurs who were pitching for funding gradually became a national pastime. Entrepreneurship thus became a mainstream endeavour – something that smart and ambitious people do.[8]

In fact, data from the government now suggests that in urban areas, entrepreneurship is now almost as common a source of livelihood as salaried employment. As Figure 11.3 shows, 39 per cent of urban households are dependent on self-employment whereas 47 per cent earn their livelihood from a regular salary.[9]

What is also evident is that while AI can substitute the office worker doing routine cognitive tasks, for small businesses AI is (more often than not) a complementary tool. Specifically, AI can help all three models of entrepreneurship highlighted earlier in this chapter by:

- coordinating activities that have been hard to coordinate historically, e.g., demand forecasting, inventory management;[10]
- reducing the cost of doing repetitive tasks, e.g. preparing the monthly accounts of a small business, using chatbots to deal with routine customer queries; and
- automating the online marketing activities of businesses, both in terms of content creation and in terms of executing the campaign on social media platforms (after automatically using predictive analytics).[11]

| Occupation of Chief Wage Earner (CWE) | % of households in rural/urban dependent on each occupation | |
|---|---|---|
| | Rural India | Urban India |
| Self-employed in agriculture (farm owner/renter/agri business) | 48 | – |
| Self-employed in non-agriculture | 11 | 39 |
| Total self-employed | 59 | 39 |
| Total casual labour | 27 | 14 |
| Regular wage/salary (mostly informal) | 14 | 47 |

**Figure 11.3**: Nature of rural and urban occupations

**Source**: NSS Annual Report Periodic Labour Force Survey, July 2022–June 2023

By reducing the grunt work and drudgery associated with entrepreneurship, AI has made it a more attractive career option. Moreover, alongside the rising aspirational quotient of entrepreneurship has come funding for entrepreneurs – both from the government and from the private sector.

The GoI has sought to support start-ups in three different ways. Firstly, since 2016, 53 regulatory reforms have been enacted to boost the startup ecosystem in India. The latest reform recognizes any entity or business as a startup for 10 years since its incorporation, with a turnover of less than ₹100 cr. Moreover, startups can avail of tax rebates on profits for three consecutive years of the 10 years, if incorporated before March 2024.[12]

Secondly, the government provides around ₹10,000 crore ($1.1 billion) of equity capital for a fund of funds (FoF) managed by Small Industries Development Bank of India. This FoF in-turn invests in venture capital funds which further – as discussed below – invest in startups.

Thirdly, the government tries to reduce the cost of borrowing for startups by providing credit guarantees for loans extended to recognized startups by banks and non-banking financial companies[13] and by facilitating bank loans between ₹10 lakh to ₹1 crore for setting up new ventures.[14] Under the Micro Units Development and Refinance Agency (MUDRA), the government provides loans (through public sector banks) of up to ₹10 lakh to MSMEs without collateral.[15]

Private sector funding for entrepreneurs comes from an ever-growing network of 'angel investors' (wealthy individuals who invest modest sums of money – from a few lakh to a few crore – in return for an equity stake in a start-up), and from venture capitalists (professionally organized investment firms that invest upwards of a few crore to buy an equity stake in a startup).

Funding from angel investors has grown more than fourfold over the past decade from around \$3 billion to around \$13 billion. 'Angel investors, often experienced entrepreneurs, or high-net-worth individuals, are considered "the lifeblood of early-stage startups". They provide crucial financial backing and mentorship, instrumental in navigating challenges from product development to market expansion.'[16]

Venture capital funding in India has grown significantly over the past decade, rising from approximately \$15 billion in 2014 to about \$43 billion in 2024.[17] Between the angel investors and the venture capitalists, over 3,000 startups are getting equity funding each year in India. This number too has quadrupled over the past decade. While in the context of a country in which a million new enterprises are being started each year, 3,000 might not look like a large number, it is large enough to keep hundreds of thousands of young graduates interested in setting up a new venture.

With the best part of a million Indians becoming entrepreneurs each year, and with more than \$50 billion of equity funding going into startups each year (from angels, venture capitalists and the government), the salaried person is gradually ceding space – financially, socially and politically – to the entrepreneur.[18] Does of all this then imply that India's labour market transition – from office jobs to gigs and entrepreneurship – will be a relatively smooth ride? Unfortunately, basis the current data, the answer is no because Indian entrepreneurs simply aren't earning enough and that is a problem which will need fixing if India is to beat the middle income trap we highlighted in Chapter 9.

## High Risks for Low Returns

In Figure 11.3, we highlighted that in urban India almost as many people are now earning a living from self-employment as from salaried employment. However, the data on the most affluent 40 per cent of households in India shows that entrepreneurs (represented in Table 11.1 by 'own business – non-agricultural') are under-represented in the upper echelons of India's income distribution. Of the most affluent 40 per cent of Indian households, entrepreneurs account for a modest 17 per cent, whereas salaried workers account for 39 per cent.

**Table 11.1**: Occupation profile of the richest 40 per cent of Indian households (Q5 and Q4); percentage of quintile dependent on each occupation

| Occupation Profile of the Richest 40 per cent of Indian Households | | |
|---|---|---|
| **Occupation of Chief Wage Earner** | **Richest 20% (Q5)** | **Next 20% (Q4)** |
| Own agriculture business | 17 | 23 |
| Regular salary/wage – public | 17 | 7 |
| Regular salary/wage – private | 33 | 22 |
| Own business – non-agricultural | 17 | 16 |
| Wage labourer – agriculture/allied | 1 | 5 |
| Wage labourer – non-agricultural | 2 | 15 |
| Retired/pension/rent on properties, etc. | 10 | 9 |
| **Total** | **100** | **100** |

**Source**: Rama Bijapurkar, *Lilliput Land: How Small Is Driving India's Mega Consumption Story*, Penguin, 2024.

In fact, Rama Bijapurkar's outstanding book on this subject goes on to show that in the richest 10 per cent of Indian households, a mere 14 per cent are 'non-agricultural self-employment' whereas 58 per cent of this elite stratum of Indian society are 'salaried individuals'.[19]

This data on the sub-par returns on Indian entrepreneurship is supported by data from the tax department, which shows that over the past decade, Indian companies with PAT less than ₹10 lakh have barely grown their profits. In fact, even companies with PAT less than ₹1 crore have barely grown their profits in real terms (i.e., after adjusting for inflation) over the past decade. As highlighted in Chapter 4, such firms account for over 80 per cent of the companies registered in India to pay corporate tax.

Leaving aside the issues around red tape highlighted in in Chapter 4, there are three other sets of factors that make life difficult for Indian entrepreneurs. Firstly, land for setting up factories in India is expensive and hard to get. Secondly, the cost of working capital remains high in India, even as availability of equity capital has improved. And thirdly, the mental skill sets and psychological resources to shift from employment to entrepreneurship are difficult to acquire. We now delve into each of these issues in more detail.

## Land Is Hard to Get

While setting up a services business that works out of low-cost office space in the suburbs of India's metros has become much easier over the past decade (as we discovered when we set up Marcellus in 2018), setting up a manufacturing business remains a tricky proposition due to the difficulty of getting industrial land. Not just startups, even Marcellus' investee companies – that are listed enterprises with revenues in excess of ₹1,000 crore – struggle to get industrial land in the manufacturing belts of Maharashtra or Gujarat.

Not only is it hard to get industrial land, but even if an entrepreneur were fortunate enough to find a seller, the price of land in India is high as compared to its fundamental value. In fact, 'it is also high relative to the market price of land in several advanced countries such as the Netherlands and other parts of Europe'. Why so? Because what has been dubbed the 'licence-permit-quota' raj ensures that through zoning laws and urban development permits, the supply of land is subject to excessive restrictions, thus giving those who set these rules an opportunity to earn 'rents'.[20]

Other developing economies also suffer due to such rent-seeking activity, but the combination of three levels of government – Centre, state and municipal corporation or panchayat – that can interfere with the land acquisition process through a variety of rules and regulations means that compared to countries like Vietnam, rent on industrial land in India can be 40 per cent more expensive.[21]

Price considerations aside, trying to buy land in India can be costly along another dimension – nearly one in five murders in India are caused by property disputes.[22] With the legal system comprehensively jammed when it comes to property disputes (over 30 million property disputes are pending in India's courts), the temptation for litigants to take matters into their own hands grows by each passing year.[23]

## Working Capital Is Expensive

As highlighted earlier in this chapter, the good news is that the cost of equity capital has fallen meaningfully in India over the past decade, thanks to greater availability of angel investors and venture capital funding. Using data on large-listed firms as a proxy, we estimate that the cost of equity has dropped in India over the past decade by 3–4 percentage points. However, other than equity capital, businesses also need working capital to fund things like the time gap between incurring expenses to manufacture a product and receiving revenues from the customer upon sale of the product, for example. This is where life gets difficult for small businesses in India.

The cost of working capital for small businesses in India is north of 10 per cent. In contrast, not only in China[24] but also in Vietnam small businesses can access working capital at rates starting from 3 per cent.[25]

India's punitively high cost of working capital makes it extremely difficult for Indian manufacturers to be competitive in the global market and that's why it is hard to find successful start-ups in India that are able to crack open the global market in manufactured goods.

## Psychological Challenges: Employee Mindset versus Entrepreneurial Mindset

If India's job creation is going to come from thousands of small firms rather than a handful of industrial giants, then the mindset of the workforce will have to shift. The old model of lifetime employment – joining a bank as a probationary officer and retiring as a deputy MD – is fading. However, even though the economic forces point towards entrepreneurship, professionals do not automatically leave the comfort of India Inc for the uncertainty of starting something of their own. The reason is simple: the mindset that makes you successful in a large hierarchical company is often the opposite of what carries an entrepreneur forward.

In corporate life, achievement comes from meeting targets consistently, avoiding surprises and keeping the machine running smoothly. Thinking and doing are separated by layers of hierarchy. When a crisis occurs, you look upwards for the strategy. Entrepreneurs have no such fallback. They must imagine the plan, revise it constantly and execute it personally. As Nandan Nilekani once described it, the entrepreneur is both the thinker and doer, toggling between the two continuously. Crises are not unusual events; they arrive annually, sometimes monthly. The ability to improvise, decide and act becomes central.[26]

This difference shows up strongly in personal development. Large organizations reward the outer scorecard – titles, ratings, visible symbols of upward mobility – because committees determine promotions. Conformity is safe; unconventional risks are not. Entrepreneurship, on the other hand, is guided by the inner scorecard Warren Buffett speaks of: the quiet accumulation of capability, curiosity and judgement.[27] Godrej Consumer CEO and author of *The CEO Factory*, Sudhir Sitapati's description of how insights are formed – through constant observation, wide reading and making lateral connections – captures the kind of self-driven learning that entrepreneurs rely on. Many of India's understated promoters reflect this instinct.[28] The Dhingra family of Berger Paints, for instance, built an exceptional company not by cultivating status but by staying grounded and strengthening the substance of their business year after year.[29]

Risk is where the mindsets diverge most sharply. In a corporate setting, the safest option is often to fail conventionally, rather than try something new and risk visible embarrassment. Committees are not built to reward brave failures. Entrepreneurs live in the opposite world. Every important decision is a risk, and setbacks are constant. Harsh Mariwala has said that in entrepreneurship 'sometimes you win, sometimes you learn', a sentiment shaped by his own experience of mistakes made without formal training or mentors.[30] For a founder, failure is not reputational damage; it is part of the apprenticeship.

Time horizon deepens the divide. Corporate India operates on short cycles – most CEOs last three or four years – and strategic plans reflect those rhythms. Careers evolve around these cycles, which naturally limits experimentation. Entrepreneurs, in contrast, often think in decades. Some of India's most durable enterprises were built by founders who believed they were constructing institutions, not merely businesses. Jamsetji Tata's partnership firm from 1868, now the Tata Group, illustrates how a long-term mindset anchored in purpose can shape an organization that thrives for over a century.[31]

Taken together, these differences point to a new entrepreneurial mindset India must cultivate: improvisational, internally driven, comfortable with risk, frugal and oriented towards building something that lasts. It is a shift from asking 'what is expected of me?' to 'what can I build here?', from playing within a three-year cycle to thinking across decades. As India's economy becomes more dispersed and dynamic, this owner mindset – rather than the traditional middle-class employee mindset – will increasingly determine who succeeds.

If the real world was the world described by economics textbooks, then – given the dynamics we have described in the preceding chapters – we would expect to see a rapid flow of educated professionals migrating from the air-conditioned offices and bountiful canteens of India Inc into the entrepreneurial sphere. However, the real world is not that simple. There are a number of skills and mindset differences between what helps one succeed in a large Indian corporate versus what helps an Indian entrepreneur succeed. These skill differences make it difficult for employees of large companies to become entrepreneurs or entrepreneurial gig workers. The table below (Table 11.2) is our attempt to capture some of the more important differences.

**Table 11.2**: 10 Attributes that Determine an 'Employee' Mindset vs an 'Entrepreneur' Mindset

| | Attribute | 'Employee Mindset' | 'Entrepreneur Mindset' |
|---|---|---|---|
| 1 | Mental orientation | Goal-oriented with structured planning and research | Means-oriented and open to improvisation as the business evolves |

| | Attribute | 'Employee Mindset' | 'Entrepreneur Mindset' |
|---|---|---|---|
| 2 | Belief | Accept the world as it is given to you. Ask 'What can my country do for me?' | Change the world (or at least the sector in which you operate). Ask 'What can I do for my country?' |
| 3 | Basis for action | 'What should I do? What is expected of me in my role?' | 'What can I do? What are the NPV* positive bets available to me? |
| 4 | Attitude towards surprises and risks | Avoid them and don't rock the boat | Seek them out because that's how new opportunities arise |
| 5 | Budgeting and spending | Seek bigger budgets | Spend frugally |
| 6 | Planning | Someone more senior will give you the plan for a year or two at a time | Create the plan (and if need be, re-plan) for long term horizons |
| 7 | Vector for upwards mobility | Look for a job that pays more than your current one | Look for the next NPV positive opportunity that your firm can exploit |
| 8 | Attitude towards failure | Failure can be career limiting | Failure is an essential building block of learning and success |
| 9 | Time management | Ensure that you put in long hours (and ensure that people in the office are aware of this) | Take time to refresh and recharge (so that you can be on top of your game) |
| 10 | Scorecard (outer vs inner) | Outer scorecard focus: Credentials, rank, title and status markers are important | Inner scorecard focus: Seek accumulation of knowledge and insights on a range of subjects, and strive to apply it to the world at large |

**Note:** *Net present value

**Source:** Marcellus Investment Managers, inspired by a table given in Mukesh Sud and Priyank Narayan, *Leapfrog: Six Practices to Thrive*, Penguin Random House India, 2022.

## deAsra: Ramping up Ambition on a National Scale

It is unlikely that structural issues like the high cost of land and stubbornly high cost of working capital can be resolved anytime soon. However, given the pressing need to ramp up entrepreneurship in India – not in the least to deploy the 8 million graduates who are emerging from university every year – waiting for structural problems to be resolved is not going to improve the situation. Over a decade ago an entrepreneur in Pune decided to see what he could do to move things forward.

Anand Deshpande, founder and chairman of Persistent Systems, a $9 billion market cap IT services company headquartered in Pune is the man behind deAsra. Nandita met him in his office in Pune's bustling area of Senapati Bapat Road on a rain-soaked afternoon to understand how this tech entrepreneur had ventured into the world of helping small businesses.

Anand explained that in 2012, as he turned 50, sitting in the very office where he sat today and sees the city of Pune blaze past, a thought struck him. Since the beginning of his career he had worked with the motto of 'learn, earn, return'. With the first two objectives from the principle achieved, he was now thinking hard about how he could return something to the ecosystem, to the country that had supported him and his ambitions, helped him grow and make his mark.

He realized in 2012 that India would face a massive challenge with job scarcity, as demographic shifts would result in labour supply far outstripping demand. Anand explained that while India needed fewer number of jobs per year 10 years ago on an absolute basis (~10–15 million in 2014–15 vs 18 million required today), the imbalance between massive supply of and limited demand for labour was no better then than it is today. With clarity of thought built around the scale of the jobs problem, deAsra was born.

Being a pragmatic man, he knew that working towards creating more jobs in the conventional way was a lost cause, both from a capability perspective and due to the constant evolution of ground realities in India. As a result, Anand decided that deAsra will help people get mentored to start their own small businesses, potentially being able to employ others.

Anand's idea was very simple – he wanted Indian families to be able to earn at least ₹30,000 per month for them to be able to live a life of decent quality. He came up with an idea called 'Business in a Box' – which could allow anyone to create a business by themselves. A document with a 6x6 grid was created detailing the things that would be required to create a business. Unfortunately, deAsra didn't get the response Anand was hoping for. Entrepreneurs at the early stage of their venture's existence tend to be more spontaneous and don't necessarily plan as extensively as the 'Business in a Box' construct had envisaged.

Anand then came at the issue from another angle – deAsra approached National Skill Development Council (NSDC) to tap into the group of potential entrepreneurs who are acquiring skills. What Anand soon realized was that the people deAsra was reaching out to, who use formal skill development or educational institutes, were gearing themselves towards employment and not entrepreneurship.

The unsuccessful experiments of 2013–16 resulted in Anand learning three important lessons that would determine how deAsra would evolve over the next decade:

- By 2016, deAsra had helped ~3,000 businesses. While to a layperson, this seems like a solid number, Anand was not at all happy with this figure. That's when he decided to change deAsra's focus.
- The experience with NSDC had helped Anand understand that skill acquisition is *not* the key for entrepreneurship. He explains that this is the crux of the problem with our education system – 'we train people to "seek" jobs and not "create" them'. And not much has changed on this front; even those pursuing MBA degrees in India do so with the aim of getting a job rather than to manage a business.
- Most micro businesses in the country are working on a sustenance basis, and real impact will come from such businesses who have achieved a bit of scale in their revenues and whose owners are serious about growing their business.

Thanks to these three insights, deAsra decided to disaggregate their services and help businesses in specific functions where they required help. This turned out to be a pivotal moment for them. By using technology and specific tasks as end goals for businesses, deAsra was able to locate pain points for small businesses and then resolve these problems effectively.

Furthermore, they realized that approaching students/ people getting skills for business creation was a futile exercise, as the focus for such candidates is usually on finding a job somewhere. Instead, what the team at deAsra did was to focus on those people who want to scale their businesses. The authors of this book reached the same conclusion as the team at deAsra – helping people who are already sold on the idea of entrepreneurship is far easier than helping someone who is looking for a job – while traversing vastly different journeys to reach that conclusion.

This pivot enabled deAsra to focus on small entrepreneurs who usually don't get support from anywhere. For instance, the smallest of firms or enterprises usually get government-led grants and the larger businesses have enough resources in their kitty to ensure they scale further. It's usually those in the middle – with revenues between ₹5 lakh to ₹1 crore – who are aspirational but lack know-how on how to scale efficiently. These businesses were the ones deAsra decided to focus on.

In 2018, the scale of their operation really took off when they started doing Google Ads. This is when word started to spread and as a result of this change in mindset, attitude and actions, deAsra has been able to successfully touch 4,28,000 lives since its inception across multiple sectors like food, education, fashion, etc.

While it is evident that India needs more entrepreneurs as the sun sets on the Indian salaried employee, how easy is it to become an entrepreneur in India especially if you are competing against much larger companies?

Our final case study highlights the remarkable rise of a colossal national network of self-employed distributors of financial services products, headquartered in Surat, Gujarat (Figure 11.5).

## Case Study: Neeraj Choksi and Jignesh Desai, NJ

**Figure 11.5**: Left to right: Jignesh Desai, Neeraj Choksi and the team at NJ

**Source**: NJ Group

Getting off the train at Surat railway station has always been a chaotic affair. After all, the city's famous textile and apparel trading hub is right next to the station, and sometimes the hubbub of the tens of thousands of Surati traders can leave a visitor from suburban Mumbai feeling overwhelmed. But now that the station in Surat is in the process of being transformed into a major shopping-cum-entertainment complex, there is construction activity everywhere in the station. Thus, getting off the train at Surat with the jackhammers drilling away feels like an entry into a city whose pulse-pounding chaos captures the essence of Indian capitalism.

As you leave the hubbub of the main city of Surat and enter the nearby industrial town of Udhna, it gets quieter. The colossal textile traders' hubs make way for conventional office blocks. In the middle of this industrial town stands Udhna Udyog Nagar Sangh Commercial Complex, a nine-storey part-glass part-concrete façade building. This is the headquarters of NJ, a financial services firm that has now become synonymous with the ascent of India's mutual fund industry.

For those who are a part of the ₹75 trillion Indian mutual fund industry, a regular visit to Surat to meet NJ – founded by Neeraj Choksi and Jignesh Desai – is par for the course. Founded in June 1994, when Neeraj bhai and Jignesh bhai were a year or two out of college, the firm was known as NJ Capitalstocks in those days.[32]

Choksi and Desai were college roommates in Vallabh Vidyanagar, a small town in Anand district of Gujarat, where Desai was studying engineering and Choksi was a business management student. After graduation, they decided to work together and began their careers by selling financial instruments as brokers and distributors.

Building a financial services distribution in the India of the 1990s was tough. The market was trying to recover from the 1992 Harshad Scam when the East Asian crisis and an economic downturn struck in the mid-1990s. In that era, the two young graduates from Vallabh Vidyanagar, aside from trying to sell mutual funds out of their 3,000 sq. ft office in Surat, also tried their hands at being sub-brokers in the Indian stock market (where they bought and sold equity shares and initial public offerings for their clients), selling fixed deposits and car financing.

The first Indian mutual fund was launched in 1963 by the Unit Trust of India. The year 1987 marked the entry of public sector mutual funds set up by public sector banks and insurers. However, it wasn't until the 1990s that private sector companies entered the industry. The erstwhile Kothari Pioneer (now merged with Franklin Templeton MF) was the first private sector mutual fund to register itself with the then newly created regulator, SEBI, in July 1993.[33]

By the mid-1990s, 11 private-sector fund houses had entered the mutual fund industry. Neeraj bhai and Jignesh bhai vividly remember selling Birla Sun Life Funds, Birla Advantage Fund (Birla's asset management company had at that point in time a joint venture with Capital International, the Los Angeles – headquartered American mutual fund giant) and ITC Threadneedle Top 200 Fund (IT200: now, HDFC Large Cap Fund).

'We had assembled around 100 people for a presentation that a senior person from ITC Threadneedle had come down to Surat to give. Eventually, we got just three applications totalling ₹13,000 for IT200,' Neeraj bhai said. The other mutual fund schemes they sold in those days got a similar response.

One of the most difficult challenges for entrepreneurs who are just starting out in life is to figure out how to eliminate distractions and focus their attention on growing one line of business. As mentioned above, at the outset the founders of NJ were selling a variety of financial products. After a couple of years of experimentation, Choksi and Desai became convinced about the upside potential of mutual funds. In the years ahead, the duo kept their focus on mutual funds, unlike many other large distributors in those days who moved their focus to selling other products.

'In those days, it was unusual for even fund houses to have a full-fledged sales machinery on the roads talking about mutual funds. So mutual fund houses used to find it strange to run into people like Jignesh and me, who were willing to talk mutual funds to an audience,' said Neeraj bhai, who remembers senior officials from the mutual fund industry in Mumbai like Pankaj Razdan (former CEO and MD at Birla Sun Life Insurance Ltd), Prashant Jain (former CIO, HDFC AMC) and Nilesh Shah (now MD, Kotak AMC) visiting their office in Surat.

'We used to take them to potential customers' homes; people used to like meeting them and listening to them; some even used to ask for stock tips. But many never invested (in mutual funds). We kept going to their homes for as long as two years before they wrote their cheques. We didn't have much to do back then, so we had lot of time,' said Neeraj bhai with a laugh. 'Today,' he added, 'many of those early customers of NJ are *crorepatis* [multimillionaires] thanks to their investments in mutual funds, which they eventually made, and still do, with NJ.'

Even as founders of NJ put in the hard yards taking mutual fund managers to their customers' houses in Surat, they hit upon a pioneering operational improvement in their business model.

In the year 2003, NJ started building a network of partners. Typically, distributors who wish to expand hire people to work for the firm and pay them a fixed salary. But NJ found it better to build a network of partners and share commissions with them. Otherwise called sub-brokers, NJ's partners were free to sell products that NJ did not at the time. They were also likely to have other professions (e.g., running a kirana store). 'At that time, we had limited capital; we couldn't afford people to take a salary. A distributor network that could plug and play into NJ would work better since we would keep a share of commissions and pass on the rest to our partners,' Neeraj bhai said.

In parallel to this buildout of the distributor network, NJ also began leveraging technology proactively during this time. For example, NJ was at the forefront when the units of mutual funds were made available to be transacted through stock exchanges in 2010. A few years later, NJ was the among the first financial services firms in India to launch an Aadhaar based e-mandate.

The hard work that Neeraj bhai and Jignesh bhai put in between 1994 and 2004 paid off in the bull market that gripped India between 2003 and 2010. As the Sensex rose from 3,000 to 21,000, NJ's assets under management surged from ₹342 crore in March 2004 to ₹7,508 crore by March 2010 (implying 22x growth, versus the 7x growth seen in the underlying benchmark index). Revenues rose from ₹8.82 crore to ₹86.3 crore (approximately 10x growth) in the same period, while PAT jumped from ₹1.04 crore to ₹8.5 crore (8x growth). This incredible seven-year surge in scale and profitability – the foundations of which were built through ten years of entrepreneurial vigour from 1994 to 2004 – put NJ at the forefront of the rise of India's mutual fund industry.

Other than constructing a mutual fund distributor network, they also pioneered a corporate structure that can successfully manage such a network. Unit managers at NJ are meant to recruit distributors (each manages around 60 distributors), bring them into the NJ fold, train them and make them self-reliant. A distributor's performance is the unit manager's responsibility. Hence the unit manager's set the distributors demanding targets so that distributor can end a decent income within his first three years as part of the NJ ecosystem.

Unit managers are right at the bottom rung of the hierarchy in the sales division at NJ. They report to branch managers, who report to regional managers, who then report to zonal managers. All zonal managers report to the NJ veteran of over two decades, Misbah Baxamusa, CEO of NJ Wealth.

While our description of how NJ and its mutual fund distributor network might sound prosaic, it is hard to overstate just how difficult it is to get this type of operational model right. Juggling expansion in scale without diluting entrepreneurial vigour, and without encouraging unfair trade practices (which disadvantage the customer while pursuing near term profitability), is a difficult balancing act in any country. In the turbulent evolution of the Indian stock market, NJ's steady expansion over the past 30 years is a tribute to Neeraj Choksi and Jignesh Desai's clarity of thought and persistence.

With its pioneering operational model now being widely emulated by multiple firms in different parts of the country, NJ is today the largest privately owned distributor of mutual funds in India. In fact, across the public and private sector, the only institution that distributes more mutual funds than NJ is the colossal GoI undertaking, the State Bank of India.

In FY2025, inflows into the Indian mutual fund industry were ₹4.2 trillion.[34] Out of that amount, NJ accounted for 10 per cent. Thanks to their firm's ability to channel colossal sums of money year after year, Choksi and Desai are now among the wealthiest men in India.[35]

> Over the years, NJ Group [...] expanded from mutual funds into other areas like insurance and asset management. Today, NJ Group manages over Rs 2.7 trillion in assets and has more than 2,400 employees across 230 locations in India. Their flagship business, NJ Wealth, has over 47,875 active distributors, all working hard to spread financial awareness and provide access to mutual funds. [...] Neeraj and Jignesh are excited about the potential for growth in the mutual fund industry. They encourage young people to see this as a career opportunity, emphasizing that the stage is set for a financial revolution. Their journey is not just about building a business; it's about making a real impact on society.[36]

**Note**: Our description of Neeraj Choksi and Jignesh Desai's build out of NJ is based on our interviews with the two founders and from a long article on NJ, which was published in *Livemint* on 16 August 2017.[37]

# 12

# Conclusion: India at the Breakpoint

*[...] India was, in the simplest way, on the move; that all over the vast country, men and women had moved out of the cramped ways and expectations of their parents and grandparents, and were expecting more. This was the 'million mutinies' ...**

## A Massive Labour-Market Transition Looms

For two decades, we watched factory jobs in India disappear into automation as employers systematically invested more in machines than in workers. What we are witnessing in the post-Covid-19 era is the same phenomenon spreading through India's offices. In this latest wave of job destruction, not only are routine cognitive roles like bookkeeping and clerical tasks vanishing, but even sophisticated cognitive work (including coding) is being phased out by AI.

---

* V.S. Naipaul, 'The Long Way Round', *The Guardian*, 10 March 2007, https://tinyurl.com/y8rxyx4y.

Many of India's largest private sector employers have told us they are aiming to use AI to reduce their salary bills by up to a third. The stagnation in their employee numbers, even as revenues and profits grow at double digits testifies to their commitment to not hire more people. Employees in these firms tell us repeatedly about job losses and management's determination to replace humans with bots. This trend extends beyond India's borders – Microsoft, Alphabet and Oracle are laying off tens of thousands of highly qualified tech workers despite generating billions in profits.

The scale of disruption becomes clear when we compare workforces: while Microsoft employs 2,28,000 people and OpenAI operates with roughly 3,500 employees, DeepSeek employs just 200 people (as mentioned earlier). This stark contrast suggests the day of reckoning will arrive sooner rather than later, especially for Indians in jobs involving relatively repetitive tasks.

Yet within this gathering storm, three bright lights shine: policy initiatives announced by the government, AI's potential to create (not just destroy) jobs and the rise of entrepreneurialism in India. The interplay among these forces will determine whether India navigates this transition successfully or stumbles into prolonged economic distress.

## Policy Initiatives: Addressing the Consumption Crisis

Throughout 2024 and 2025, the GoI demonstrated awareness of the consumption slowdown documented in this book.

Income tax cuts, GST reductions and the RBI's 125 basis points of interest rate cuts (at the time of writing this book) were welcome measures. Even more encouraging was the government's October 2025 ban on online money gaming – an activity that, by our estimates, was siphoning ₹70,000 crore annually from productive consumption into the pockets of gaming platforms and their elite backers.

A similar crackdown on retail investors' F&O trading is warranted. The SEBI's data shows more than $10 billion being transferred each year from retail investors to institutional investors and Wall Street – a wealth transfer that confers no economic benefit to India. This money, had it not been speculated away, could have supported consumption of goods and services, creating genuine economic activity and employment.

But beyond specific interventions, a broader policy course correction is required: India must liberalize its labour markets to the same extent it has liberalized its capital markets. Post 1991, every government has steadily opened India's financial markets to the point where the country now boasts one of the world's most advanced stock markets with booming retail participation. The cost of equity for listed Indian companies has fallen to around 10 per cent – the lowest it has ever been.

The cost of labour, however, remains artificially elevated by regulations and minimum wage rules that set wages at two to three times Bangladesh's levels despite similar per capita incomes. With capital costs falling and labour costs remaining rigid, Indian promoters logically invest more in machines and technology while economizing on labour. This is the central driver behind India's jobless growth.

Labour market liberalization inevitably raises concerns about exploitative employers who might squeeze workers, and hire and fire on short notice. These concerns, amplified in democratic discourse, cannot be ignored by politicians. The answer lies in strengthening India's social security measures beyond what direct benefits transfer has already delivered. A robust social security ecosystem would provide the safety net that makes labour market flexibility politically palatable.

The consumption pickup in late 2025 demonstrated that when the government cuts taxes significantly, the heavily indebted Indian middle class – with its high propensity to spend – responds by consuming more. As the AI transition accelerates, further tax cuts combined with meaningful social security for those earning above ₹5 lakh per annum will cushion the disruption facing India's middle class.

## Job Creation through AI: From Substitution to Complementarity

The current gloom centres on AI's 'substitution effects' – particularly evident in tech and customer experience roles, where bots are replacing humans at scale. But if AI is truly as revolutionary as its proponents claim, then like electricity before it, its 'complementarity effects' will prove manifold and largely unpredictable from today's vantage point.

Already, in specific domains like data collection, cleaning, labelling and bot training, India is creating hundreds of thousands of new jobs. Even more encouragingly, many of these jobs are not in India's overcrowded metropolitan cities. In smaller towns and tier-two cities, some of the world's most advanced algorithms are being trained and validated by local workers earning decent incomes.

Over the next five years (till 2030), AI will likely eliminate a fifth of existing tech and customer experience jobs. But it seems equally feasible that AI could create 100 million jobs in training, validation and real-time handling of AI systems. In effect, while the US continues leading in AI intellectual property creation, India's youthful workforce and low-cost mobile data connectivity position it to capture much of the 'farming' work related to AI – the unglamorous but essential labour of teaching machines to think.

The same dynamic applies to blockchain and cryptocurrency. Any global technology that does not care about workers' nationality will gravitate towards India, potentially turning the country's annual production of 8 million graduates from a demographic burden into an economic blessing. Of course, we must acknowledge that this same logic applies to darker activities on the dark web, where cryptocurrencies increasingly facilitate illegal transactions.

## The Rise of Indian Entrepreneurship: From Mutiny to Enterprise

Over the past decade, we have witnessed a renaissance in Indian entrepreneurship. The middle class's children, accustomed to greater comfort than their parents enjoyed, ironically face both far greater need to become entrepreneurs (thanks to job scarcity) and far greater resources – financial and psychological – with which to pursue business ventures.

While it has become fashionable to celebrate this entrepreneurial upsurge, it's worth remembering V.S. Naipaul's assessment of India on the eve of its 1991 economic liberalization:

> People everywhere have ideas now of who they are and what they owe themselves. The process quickened with the economic development that came after independence ... The liberation of spirit that has come to India could not come as release alone. In India, with its layer below layer of distress and cruelty, it had to come as disturbance. It had to come as rage and revolt. India was now a country of a million little mutinies.[1]

Forty years ago, the economic resources at an ordinary Indian's disposal were a fraction of today's. At that point in India's journey, rage and revolt were the only outlets for frustration. Today, that same rage and revolt are being channelled into something far more constructive. India's mutineers have become the country's entrepreneurs.

Our lived experience suggests that the ongoing entrepreneurial upsurge arises from both economic need and considerable rage against the system. As the 2024–25 Economic Survey acknowledged, the bureaucratic system itself works to suffocate entrepreneurial endeavour through red tape, Inspector Raj and arbitrary regulations. Meanwhile, the broader social system remains fractured and cruel, made more so by polarized social media commentary.

However, increasingly, as financial compulsion pushes Indians towards entrepreneurship, digitalization helps entrepreneurs cope with bureaucratic excesses while social support systems enable them to handle the unrelenting demands of running small businesses. Nearly a million meaningful enterprises are being created annually – solopreneurs like the boutique owners in Delhi's markets, Bollywood model collaborations of freelancers working on project-based gigs, and network model operations where hundreds of thousands of independent operators function as spokes in vast national networks.

This entrepreneurial boom has attracted over $50 billion in annual funding from angel investors, venture capitalists and government programmes. Shows like *Shark Tank India* have transformed entrepreneurship from a risky outlier career into an aspirational mainstream choice. In urban India, 39 per cent of households now depend on self-employment compared to 47 per cent earning regular salaries – a rapidly narrowing gap.

However, the returns to entrepreneurship remain disappointingly modest. Among the richest 40 per cent of Indian households, entrepreneurs account for just 17 per cent, while salaried workers comprise 39 per cent. In the top 10 per cent, a mere 14 per cent are self-employed while 58 per cent are salaried. Over 80 per cent of registered companies in India have barely grown their profits in real terms over the past decade, hobbled by expensive and scarce industrial land, working capital costs exceeding 10 per cent (versus 3 per cent in Vietnam and China) and the psychological challenges of shifting from employee to owner mindset.

These obstacles are formidable but not insurmountable. If India can liberalize land acquisition, bring down the cost of working capital through banking sector reforms and cultivate entrepreneurial mindsets through education reform, the current trickle of successful ventures could become a flood.

## India at the Crossroads: The Privilege and Peril of the Breakpoint

This bittersweet trifecta – policy awakening, AI's dual nature and entrepreneurial resurgence – has convinced us that working in the world's largest democracy is no small privilege. To live and work in India at this 'breakpoint' is to witness the world's youngest democracy dealing with its greatest economic disruption in a generation.

The old certainties are crumbling. The Indian middle class, once defined by stable salaried employment, rising incomes and aspirational consumption, now faces stagnant wages, disappearing jobs and crushing debt burdens. In FY2023, net household savings (as a percentage of income) plunged to their lowest levels since 1977 – not because Indians are spending more, but because they are borrowing more to maintain consumption levels their incomes can no longer support. Nearly 40 per cent of household income now goes to debt servicing, with between 5 and 10 per cent of retail borrowers trapped in a vicious cycle of taking new loans to service old ones.

The consumption crisis manifests across India's economy. The FMCG volume growth has collapsed from 10 per cent annually to 3 per cent. Car sales are actually declining year after year. Nestlé India's managing director observed that 'the middle segment ... the middle class of the country[...]seems to be shrinking'.[2] When middle-class Indians do spend, they increasingly borrow to do so – not for productive assets but for holidays (the most common reason for personal loans), smartphones and lifestyle upgrades financed through EMIs that obscure true costs until interest kicks in after the initial zero-rate periods.

The jobs crisis underlying this consumption collapse is equally stark. Among graduates under 25, unemployment exceeds 40 per cent. Those fortunate enough to find work face wages that have stagnated in real terms for over a decade. A software engineer's starting salary in 2010 was ₹3.5 lakh; today it remains ₹3.5 lakh despite prices doubling. Entry-level consultants earned ₹14 lakh in 2014; they earn the same today. Meanwhile, companies like TCS, Infosys and Wipro – which employed 1.4 million people combined – have stopped growing their workforces despite revenue and profit growth continuing unabated.

The causes are multiple and reinforcing. Artificial intelligence is eliminating not just routine tasks but sophisticated cognitive work. Companies explicitly tell us they aim to cut salary bills by a third through AI deployment. Meanwhile, India's labour market regulations make formal employment expensive and risky, encouraging companies to invest in machines rather than people. The education system produces 8 million graduates annually, but their skills often don't match market needs – particularly as the market itself transforms at bewildering speed.

Against this backdrop, how India treats its entrepreneurs will determine its place in the twenty-first century world order. If policymakers can liberalize labour markets, reduce the cost of working capital, simplify land acquisition, strengthen social security and cut taxes further to support consumption during the transition, India's entrepreneurial energy could power the next phase of growth. The country's vast domestic market, youthful population and improving digital infrastructure provide genuine advantages.

But if vested interests block reform, if bureaucratic red tape continues strangling small businesses, if the education system fails to evolve and if AI's job destruction outpaces new job creation, India risks sliding into prolonged stagnation – a middle-income trap where per capita incomes plateau while social tensions mount.

The stakes could not be higher. India houses one-sixth of humanity. Its success or failure in navigating this labour market transition will reverberate globally. For investors like us, this moment presents both profound opportunity and significant risk. Companies that help Indians earn livelihoods in new ways – whether through gig platforms, entrepreneurial financing, skill development or AI tools that complement rather than replace human work – will likely thrive. Those dependent on old models of salaried middle-class consumption may struggle as that consumption base erodes.

We remain cautiously optimistic, not because the path ahead is clear or easy, but because we have seen up close the resourcefulness, determination and, increasingly, the desperation of ordinary Indians seeking better lives. That combination – aspiration meeting necessity – has historically proven a powerful force for transformation. Whether India's million mutineers can evolve into a 100 million successful entrepreneurs remains the defining question of this decade. The answer will shape not just India's future, but the economic and geopolitical landscape of the entire twenty-first century.

To work in India now is to stand at a breakpoint in history – the moment when an old order built on secure employment and steady consumption gives way to something new and uncertain. It is uncomfortable, occasionally frightening, but always exhilarating. We are privileged to witness it.

# Acknowledgements

We spent two years reading, travelling, meeting a variety of experts and crunching data to pull together the core insights contained in this book. Saurabh is grateful to Nandita for driving the data collection, analysis and research-related trips with rigour and enthusiasm. For both Nandita and Sapana, the workload imposed by this book came over and above their day job. Given the complexity of the research taken to pull together this book, Saurabh is thankful that his co-authors not only kept up with the pace required to meet Juggernaut's deadline but also spurred Saurabh to push himself harder.

The authors are very grateful to the following experts and company owners, who not only spared time from their busy schedules to meet the authors but often made follow-on introductions which were just as useful: Abhilasha Singh, Aditi Phadnis, Akash Prakash, Ambarish Raghuvanshi, Amit Kapale, Amitabh Chaudhry, Anand Deshpande, Anand Godse, Anirudha Dutta, Anupam Gupta, Ashok K. Bhattacharya, Balram Yadav, Bhaskar Bhat, Chintan Thakkar, Chris Kay, Devangshu Dutta, Dharmendra Gangwar, Gaurav Trivedi, Girish K., Govardhan Gedela, Hitesh Oberoi, Jignesh Desai, Laveesh Bhandari, Manish Sabharwal, M.K. Venu,

Mohandas Pai, Montek Singh Ahluwalia, M.R. Madhavan, N. Srinivasan, Nandan Nilekani, Neeraj Choksi, Noel Tata, Patrick Foulis, Pirojsha Godrej, Prashant Pandey, Priyank Narayan, Pronab Sen, Raj Shamani, Rajeev Jain, Raoul Kapoor, Ravindra Kumar Kundu, R.G. Chandramogan, Rohit Rajendran, Sandeep Bakhshi, Sanjeev Bikhchandani, Sanjoy Bhattacharyya, Sankaran Naren, Sashidhar Jagdishan, Sathish Kumar, Sayalee Marathe, Shankkar Aiyar, Shankar Maruwada, Sharmila Banwat, Shekhar Gupta, Shweta Shah, Soniya Rangole, Soumendra Nath Lahiri, Sudarshan Venu, Sudipa Sarkar, Sunil Reddy, Swati Rohit, T.N. Ninan, V. Anantha Nageswaran, V. Swaminathan, Vellayan Subbiah, Vineet Ranjan, Vinod Rai, Vipin Shirsat and Vishvajit Kadam.

Our editor at Juggernaut, Chiki Sarkar, was a hard taskmaster as she pushed us to clarify our thinking and refine our arguments. While a neuron or two in our brains might have got fried as we dealt with Chiki's laser-sharp focus on writing clearly, we loved working with and learning from her. As intellectual adventures for office workers (in the age of AI) go, this one will rank close to the top for us.

Our colleagues at Marcellus provided much of the research material that went into the book. Thanks in particular to Tej Shah, Keshav Binani, Vishnu Gopal, Omkar Sawant, Ashvin Shetty, Jaibir Singh Sethi, Manish Hemnani and Salil Desai.

The authors would like to thank Jeet Mukherjee for editing and formatting the charts and tables in this book and for providing incisive inputs on what material could be deleted to make the book more readable.

While Saurabh wrote this book, his better half, Sarbani, piloted their children's admission into university (for the older one) and high school (for the younger one). Sarbani also travelled to different parts of the world to look after both sets of parents, while continuing her professional engagements. Without Sarbani holding the fort on multiple fronts, Saurabh would not have been able to write this book. And therefore, Saurabh's biggest 'thank you' is reserved for the woman who holds him back from the Breakpoint.

Nandita's parents, Chetan and Dhanashree Rajhansa, deserve credit of the highest order for not only keeping her sane but also encouraging her to push her boundaries – be it for travel to the remotest parts of the country or for powering through some of the most gruelling days, when stock-level research, macroeconomic research and work for the book all coincided. Equally supportive were her grandparents in Mumbai, Vaidehi and Vijay Erande, who ensured that she travelled safely across the country and ate nutritious food to power through multiple tasks. She is also grateful to her colleagues at Marcellus, particularly Ashvin Shetty who supported her immensely. Last but not least, she is and will be eternally grateful to Sakshi Sohoni – a classmate from her university, a fierce friend and her biggest cheerleader – with whom Nandita could discuss all that is, was and might have been.

Sapana would like to thank her parents, Sanjivani and Anil Bhavsar, and her sister Dr Deepali for their persistent faith and encouragement. Her spouse, Ashish Parab, deserves special mention for adding humour and wisdom to her career and life, and for being the doting pet parent to their cats, Stark and Sherlock. She is also grateful to her colleagues at Marcellus, and friends in the HR fraternity for being guides and thought partners.

# Notes

## Introduction

1. Name changed to protect his identity.
2. Anup Roy, 'Young Indians More Likely to Be Jobless If They Are Educated: ILO Data', *Business Standard*, 29 March 2024, https://tinyurl.com/45hyfsew.
3. Naukri Jobspeak Index
4. Financial years in India run from April of the preceding year to March of the year that is mentioned. For example., FY2025 runs from 1 April 2024 to 31 March 2025.
5. Ibid.
6. Ibid.
7. IQVIA database
8. Lakshima Sareen, 'Suicides Surge in IITs, IIMs and Other Elite Institutions: Will SC Intervention Put Safety before Reputation?', *The Times of India*, 14 October 2025, https://tinyurl.com/mwnypaam.
9. 'Comparative Study of Growth in Equity Derivatives Segment vis-à- vis Cash Market after Recent Measures', *SEBI*, 7 July 2025, https://tinyurl.com/brbv3way.
10. Monika Yadav, 'AI Impact May Affect 2 Million Jobs in India's Tech Sector: NITI Aayog', *Business* Insider, 11 October 2025, https://tinyurl.com/39ee2p95.

11. Niyaatii Swami and Vinita Rakheja, 'India's Graduate Skills Index 2025', Mercer | Mettl India, 2025, https://tinyurl.com/2h2n5a4e.
12. Pankaj Vashisht and Jay Dev Dubey, 'Changing Task Contents of Jobs in India: Implications and Way Forward', Indian Council for Research on International Economic Relations, New Delhi, No. 355, March 2018, https://tinyurl.com/jz6fmxta.
13. 'Diwali 2025 Blockbuster – A Festive Tale for India Inc and Shoppers Directed by Tax Magic', *The Economic Times*, 21 October 2025, https://tinyurl.com/5n756nh7.

**1. Who Are the Middle Class Anyway?**

1. M.G. Arun and Sonal Khetarpal, 'Middle Class | The Big Squeeze', *India Today*, 27 January 2025, https://tinyurl.com/yt9jxedu.
2. Ibid.
3. 'Largest Electorate for General Elections - Over 96.88 Crore Electors Registered Across the Country', *PIB*, 9 February 2024, https://tinyurl.com/59h65cfw.
4. Anna Fleck, 'Agriculture Is the Biggest Employer in India', *Statista*, 15 May 2024, https://tinyurl.com/2htb3vya.
5. Yogima Seth Sharma, 'Number of EPFO Subscribers up 7.6% at 73.7 Million in 2023–24', *The Economic Times*, 10 November 2024, https://tinyurl.com/ms88npk3.
6. 'ILO Reaffirms What We All Knew: Indians Are Crazy About Govt Jobs', *The Times of India*, 2 April 2024, https://tinyurl.com/3djf9u3m.
7. Abhishek Wagmare, 'Employment in India', *Data for India*, 18 March 2024, https://tinyurl.com/y9ytk4uk.
8. *Survival of the Richest: The India Story*, Oxfam India, 2023, https://tinyurl.com/3rzjkhf3.
9. Income Tax Department, Ministry of Finance, Government of

India, https://tinyurl.com/2u9juaf3.

10. 'Local Multipliers', *What Works Growth*, 1 July 2025, https://tinyurl.com/yc5e7eh8.
11. '"Let's Stop Pretending India Has a Huge Middle Class" – Redditor Questions Traditional Definitions, Triggers Debate', *Business Today*, 24 March 2025, https://tinyurl.com/5fvsvw5b.

## 2. Education: No Longer a Fail-Safe Option

1. 'India's Two Realities: The Promise of Growth & the Crisis of Graduate Unemployment', *BW Businessworld*, 4 November 2025, https://tinyurl.com/y9avhncv.
2. 'IIT Bombay's Lowest Pay Package Falls to Rs 4 Lakh from Rs 6 Lakh pa, 25% Left with No Placements', *Business Today*, 3 September 2024, https://tinyurl.com/ysrzrdwd.
3. Basharat Peer, 'A Friendship, a Pandemic and a Death Beside the Highway', *The New York Times*, 31 July 2020, https://tinyurl.com/bdp64prt.
4. 'Police Constable Salaries', *Glassdoor*, https://tinyurl.com/53d8z4r9.
5. 'UP's Mammoth Police Exam Begins 48 Lakh Vie for 60K Posts', *The Times of India*, 24 August 2024, https://tinyurl.com/ykcax3z3.
6. 'IITs Witness Drop in Placement Rate and Minimum Pay, 8,000 IITians Remain Unemployed', *APAC Media*, 5 September 2024, https://tinyurl.com/4mk3bun2.
7. *Three Hundred and Sixty Fourth Report: Demands for Grants 2025–26 of the Department of Higher Education*, Rajya Sabha Secretariat, New Delhi, March 2025, https://tinyurl.com/5dx6n8hr.
8. Mohammad Haris, 'Only 10% of India's 1.5 Million Engineering Graduates Set to Secure Jobs This Year: Report', *News18*, 13 September 2024, https://tinyurl.com/44chxmfu.

9. Shivani Shinde, '83% Engineering Graduates Have No Jobs, Internship Offers: Report', *Business Standard*, 21 March 2025, https://tinyurl.com/2t8w9m4x.
10. PTI, 'Semiconductor Sector to Create 1 Million Jobs in India by 2026: Report', *Business Standard*, 11 November 2024, https://tinyurl.com/5e8bxt5f.
11. Rama Bijapurkar, *Lilliput Land: How Small Is Driving India's Mega Consumption Story*, Penguin, 2024; author's emphasis.
12. Anup Roy, 'Young Indians More Likely to Be Jobless If They Are Educated: ILO Data', *Business Standard*, 29 March 2024, https://tinyurl.com/45hyfsew.
13. 'How Many Students Appeared for JEE Mains 2024? Key Statistics and Insights', *VHTC*, 8 January 2025, https://tinyurl.com/3matzpts.
14. Ibid.
15. Nemmani Sridhar, 'Quality of Students from IITs Coming Down?', *The Hindu*, 10 October 2011, https://tinyurl.com/3x7z97dc.
16. Niyaatii Swami and Vinita Rakheja, 'India's Graduate Skills Index 2025', Mercer | Mettl India, 2025, https://tinyurl.com/2h2n5a4e.
17. Deepto Banerjee, 'Pursuing Engineering Once a Fad, Now a Dilemma: Only 10 Percent of 15 Lakh Graduates Likely to Land Jobs This Year', *The Times of India*, 29 October 2024, https://tinyurl.com/282kaysb.
18. Ibid.
19. 'Only 45% Job Seekers Employable in Indian IT-Tech Sector amid Skill Crunch', *HRWorld*, 19 December 2023, https://tinyurl.com/2p8xsstf.
20. Debanjali Biswas, 'Infosys: The Job That Millions of India's Engineering Grads Took for Granted Is Now a Tough Sell', *The Ken*, 14 May 2025, https://tinyurl.com/mw9ammhc.

21. ANI, 'India's Semiconductor Industry Faces Supply Chain and Limited Talent Challenges: Jefferies Report', *The Economic Times*, 25 March 2025, https://tinyurl.com/yzvmx6nz.
22. Stephen Ezell, *Assessing India's Readiness to Assume a Greater Role in Global Semiconductor Value Chains*, ITIF, February 2024, https://tinyurl.com/vd9hz9wc.
23. Ibid.
24. 'Semiconductor Sector to Create 1 Million Jobs in India by 2026: Skilled Workforce in High Demand', *Business Standard*, https://tinyurl.com/3ymfvzy6.
25. ANI, 'India's Semiconductor Industry Faces Supply Chain and Limited Talent Challenges: Jefferies Report', *The Economic Times*, 25 March 2025, https://tinyurl.com/yzvmx6nz.
26. Ibid.
27. NITI Aayog, *Roadmap for Job Creation in the AI Economy*, October 2025, https://tinyurl.com/4n7ddpzy.
28. Niyaatii Swami and Vinita Rakheja, 'India's Graduate Skills Index 2025', Mercer | Mettl India, 2025, https://tinyurl.com/2h2n5a4e.
29. David H. Autor, Frank Levy and Richard J. Murnane, 'The Skill Content of Recent Technological Change: An Empirical Exploration', *The Quarterly Journal of Economics*, November 2003, https://tinyurl.com/3j5xj9tc.
30. Daniel Susskind, *A World Without Work: Technology, Automation and How We Should Respond*, Metropolitan Books, 2020.
31. Sudipa Sarkar, 'Employment Change in Occupations in Urban India: Implications for Wage Inequality', University of Warwick, *SSRN*, January 2017, https://tinyurl.com/yc8xpk5b.
32. Ibid.
33. Pankaj Vashisht and Jay Dev Dubey, 'Changing Task Contents of Jobs in India: Implications and Way Forward', Indian Council for Research on International Economic Relations, New Delhi, No. 355, March 2018, https://tinyurl.com/jz6fmxta.

34. Shiva Rajora, 'Managerial Roles Waning in Formal Manufacturing Sector, Shows ASI Data', *Business Standard*, 5 November 2024, https://tinyurl.com/4mdwnsbz.
35. Ibid.
36. Manisha Pande, *Middle Class India: Driving Change in the 21st Century*, Aleph Book Company, 2024.
37. Pavan Varma, *The Great Indian Middle Class*, Penguin, 2007.
38. Manisha Pande, *Middle Class India: Driving Change in the 21st Century*, Aleph Book Company, 2024.

## 3. AI: The New Disruptive Force in the Job Market

1. Firstpost, 'AI Models Spark Backlash as AI Transforms Film and Fashion | Vantage with Palki Sharma | N18G', *YouTube*, 7 July 2025, https://tinyurl.com/mp46bnc.
2. Shubhangi Misra, 'Private Security Is a Top Job Creator in India. It's a Booming, Recession-Free Business Empire', *ThePrint*, 10 July 2024, https://tinyurl.com/3kh79s56.
3. Monika Yadav, 'AI Impact May Affect 2 Million Jobs in India's Tech Sector: NITI Aayog', *Business* Insider, 11 October 2025, https://tinyurl.com/39ee2p95.
4. Shubhangi Misra, 'Private Security Is a Top Job Creator in India. It's a Booming, Recession-Free Business Empire', *ThePrint*, 10 July 2024, https://tinyurl.com/3kh79s56.
5. Ibid.
6. Ibid.
7. Tim Bajarin, 'Generative AI's Unprecedented Adoption Cycle', *Forbes*, 22 July 2025, https://tinyurl.com/mvnpx6xr.
8. Gunjan Samtani and George Lee, 'AI Will Define the Next Era: Will India Capitalize on the Opportunity?', *Goldman Sachs*, 26 June 2025, https://tinyurl.com/ybc4er2w.
9. Francis Kuriakose and Deepa Kylasam Iyer, 'Automation and

the Future of Jobs in India', *CASI*, 5 November 2018, https://tinyurl.com/5b2djrsd.

10. Ibid.
11. NITI Aayog, *Roadmap for Job Creation in the AI Economy*, October 2025, https://tinyurl.com/4n7ddpzy. CX stands for 'customer experience' and refers to staff working in call centres and in sales jobs.
12. 'Sundar Pichai Says AI Generates More than 25% Codes at the Company: "This Helps Our Engineers Do...."', *The Times of India*, 30 October 2024, https://tinyurl.com/2x9xmxvy.
13. Debangana Ghosh, Reshab Shaw and Chandra R. Srikanth, 'TCS to Cut 2% of Workforce, Affecting 12,000 Employees amid Skill Gap and Tech Shift', *Moneycontrol*, 27 July 2025, https://tinyurl.com/5n7ffntn.
14. '"Target 2X Revenue with Half the Workforce": HCL Tech CEO Wants Indian IT Firms to Adopt "Paranoid" Mindset for Growth', *The Economic Times*, 3 March 2025, https://tinyurl.com/bdefrx4f.
15. Shiva Rajora, 'GenAI Led to 20% Fall in White-Collar Job Listings in S Asia: World Bank', *Business Standard*, 7 October 2025, https://tinyurl.com/5h232mcc.
16. 'Why AI-Led Layoffs Are Bad Not Just for the Laid Off: Big Reality Check Coming for Indian Economy', *The Economic Times*, 29 October 2025, https://tinyurl.com/3ujvezr2.
17. *Economic Survey 2024–25*, Government of India, Ministry of Finance, Department of Economic Affairs, January 2025, https://tinyurl.com/yhvepck9.
18. Scott Dresser, 'Amazon Launches a New AI Foundation Model to Power Its Robotic Fleet and Deploys Its 1 Millionth Robot', *Amazon*, 30 June 2025, https://tinyurl.com/57w3rtxa.

## 4. Job Growth Is Stagnating

1. https://tinyurl.com/6dkwwxy8.
2. 'Silent Cries: Why Rising Suicide at IITs Turning into Epidemic', *TwoCircles.net*, 3 October 2024, https://tinyurl.com/52tznpfa.
3. Dheeraj Singh, 'India Today Rajdeep Sardesai on IIT Suicides', *YouTube*, 7 March 2025, https://tinyurl.com/4aasb35u.
4. 'Silent Cries: Why Rising Suicide at IITs Turning into Epidemic', *TwoCircles.net*, 3 October 2024, https://tinyurl.com/52tznpfa.
5. Ibid.
6. 'How Many Students Appeared for JEE Main – Year-Wise Trend Analysis', *Testbook.com*, https://tinyurl.com/5n6zab2m.
7. Rahul Kumar, 'Job Crisis at IITs: 38% Students Unplaced amid Rising Unemployment', *NDTV Education*, 23 May 2024, https://tinyurl.com/365bsve8.
8. Ibid.
9. Naukri Jobspeak Index (several years)
10. Hitesh Vyas, George Mathew and Sandeep Singh, 'Write-off Era Over, Asset Quality Review Served Banking Well: SBI Chairman', *The Indian Express*, 18 December 2023, https://tinyurl.com/5yaave2h.
11. RBI Sectoral credit (banking) data, collated by Ambit Capital
12. Shruti Rajagopalan and Kadambari Shah, 'Why Indian Firms Don't Scale: Labor Edition', India Political Economy Program, Mercatus Policy Research, Mercatus Center, September 2024.
13. Saurabh Mukherjea and Nandita Rajhansa, *Behold the Leviathan: The Unusual Rise of Modern India*, Penguin Business, 2024.
14. 'CBDT Releases Direct Taxes Data', *Income Tax Department*, https://tinyurl.com/m6r5kx2y.

15. *Economic Survey 2024–25*, Government of India, Ministry of Finance, Department of Economic Affairs, January 2025, https://tinyurl.com/yhvepck9.
16. *Kinds of Business Eligibility: Latest*, FSSAI, https://tinyurl.com/5acmawf9.
17. *Economic Survey 2024–25*, Government of India, Ministry of Finance, Department of Economic Affairs, January 2025, https://tinyurl.com/yhvepck9.
18. Ibid.
19. Ibid.
20. *Roadmap for Job Creation in the AI Economy*, NITI Aayog, October 2025, https://tinyurl.com/4n7ddpzy.
21. Company annual reports (several)
22. Company annual reports (several)

## 5. Real Wages Are Stagnating

1. Harshad Shah, 'White-Collar Workers Earning Less Than Construction Workers in India', *LinkedIn*, July 2025, https://tinyurl.com/mhxu9nac.
2. 'CBDT Releases Direct Taxes Data', *Income Tax Department*, https://tinyurl.com/m6r5kx2y.
3. Shiva Rajora, 'Real Wages Rose Most for Managers, Declined for Clerks: CSEP Study', *Business Standard*, 27 June 2025, https://tinyurl.com/4fefj85r.
4. 'India's Middle Class is Losing Ground to the Rich & the Poor', *Marcellus*, 23 January 2025, https://tinyurl.com/y5353kub.
5. 'CBDT Releases Direct Taxes Data', *Income Tax Department*, https://tinyurl.com/m6r5kx2y.
6. Koustav Das and Vani Gupta, 'The Great Indian Salary Crisis', *India Today*, https://tinyurl.com/mrx5629y.

7. Sruthi Balaji and Vignesh Radhakrishnan, 'Cost of Meals Rose by 71% in Five Years, Salaries by Just 37%: Data', *The Hindu*, 10 May 2024, https://tinyurl.com/54cxu7ec.
8. 'Why Is No One Buying Small Cars?', *Market Brew*, 6 June 2025, https://tinyurl.com/5347973b.
9. 'Medical Inflation in India: Current Rate, Causes and Impacts', *Onsurity*, 29 November 2024, https://tinyurl.com/yuhd37ks; 'India's Healthcare Inflation Runs at 12–15%, Higher than General Inflation', Medical Buyer, 3 October 2025, https://tinyurl.com/2apvjcwt.
10. Bloomberg.
11. Fareeha Ifthikar, 'Cost of Higher Education in India Is Leaving Parents Drained, in Debt. "We Put Our Own Dreams on Hold"', *The Print*, 21 November 2024, https://tinyurl.com/mrxcp9th.
12. M.G. Arun and Sonal Khetarpal, 'Middle Class | the Big Squeeze', *India Today*, 27 January 2025, https://tinyurl.com/yt9jxedu.
13. Ibid.
14. 'CBDT Releases Direct Taxes Data', *Income Tax Department*, https://tinyurl.com/m6r5kx2y.
15. Ibid.

## 6. Debt Is Skyrocketing

1. Hosuehold borrowing data collated by MOFSL
2. 'RBI Releases the Financial Stability Report, December 2024', *Reserve Bank of India*, 30 December 2024, https://tinyurl.com/3me3z9va.
3. *How India Spends: A Deep Dive into Consumer Spending Behaviour*, PwC, 2024, https://tinyurl.com/3ca763s3.
4. 'Breaking Down RBI's Financial Stability Report', *Upstox*, 10 January 2025, https://tinyurl.com/mshyrdz9.

5. 'Are Indians Taking Loans to Improve Their Lifestyle?', *Home Credit*, https://tinyurl.com/2xkwm8av.
6. 'RBI Releases the Financial Stability Report, December 2024', *Reserve Bank of India*, 30 December 2024, https://tinyurl.com/3me3z9va.
7. 'What Is a Dept Trap?', Bajaj Finance, https://tinyurl.com/47tdp36p.
8. 'Breaking Down RBI's Financial Stability Report', *Upstox*, 10 January 2025, https://tinyurl.com/mshyrdz9.
9. 'Share of Borrowers Rated Prime+ on Rise, Shows Transunion CIBIL Data', *The Economic Times*, 23 September 2024, https://tinyurl.com/ye2wd4pt.
10. 'Breaking Down RBI's Financial Stability Report', *Upstox*, 10 January 2025, https://tinyurl.com/mshyrdz9.
11. Abhishek Sharma, 'India's Middle Class: A Debt-Fueled Time Bomb Waiting to Explode', *Business World*, 9 December 2024, https://tinyurl.com/yc6rw23u.
12. 'Share of Borrowers Rated Prime+ on Rise, Shows Transunion CIBIL Data', *The Economic Times*, 23 September 2024, https://tinyurl.com/ye2wd4pt.
13. 'Breaking Down RBI's Financial Stability Report', *Upstox*, 10 January 2025, https://tinyurl.com/mshyrdz9.
14. In conversation with the authors
15. In conversation with the authors
16. K.R. Srivats, 'India's Lower-Middle Class Moves Beyond Survival Borrowing, Embracing Digital Credit Tools', *Business Line*, 18 October 2024, https://tinyurl.com/3jp9h5az.
17. Ibid.
18. K.R. Srivats, 'India's Lower-Middle Class Moves Beyond Survival Borrowing, Embracing Digital Credit Tools', *Business Line*, 18 October 2024, https://tinyurl.com/3jp9h5az.
19. Sunainaa Chadha, 'Consumer Loan Trends: Borrowing for

Smartphones Skyrockets to 37% in 2024', *Business Standard*, 18 October 2024, https://tinyurl.com/y8ade25m.

20. Abhishek Sharma, 'India's Middle Class: A Debt-Fueled Time Bomb Waiting to Explode', *Business World*, 9 December 2024, https://tinyurl.com/yc6rw23u.
21. Ibid.
22. K.R. Srivats, 'India's Lower-Middle Class Moves Beyond Survival Borrowing, Embracing Digital Credit Tools', *Business Line*, 18 October 2024, https://tinyurl.com/3jp9h5az.
23. 'University Education and the Illusion of Learning', *Marcellus*, 3 January 2025, https://tinyurl.com/ym4ab64x.
24. George Mathew, 'Education Loan AUM of NBFCs to top Rs 60,000 Crore this Fiscal', *The Indian Express*, 4 September 2024, https://tinyurl.com/487hh27h.
25. 'Student Loan Debt in India: Facts and Figures', *Varthana*, 22 July 2024, https://tinyurl.com/e877jtaf.
26. ANI, 'More than 560 Mn Jan Dhan Accounts Opened in Last 11 Years: Sitharaman', *Business World*, 28 August 2025, https://tinyurl.com/5x5tvycm.
27. 'India's Smartphone Market Becomes Second Largest Globally by Unit Volume', *IBEF*, 8 November 2024, https://tinyurl.com/3d9683aj.

## 7. Job, Wages, Debt ... How All of this Impacts Consumption

1. Raghav Aggarwal, 'Shrinking Middle Class Hitting FMCG Firms: Nestle India', *The Financial Express*, 23 October 2024, https://tinyurl.com/2s3hr2aw.
2. 'India Historical Inflation Rates', *Inflation Tool*, https://tinyurl.com/4b9jret6.

3. 'Exports of Goods and Services (% of GDP) – Japan', *World Bank Group*, https://tinyurl.com/536efj2y.
4. 'Exports of Goods and Services (% of GDP) – China', *World Bank Group*, https://tinyurl.com/yx7j722y.
5. Manish Pandey and Xiao-yuan Dong, 'Manufacturing Productivity in China and India: The Role of Institutional Changes', *China Economic Review*, Vol. 20, No. 4, December 2009, pp. 754–66, https://tinyurl.com/5acuexz7.
6. Manisha Pande, Middle Class India: Driving Change in the 21st Century, *Aleph Book Company*, 2024, pp. 185–86.
7. Ibid.
8. Karandeep Singh, 'Why India's FMCG Sector Struggling Despite Strong Market Growth?', *Ind Money*, 1 July 2025, https://tinyurl.com/4t9fhpuv.
9. Raghav Agarwal, 'Shrinking Middle Class Hitting FMCG Firms: Nestle India', *Financial Express*, 23 October 2024, https://tinyurl.com/4naj584a.
10. 'India Food Inflation', *Trading Economics*, https://tinyurl.com/2hctcrmr.
11. Mohil Detroja, 'The Hidden Reasons Behind FMCG's Slowdown in India', *Erigo India*, 4 August 2025, https://tinyurl.com/ybrjhdr3.
12. 'India's FMCG Growth Is Slowing', *The Daily Brief by Zerodha*, 5 February 2025, https://tinyurl.com/mr9retm6.
13. Surabhi Upadhyay and Nigel D'Souza, 'Why Rising Incomes Aren't Sparking a Car Demand Recovery—RC Bhargava Explains', *CNBC TV 18*, 30 October 2024, https://tinyurl.com/h3nbs2ur.
14. Sohini Das, 'Average Selling Price of Passenger Vehicles in India up by 50% in 5 Years', *Business Standard*, 21 January 2024, https://tinyurl.com/4e7fyvz9.
15. Nishan Kumar, 'Unraveling the High Costs of Indian Cars:

Reasons and Insights', *Blue D Air Control*, 31 December 2024, https://tinyurl.com/58ktw94b.
16. Sohini Das, 'Average Selling Price of Passenger Vehicles in India up by 50% in 5 Years', *Business Standard*, 21 January 2024, https://tinyurl.com/4e7fyvz9.
17. Ibid.
18. Ajit Dalvi, 'SUVs Power UV Share of PVS to 65% in FY2025, Car and Sedan Share Plunges to 31%', *Autocar Professional*, 17 April 2025, https://tinyurl.com/3znzf3p4.

## 8. The Side Effects of Social Media

1. 'India Population (2025)', *Worldometer*, 2025, https://tinyurl.com/yx79yzvk.
2. 'Internet Cost Ranking by Country', *Global Relocate*, https://tinyurl.com/2ruhdu9w.
3. 'Internet Penetration Rate in India from 2015 to 2025', *Statista*, 10 December 2025, https://tinyurl.com/ye9f7xvt.
4. Gourab Das, 'Indians Spent 1.1 Lakh Crore Hours Staring at Smartphones to Make Many Richer', *The Economic Times*, 28 March 2025, https://tinyurl.com/mszrrcbp.
5. In conversation with the authors
6. *2002 Annual Report*, Berkshire Hathaway Inc., 2003, https://tinyurl.com/3e6ntaka.
7. 'Retail Investors', *Angel One*, https://tinyurl.com/mtyusb3z.
8. *Analysis of Profit and Loss of Individual Traders Dealing in Equity F&O Segment*, SEBI, 25 January 2023, https://tinyurl.com/ycxpum9b.
9. Sachin Gupta, 'Retail F&O Losses Rose to over ` 1 Lakh Crore: Trader Participation Dropped 20%', *Angel One*, 9 July 2025, https://tinyurl.com/38pchzdh.
10. 'Union Education Minister Lauds Historic Budget 2025–26',

*PIB*, 1 February 2025, https://tinyurl.com/2vabz4j4.

11. 'Comparative Study of Growth in Equity Derivatives Segment vis-à- vis Cash Market after Recent Measures', *SEBI*, 7 July 2025, https://tinyurl.com/brbv3way.
12. Sandeep Jethwani, 'The Alarming Rise of Retail Losses in F&O Trading', *DEZERV*, 8 October 2024, https://tinyurl.com/5n836t6m.
13. Vivek Kaul, 'How Futures and Options Became India's Favourite Game: Lessons from the Soviet Union', *Mint*, 17 July 2024, https://tinyurl.com/4wkmua64.
14. Khushboo Tiwari, 'Less than 2% Dare to Go Only-Derivatives: NSE's Market Pulse Report', *Business Standard*, 23 October 2025, https://tinyurl.com/3uppfw2w.
15. 'Option Buying: The Riskiest Trade Out There', *Zerodha*, 1 July 2021, https://tinyurl.com/5n948zkd.
16. Ibid.
17. Piyush Jhunjhunwala, 'Options Trading Makes Three Fourth of NSE's Revenue', *Stockify*, 5 July 2025, https://tinyurl.com/49dej785.
18. 'National Stock Exchange (NSE) FY25 Results, Revenue, PAT, and Key Highlights', *Unlisted Zone*, 3 June 2025, https://tinyurl.com/33cdrsm4.
19. Deepak Shenoy, 'The Saga of the Jane Street Trading Scandal', *Capital Mind*, 10 July 2025, https://tinyurl.com/4myu9stt.
20. 'F&O Trading Volumes See 8-Month High in July, Despite Ban on Jane Street', *Angel One*, 5 August 2025, https://tinyurl.com/yhwcv6bs.
21. 'Jane Street vs Millennium: A US Tech Feud Sparked India's Biggest Market Probe', *The Economic Times*, 5 July 2025, https://tinyurl.com/537ebmfs.
22. Ibid.
23. Samridhi Tewari, 'Profit in NY, Loss in UP—What Jane Street

'Market Manipulation' Did to Tier 2 & 3 India', *ThePrint*, 12 August 2025, https://tinyurl.com/3fpknubh.

24. Ibid.
25. Ibid.
26. Ibid.

## 9. The Policy Response

1. Sybilla Gross, Preeti Soni, Jack Ryan, Yvonne Yue Li, and Jack Farchy, 'Sold Out in India, Panic in London: How the Silver Market Broke', *The Economic Times*, 20 October 2025, https://tinyurl.com/2eemajxs.
2. Ibid.
3. Ibid.
4. Eshita Gain, 'India's Auto Sector Eyes Record Festive Sales; Maruti Reports 50% Increase, Tata & Others Post Robust Growth', *Mint*, 19 October 2025, https://tinyurl.com/3a9trv5m.
5. Shine Jacob, 'Dhanteras Engine Fires Up Auto Market: Over 100K Cars Delivered in 24 Hours', *Business Standard*, 19 October 2025, https://tinyurl.com/yx73c3e9.
6. 'CBDT Releases Direct Taxes Data', *Income Tax Department*, https://tinyurl.com/m6r5kx2y.
7. '2025–26', *PRS Legislative Research*, https://tinyurl.com/p22prcvn.
8. Ruchika Chitravanshi, 'Road, Rail and Defence Lead FY26 Capex Surge; Overall Spend at 52%', *Business Standard*, 5 November 2025, https://tinyurl.com/3ed7bxs8.
9. 'First Advanced T-90 Mark-III Delivered to Indian Army by Heavy Vehicles Factory, AVADI', *Indian Defence News*, 27 May 2024, https://tinyurl.com/3mx46ayf.
10. 'Summary of Union Budget 2025–26', *PIB*, https://tinyurl.com/4d654fcu.
11. 'Household Savings to Recover in H1 FY25 as Debt Load

Eases', *The Times of India*, 16 January 2025, https://tinyurl.com/3zh8cxtp.

12. This ₹2 trillion per annum figure is arrived at using FY25 GST collections of about ₹22 trillion. With collections for all the categories that have either witnessed a tax rate reduction or rise, adjusted for impact of cess and foregone input tax credit benefit, the total cut comes to ₹2 trillion, something which was also confirmed by the finance minister.
13. Rishika Agarwal, 'GST Reforms Infused ₹2 Trillion in Indian Economy: Nirmala Sitharaman', *Business Standard*, 17 September 2025, https://tinyurl.com/y2yczbvb.
14. Abhik Deb and Nikita Yadav, 'From Boom to Ban: The Rise and Fall of India's Betting Apps', *BBC*, 28 August 2025, https://tinyurl.com/yc4rzjam.
15. The government has said that banning online games will create a ₹20,000 crore hit to the Exchequer, of which ₹16.5k GST taxed at 28 per cent rate and ₹3.5k TDS taxed at 30 per cent suggests ₹71,000 crore of annual spend on gambling by participants.
16. 'Real Money Gaming Ban to Be Formally Notified on Oct. 1: Vaishnaw', *The Hindu*, 18 September 2025, https://tinyurl.com/5n7hct34.
17. Lily Jamali, 'Microsoft to Cut up to 9,000 More Jobs as It Invests in AI', *BBC*, 3 July 2025, https://tinyurl.com/4j3ksmn4; Unnati Gusain, 'Accenture Lays off 11,000 Employees, Warns More Job Cuts Are Coming Due to AI: Story in 5 Points', *India Today*, 28 September 2025, https://tinyurl.com/3wcmcyex.
18. Nitin Seth, *Human Edge in the AI Age: Eight Timeless Mantras for Success*, Penguin Business, 2025, pp. 146–47.
19. Sanjay Maurya, '137 Indian Institutions in QS Rankings but None in

Top 50', *Hindustan Times*, 5 November 2025, https://tinyurl.com/yc84hbv9.

20. '"Middle-Income Trap" Hinders Progress in 108 Developing Countries', *World Bank Group*, 1 August 2024, https://tinyurl.com/2f2kz398.

## 10. AI: New Opportunities in the Brave New World

1. 'Fast Company', *MIT News*, 2 April 2024, https://tinyurl.com/4mpvx2jh.
2. 'Future of Workforce: Decoding the Gig Workforce 2.0', *Nasscom*, https://tinyurl.com/yv7rr9t5.
3. David Autor, 'The Labor Market Impacts of Technological Change: From Unbridled Enthusiasm to Qualified Optimism to Vast Uncertainty', Working Paper 30074, 2002, www.doi.org/10.3386/w30074.
4. 'Future of Workforce: Decoding the Gig Workforce 2.0', *Nasscom*, https://tinyurl.com/yv7rr9t5.
5. Ibid.
6. Ibid. p. 351.
7. Ibid.
8. Daniel Susskind, *A World Without Work: Technology, Automation and How We Should Respond*, Metropolitan Books, 2020.
9. Vibha Rana, 'Legal Status of Gig Workers in India: Labour Protections in the Platform Economy', *The Legal Quorum*, 23 December 2025, https://tinyurl.com/2bv4wy3f.
10. Sachin Seth, 'India's Gig Economy in 2025: Growth, Formalisation, and Financial Inclusion Explained', *LiveMint*, 25 July 2025, https://tinyurl.com/yc5abc2h.
11. 'India's Gig Economy Could Add 90 MN Jobs Enabled by Large Multinationals', *IBEF*, 29 November 2024, https://tinyurl.com/44j7paj7.

12. Daniel Susskind, *A World Without Work: Technology, Automation and How We Should Respond*, Metropolitan Books, 2020.
13. Ibid.
14. Ibid.
15. Raghavan Jagannathan, *The Jobs Crisis in India*, Pan Macmillan India, 2018.
16. IANS, '8cr Creators in India but 1.5 Lakh Able to Earn; Most Make Just Rs 16k a Month', *ETTelecom.com*, 10 October 2022, https://ettelecom.com/s/jb9fgpg.
17. Leslie D'Monte and Jayanth Kolla, *AI Rising: India's Artificial Intelligence Growth Story*, Jaico Publishing House, 2023.
18. Himanshi Lohchab and Annapurna Roy, 'Indian Gig Workers Toil at Frontlines of AI Revolution', *The Economic Times*, 6 May 2024, https://tinyurl.com/3ve67h9s.
19. Neha Arya, 'India's Data Workers: The Human Labour Making Machines Learn', *The Wire*, 11 September 2025, https://tinyurl.com/4uyjmsau.
20. 'Bot Jobs', *Naukri*, https://tinyurl.com/4ee5u7ua.
21. *Marshall Goldsmith. AI*, https://marshallgoldsmith.ai/.
22. Raghavan Jagannathan, *The Jobs Crisis in India*, Pan Macmillan India, 2018, p. 91.
23. Sunainaa Chadha, 'Blockchain Is India's Future, and If You Are a Developer You Can Earn Rs 82 Lakh a Year!', *The Times of India*, 22 December 2021, https://tinyurl.com/2urzhda4.
24. KV Kurmanath, 'Layoffs Fuel Dark Web Hiring Spree for Tech Roles', *BusinessLine*, 29 November 2025, https://tinyurl.com/mvspw4xv.
25. PTI, 'AI Jobs in India Surged 42% Over the Past Two Years Reaching 2,53,000 Positions: Report', *HRWorld*, 22 January 2025, https://tinyurl.com/5n8tbp5j.
26. Veena Mani and Shilpa Phadnis, 'GCCs Lead India's Tech Hiring,

Surpass 1 Lakh Hires in FY25', *The Times of India*, 3 March 2025, https://tinyurl.com/7tszepkj.

27. Priti Gupta, 'Micro, Medium & Small Scale Industry', *BBC*, 16 October 2025, https://tinyurl.com/y8e7csen.
28. As quoted in Raghavan Jagannathan, *The Jobs Crisis in India*, Pan Macmillan India, 2018.

## 11. Entrepreneurship in India

1. Aayushi Dubey, 'India's Startup Boom: $50 Billion in Funding in 2024 Reflects Global Confidence in Innovation - Read Now', *The Vocal Now*, 13 September 2024, https://tinyurl.com/3fypbb29.
2. 'Economic Survey 2025: Self-Employment, Entrepreneurship Lead India's Employment Surge', *Firstpost*, 31 January 2025, https://tinyurl.com/ys8myzrm.
3. Designmachinesuitslive, *Instagram*, https://tinyurl.com/384pxbwc.
4. Saurabh Mukherjea and Nandita Rajhansa, *Behold the Leviathan: The Unusual Rise of Modern India*, Penguin Business, 2024, p. 77.
5. 'Micro, Medium & Small Scale Industry', *CII*, https://tinyurl.com/hxrea9t7.
6. PTI, '83% of Indian Workforce Prefers to Be Entrepreneurs: Survey', *The Times of India*, 9 August 2017, https://tinyurl.com/2b2pxnzj.
7. Neil Ghai, 'A Third of Indian Students Want to Turn Startup Founders, Says Report', *The Economic Times*, 21 October 2024, https://tinyurl.com/7a9ncsjx.
8. Abhimanyu Mathur, 'Decoding Shark Tank India's Success: How the Show Captured the Imagination of a Business-Agnostic Country', *Hindustan Times*, 4 February 2022, https://tinyurl.com/36vz4z79.
9. 'Economic Survey 2025: Self-Employment, Entrepreneurship Lead India's Employment Surge', *Firstpost*, 31 January 2025, https://tinyurl.com/ys8myzrm.

10. Elysse Bell, 'How Small Businesses Can Use AI Tools', *Investopedia*, 8 March 2025, https://tinyurl.com/3ec43zya.
11. Darrell Tyler, 'AI for Small Business Marketing: How AI Is Revolutionizing Marketing for Small Businesses', *CallRail*, 24 August 2023, https://tinyurl.com/424yyev3.
12. 'The Role of Government Initiatives in Boosting Startups', *Invest India*, 26 March 2024, https://tinyurl.com/3v4442wz.
13. 'Credit Guarantee Scheme for Startups', *DPIIT #startupIndia*, https://tinyurl.com/4nju2zcx.
14. 'Stand-Up India', *myScheme*, https://tinyurl.com/ccefyfj6.
15. 'Top 6 Government Loan Schemes for Small Businesses', *Paisabazaar*, https://tinyurl.com/3ed5897n.
16. 'The Evolving Landscape of Angel Investing in India', *Express Computer*, 27 June 2024, https://tinyurl.com/2ckvzjwf.
17. Arpan Sheth et al., 'India Private Equity Report 2025', *Bain & Company*, https://tinyurl.com/3mrdv2k3.
18. 'India's Middle Class is Losing Ground to the Rich & the Poor', *Marcellus*, 23 January 2025, https://tinyurl.com/y5353kub.
19. Rama Bijapurkar, *Lilliput Land: How Small Is Driving India's Mega Consumption Story*, Penguin, 2024.
20. Gurbachan Singh, 'Why Is Land Expensive in India, and What Can Be Done About It?', *Ideas for India*, 29 February 2024, https://tinyurl.com/ytn7czhz.
21. 'Southern Region Faces Scarcity of New Supply of Industrial, *HKBAV*, https://tinyurl.com/4yxdr4ep.
22. Zumbish, 'Disputes over Natural Resources or Property Triggered 16.8% of All Murders in India in 2019-21: UN Report', *Down to Earth*, 20 December 2023, https://tinyurl.com/ycyx8upd.
23. Aarish Alam, 'Is Land Digitisation Enough?', *VIDHI Centre for Legal Policy*, 25 July 2025, https://tinyurl.com/57thdc2x.

24. 'China Loan Prime Rate', *Trading Economics*, https://tinyurl.com/yzdtakja.
25. 'Banking Sector Lower Lending Rates', *Vietnam Law & Legal Reform*, 26 July 2025, https://tinyurl.com/y7kan635.
26. Pankaj Mishra, *Against the Grain: Lessons from the Outliers*, Penguin Random House India, 2024, p. 141.
27. 'The Inner Scorecard: How Warren Buffett Mastered Life', *Farnam Street*, https://tinyurl.com/w7me667d.
28. Sudhir Sitapati, *The CEO Factory: Management Lessons from Hindustan Unilever*, Juggernaut Books, 2020.
29. Saurabh Mukherjea, *The Unusual Billionaires*, Penguin Random House India, 2016, p. 87.
30. Pankaj Mishra, *Against the Grain: Lessons from the Outliers*, Penguin Random House India, 2024.
31. Harish Bhat and R. Gopalakrishnan, *Jamsetji Tata: Powerful Learnings for Corporate Success*, Penguin Random House India, 2024, pp. 9–10.
32. Livemint, 'How NJ India Invest Became India's Giant Mutual Funds Distributor', *NJ Group*, 16 August 2017, https://tinyurl.com/yjv43cbf.
33. 'History of Mutual Funds in India', *Association of Mutual Funds in India*, https://tinyurl.com/589t26e2.
34. Surbhi Khanna, 'Equity Mutual Funds Saw Highest Ever Inflows of Rs 4.17 Lakh Crore in FY25: AMFI', *The Economic Times*, 19 May 2025, https://tinyurl.com/3yrmjwvt.
35. '2024 Hurun India Rich List', *Hurun India*, 29 August 2024, https://tinyurl.com/3t8f5k86.
36. PTI, 'The NJ Group Story: How Two Friends Redefined Mutual Fund Distribution in India', *The Wire*, 14 July 2025, https://tinyurl.com/bd8jxvb7.
37. Livemint, 'How NJ India Invest Became India's Giant Mutual Funds Distributor', *NJ Group*, 16 August 2017, https://tinyurl.com/

yjv43cbf.

## 12. Conclusion: India at the Breakpoint

1. V.S. Naipaul, *India: A Million Mutinies Now*, Vintage, 1991, p. 517.
2. Richa Sharma, 'Nestlé India Feels the Middle-Class Pinch', *Business Today*, 23 October 2024, https://tinyurl.com/w9eyzjrn.

# The Ultimate Middle-Class Reading List

While writing *Breakpoint*, the following were the books we found most useful in terms of identifying the Indian middle class, understanding their aspirations, zeroing in on the challenges facing this stratum of society, and then figuring out a get-out-of-jail plan for this constituency:


A.M. Gautam, *Indian Millennials: Who Are They, Really?*, Aleph Book Company, 2024.

Adam Alter, *Irresistible: Why You Are Addicted to Technology and How to Set Yourself Free*, Vintage, 2017.

Ashoka Mody, *India Is Broken and Why It's Hard to Fix*, Juggernaut Books, 2023.

Cal Newport, *Digital Minimalism: Choosing a Focused Life in a Noisy World*, Portfolio/Penguin, 2019.

Chen Qiufan and Kai-Fu Lee, *AI 2041: Ten Visions for Our Future*, Crown, 2021.

Daniel Markovits, *The Meritocracy Trap: How America's Foundational Myth Feeds Inequality, Dismantles the Middle Class, and Devours the Elite*, Penguin, 2019.

Daniel Susskind, *A World Without Work: Technology, Automation and How We Should Respond*, Metropolitan Books, 2020.

David A. Mindell, David Autor and Elisabeth B. Reynolds, *The Work of the Future: Building Better Jobs in an Age of Intelligent Mac*, The MIT Press, 2022.

Harish Damodaran, *India's New Capitalists: Caste, Business, and Industry in a Modern Nation*, Hachette India, 2018.

Harsh Mariwala and Ram Charan, *Harsh Realities: The Making of Marico*, Penguin Random House India, 2021.

Jeffrey Witsoe, *Democracy Against Development: Lower-Caste Politics and Political Modernity in Postcolonial India*, University of Chicago Press, 2013.

Jonathan Haidt, *The Anxious Generation: How the Great Rewiring of Childhood is Causing an Epidemic of Mental Illness*, Penguin Books Limited, 2024.

Lakshmi Subramanian, *India Before the Ambanis: A History of Indian Business, Money, and Economy*, Penguin Random House India, 2024.

Leslie D'Monte and Jayanth Kolla, *AI Rising: India's Artificial Intelligence Growth Story*, Jaico Publishing House, 2023.

Manisha Pande, *Middle Class India: Driving Change in the 21st Century*, Aleph Book Company, 2024.

Mukesh Sud and Priyank Narayan, *Leapfrog: Six Practices to Thrive*, Penguin Random House India, 2022.

Nir Eyal, *Hooked: How to Build Habit-Forming Products*, Penguin Publishing Group, 2014.

Nitin Seth, *Human Edge in the AI Age: Eight Timeless Mantras for Success*, Penguin Random House India, 2025.

Pankaj Mishra, *Against the Grain: Lessons from the Outliers*, Penguin Random House India, 2024.

Pavan Varma, *The Great Indian Middle Class*, Penguin, 2007.

Raghavan Jagannathan, *The Jobs Crisis in India*, Pan Macmillan India, 2018.

Rama Bijapurkar, *Lilliput Land: How Small Is Driving India's Mega Consumption Story*, Penguin Random House India, 2024.

Ramachandra Guha, *India After Gandhi: A History*, Pan Macmillan, 2023.

Sanjaya Baru, *India's Power Elite: Class, Caste and Cultural Revolution*, Penguin Random House India, 2021.

Snigdha Poonam, *Dreamers: How Young Indians Are Changing Their World*, Penguin Random House India, 2018.

Sonu Bhasin, *Unstoppable: Kuldip Singh Dhingra and the Rise of Berger Paints*, Penguin Random House India, 2021.

Sudhir Sitapati, *The CEO Factory: Management Lessons from Hindustan Unilever*, Juggernaut Books, 2020.

V.S. Naipaul, *India: A Million Mutinies Now*, Penguin, 1990.

Vishal Vasanthkumar, *The Smart and the Dumb: The Politics of Education in India*, Penguin Random House India, 2024.

William Deresiewicz, *Excellent Sheep: The Miseducation of the American Elite*, Free Press, 2014.